W9-DFL-401

THE VICTORIAN SPINSTER AND COLONIAL EMIGRATION

Landing Stage, Liverpool, 1900. Courtesy of the Prints and Photographs Division, Library of Congress.

THE VICTORIAN SPINSTER AND COLONIAL EMIGRATION

❧

Contested Subjects

Rita S. Kranidis

St. Martin's Press
New York

THE VICTORIAN SPINSTER AND COLONIAL EMIGRATION
Copyright © Rita S. Kranidis, 1999. All rights reserved. Printed in the United States of America. No part of this book may be used or reproduced in any manner whatsoever without written permission except in the case of brief quotations embodied in critical articles or reviews. For information, address St. Martin's Press, 175 Fifth Avenue, New York, N.Y. 10010.

ISBN 0-312-21605-X

Library of Congress Cataloging-in-Publication Data
Kranidis, Rita S.
The Victorian spinster and colonial emigration : contested subjects / Rita S. Kranidis.
    p. cm.
Includes bibliographical references and index.
ISBN 0-21605-X
1. Single women—Great Britain—Colonies—History—19th century.
2. White women—Great Britain—Colonies—History—19th century.
3. Women immigrants—Great Britain—Colonies—History—19th century.
4. Great Britain—Emigration and immigration—History—19th century.
I. Title.
HQ1593.K73 1999
305.48'9691—dc21   98–42901
                                                                              CIP

Design by Letra Libre

First edition: March, 1999
10 9 8 7 6 5 4 3 2 1

For Sandra

CONTENTS

ACKNOWLEDGMENTS

Many people have helped in my work on this book during the past five years.

Maura Burnett, associate editor at St. Martin's Press, has been most helpful and supportive. Writing associates and colleagues Moira Baker and Sally Sevcik offered invaluable feedback and suggestions for revising the latest drafts, and I owe a great deal of gratitude to them for offering their support and expertise so generously. Thanks also go to Scott Christianson, Tim Poland, and Paul Witkowski, who were kind enough to read early versions of this book and share their insights and advice.

I thank David Doughan, Librarian at the Fawcett Library in London, for helping me locate materials central to Victorian female emigration and for diligently maintaining such very important collections for our use. I am grateful to the women who staff the Photographs and Prints Division of the Library of Congress, who have helped me in my search of relevant images, and to the Library itself for rendering many important services. I also want to recognize Bud Bennett, the interlibrary librarian at Radford University, without whose help and persistent efforts this task would have been infinitely more difficult, and Margie Miller, secretary in the English Department at Radford University, for her ongoing help with countless tasks.

I also wish to acknowledge the Radford Foundation for the faculty development grants (1995 and 1996) that made research travel possible and then gave me release time from teaching in order to write. Michele Ren's help with my research saved me much time and hardship, and I thank Hilary Siebert for making that work possible. I am grateful to Rosemary Fithian Guruswamy, under whose chairmanship I completed this book and whose warmth and encouragement have made my work much more pleasant and rewarding. My students at Radford have participated in my work on this book during the past several years, often innocently and informally, always with much natural curiosity and interest. Former graduate students Wendy Turner, Lisa Hurst, Randall Cream, Adam Wood, and Cortney Green have helped me in thinking about some of this material through our work together.

The 1997 NEH Summer Seminar at UNC—Chapel Hill, "Literature and Values," helped me to refine many of the ideas central in this book, and I thank its organizers and participants for that.

I want to acknowledge the support of my extended family for their nurturing and for helping me to not lose sight of the truly important things.

Finally, I want to thank the "spinsters" I have known through the years. They have inspired me to be innovative with life and to revise and challenge rules that do not fit. They served to remind that women can exist outside the traditional roles and life-scripts. They have made all the difference in my own life.

INTRODUCTION

֍

The Imperial Import of the Emigrant Spinster

The exchange of women is a profound perception of a system in which women do not have full rights to themselves. The exchange of women becomes an obfuscation if it is seen as a cultural necessity. . . .

—Gayle Rubin, "The Traffic in Women"

This study arose out of an interest in Victorian women's writing, women's history, and the cultural subjectivity of the middle-class female emigrant.[1] The emigration of Victorian women was comprised of a series of events that potentially can reveal the specifics of gender's relation to nation and to empire. By looking at discussions of female emigration as a possibility and as a desirable course of action, and by locating the center of the female emigration controversies in the status of the unmarried woman and within England itself, this study examines the relationship of domestic spinsters and "superfluous" emigrant women to the production, consumption, and dissemination of "culture" in the colonial context. My approach to these matters does not necessarily take for granted the idea that geographical divisions determine cultural experience or positioning; instead it recognizes that such boundaries are often fluid.

Rather than concentrate exclusively on how emigrant spinsters were "placed" in the colonies and dominions, this investigation focuses on how such transfers in national subjects and cultural value were made possible in the first place. Hence, the focus of this study is the *domestic* side of the colonial emigration efforts. Accomplishing such an analysis requires an investigation of the following areas:

1. the processes of emigrant women's cultural commodification;
2. theoretizations of the concept of "spectacle";
3. Victorian characterizations and representations of the colonies;
4. the rhetoric of national and cultural "dangers" posed to women;
5. the foundations of imperial practice within England; and
6. literary representations of the contested arenas of hegemonic valuation, mainly in relation to gender and the nation.

One rather difficult area of consideration in studying Victorian female emigration concerns socioeconomic class. The chapters that follow delve into the implications of mass emigration movements, especially those centered on middle-class spinsters. While there are important distinctions between the different classes of female emigrants, my focus is on the category of the problematic female subject across class lines. There are several ways of understanding and constructing meaning out of the available population statistics and the emigration figures, and also different ways of thinking about the class identity of the "genteel" emigrant. Therefore, the usual implications of class membership and status may not apply to the unmarried "genteel" women, who are the subjects of my inquiry. According to Josephine Butler's pamphlet, "The Education and Employment of Women," the distinctions between the different classes of women were in sharp relief by the time of the 1851 and 1861 census:

The census of 1861 gave nearly six millions of adult Englishwomen, distributed as follows:

Wives	3,488,952
Widows	756,717
Spinsters over 20:	1,537,314
Total	5,782,983

The census also gives the numbers of women who work for their own subsistence:

Wives	838,856
Widows	487,575
Spinsters (above or under 20)	2,110,318
Total	3,436,749

Butler shows that the population of spinsters had nearly doubled between the 1851 and the 1861 census, as the number of working women increased generally. This information might explain general comments in the Victorian popular press that exhibit an intensifying concern over the growing number of spinsters and also may explain their proliferation in the "finer" literature as well.

The women who emigrated belonged to various socioeconomic classes, and the unmarried women among them were mainly working class, since they were the most motivated to seek better lives outside England. The colonies also wanted domestic servants more than any other class of women. However, the bulk of material available concerns middle-class women because their exportation was a more complicated and delicate matter, entailing intricate arguments and rationales as to why and how they might fare "better" abroad than at home. This class distinction does not minimize the fact that where gender politics and questions of moral integrity are concerned, the exportation of any woman to whom the protective gender ideology applied—even tangentially—was effected against the better judgment of many. This interesting cultural space has not been adequately addressed in the recent scholarship on Victorian women, with some exceptions that do not, however, apply directly.[2] Research in the area of Victorian women's emigration reveals the extent to which the "superfluous" woman constitutes a cultural and ideological crisis and how her removal came to be considered essential not only for her own well-being but for England's as well. Therefore, whereas duty to empire and to the welfare of the nation predominate as justifications for general emigration, the rhetoric changes dramatically when the subject is female emigration.

As marginal and disenfranchised subjects, women perforce occupied some other "place" in the imperial endeavor, although making purely theoretical predictions of what that place may have been is a dubious position to take, at best. More appropriate and useful, perhaps, is Edward Said's directive for postcolonial analysis, which elucidates that the project of reading across cultures and times is already complex: "The problem for the contemporary cultural critic is how to bring [different cultural versions] together meaningfully" (*Culture and Imperialism* 128). This is necessary, since several stories accompany female emigration's role in the imperial context, many of which are complicated by the role of gender. This approach allows dialectical relations to emerge in the process of historical analysis and permits the possibility of contradiction.

ૐ

The analysis that follows grapples with both the usefulness and inapplicability of postcolonial critic Homi Bhabha's formulations on cultural stereotypes to dislocated and disenfranchised cultural subjects such as the emigrant spinster. Hence, I make a rather unorthodox application of Bhabha's conceptions in my discussion of emigrant unmarried women who are stereotyped in a similar fashion at home. However, insofar as they are stereotyped effectively for the colonies, they also challenge this process of stereotyping and prove insubordinate toward emigration, even as they accept it. A transformation occurs in the space between the two domains of "home" and the colonies, a transformation that changes the currency of that stereotype and most explicitly refigures emigrant women as commodities. This disjunction serves as yet another illustration of Bhabha's conception of the "slippage" in signification enacted through the stereotype. Given these contentions, it may seem questionable that in examining imperial relations and the refiguring of geographic and cultural boundaries, my study should examine the other end of the equation—the experience of the established colonists—so little. This objection must be allowed to stand since certain truths pertaining to the politics of domination have been established adequately.[3] That is, apart from investigating the exchanges between the colonists' and imperialists' perceptions of emigrant spinsters, the politics of domination prevalent in colonial economies are assumed.

The main paradox encountered in pro-emigration discussions is that even as they were established as emblems of domestic bliss symbolically extending to England's very nationhood, Victorian middleclass women were systematically removed from England en masse. When we consider the prevalent rhetoric concerning women's idealized status within the Victorian hegemony, we find that the transition between cherished object to cultural and ideological "excess" is significant: It implicates modes of representation and figures of nationality and cultural legitimacy. In addition to being perceived as un[re]productive and "superfluous," the middle-class spinster as problematic excess also was constituted as "surplus" and "redundant." In Victorian discourse, the meaning and substance of the emigrant are inconsistent to the extreme. Seen as engaging in meaningless occupations that merely consume time, spinsters also are potentially capable of depleting the Victorian hegemony, thus posing a threat to the projected cultural organicity of the nation. By the same token, in being "superfluous" and unproductive, spinsters also are suggestive of British debauchery in general. The implications of middle-class Victorian women's relation to conceptions of the nation or to questions of national identity may prove most vital. This relationship may, for instance, challenge how we think about the national politics as impacted by domestic and sociocultural concerns. Redefining those essential boundaries (and others like them) helps us to reenvision the question of how the problem of gender permeates the constitution of social, cultural, and national political life. Ultimately, gender's relation to cultural excess surfaces as an instrumental force in the imperial effort.

As critic Laura Brown contends in *Ends of Empire,* gender historically has been one of the most instrumental tools for power appropriation, both domestically and in the colonial context, mainly because of woman's vested "value": "The female figure, through its simultaneous connections with commodification and trade on the one hand, and violence and difference on the other, plays a central role in the constitution of [the] mercantile capitalist ideology" (3). Yet the female figure is important not just in the figurative or vaguely "ideological" sense, but in her very materiality and in her very practical constitution in relation to other material entities, namely the colonies and the empire's established interests in them. It is fruitful, therefore, to consider the central function of Victorian gender ideology as not necessarily distinct from material and social, cultural practice. Because the imperial endeavor was couched in figurative rhetorical terms, it is all too tempting to overlook the ways gender itself figures as a concrete category in situating both the establishment of the empire and the ongoing dialectic between the category of the "nation" and its constituents. Thus Brown's observation, that in the context of the empire and colonial expansion "the function of the figure of the female arises from the connection between gender and difference—the radical heterogeneity of sexual, racial, or class dissimilarities," may be extended to encompass the very material constituency of "difference" with regard to the colonies and to women (19). That is, the women being exported to

the colonies were excessively problematic in basic economic terms
within England, since they were unemployed and—because of
gender-ideological constraints—unemployable.

Historians of women have long observed the difficulties in trying to locate women in the contexts of imperial expansion and intercultural transactions; Joan Wallach Scott explicated this most
lucidly in *Gender and the Politics of History*. According to Scott, histories that are attentive to issues of gender challenge those rigid systems that maintain that agency and "culture" are Western male
preserves, while the subversion of such systems often suggests the
impossibility of interpretation and finite meaning. Scott's conceptu-
alization of the complexities of constructing a women's history, im-
bued with contradiction and covert cultural negotiation as it is, helps
to account for the many contradictory transactions relevant to Victorian female emigration. It also provides an analytical framework
that allows for the pervasive, multivalent obfuscations of signification. When we contend, as Scott does, that gender and class are invested with ambiguous value in specific historical and cultural
moments, we encounter the need to construct "[a] theory of meaning that assumes a multiplicity of references, a resonance beyond literal utterances, a play across topics and spheres [that] makes it
possible to grasp how the connections and interactions work. When
such a theory posits the multiple and contested aspects of all definitions, it also contains a theory of change since meanings are said to
be open to interpretation, restatement, and negation" (66). This observation on class corresponds with the similarly problematic "meaningfulness" of women, enabling an analysis that pays special attention
to the ways rhetoric is counterdisposed to social practice, highlighting "the ways in which contrasts and oppositions secure meanings"
(66). Addressing Scott's question, "If significations of gender and
power construct one another, how do things change?" requires that
we shift our focus away from monolithic or linear explanations—
both the "fixate of meaning" and "the absence of meaning"—to promote a scheme of interpretation that is not limited to a unilateral
causality: "The answer in a general sense is that change may be initiated in many places" (49). Likewise, an understanding of Victorian
female emigration, both in its processes and its hegemonic meanings,
is to be found in "many places" and must constitute a convergence
of several sociopolitical and symbolic moments. These same moments and contexts consist of specific power relations that ultimately

inform the emigrant woman's place in the Victorian cultural economy and also her removal from it.

What is the cultural economy to which unmarried women's emigration makes reference and that subsumes heterogeneity? The concept of a Victorian national "hegemony" is most apt for thinking about emigration as embedded in a series of complex relationships with the cultural and material economies and with the power structures. My use of the term is specific so as to include gender politics as they relate to imperial initiatives. Part of my meaning includes the dynamic described by postcolonial feminist Trinh Minh-ha, who says in *Woman, Native, Other: Writing, Postcoloniality and Feminism* that the term "hegemony" makes reference to "the authority of certain states over others, of one sex over the other, and to the form of cultural and sexual ascendancy that once worked through direct domination but now often operates via consent" (49). Such an uneasy understanding of "hegemonies" is appropriate to investigations of imperial systems' intersections with domestic cultures and makes specific reference to power relations. In addition to this necessary emphasis on "control by coerced consent," the term "hegemony" also encapsulates the complex complicity of material and ideological relations within a given cultural economy and not privilege one over the other.

In the well-known essay "Ideology and Ideological State Apparatuses," Marxist critic Louis Althusser argues that "there is no such thing as a *purely* ideological apparatus" (*Lenin and Philosophy and Other Essays*, 1971, 145, emphasis added), and that ideology serves to reproduce social and material relations. This key premise allows for the interplay between ideology and material forms, especially so in his observation that "the category of the subject is constitutive of all ideology" and that in the functioning of this "double constitution" of subjecthood and ideology "exists the functioning of all ideology, ideology being nothing but its functioning in the material forms of existence of that functioning" (171). Such an intricate inclusiveness allows the emigrant Victorian woman to emerge as both something more and something *beyond* the proscribed categories of subjecthood that coincide with social stratification.

Given these correspondences, and understanding ideology's relation to the constitution of the category of the subject in these terms, "hegemony" is a conceptual tool that is inclusive of the many interdependent levels of correspondence between the empire's negotiations with the colonies and domestic conditions, both material and ideological. In thus adapting the significance of this term, I share Marxist critic Raymond Williams's reservations over how "hegemony" has been conceptualized; as he states, "hegemony supposes the existence of something which is truly total, which is not merely secondary or superstructural" (37). I invoke Williams's observation that "hegemony" "corresponds to the reality of social experience very much more clearly than any notions derived from the formula of base and superstructure." The latter is a model that does not apply quite easily to Victorian commodity culture and does not explain the dislocations between ideology and subject positioning so prevalent during this period. Hence, while quite fundamental in cultural analysis, the extent to which "hegemony" makes reference to material reality and is inclusive of social experience is therefore neither predetermined nor predictable. The relationship between materiality and "ideology" that the concept of "hegemony" articulates may be seen to fluctuate in meaningful ways, and this very fluctuation becomes the basis for critical analysis itself. This understanding of hegemony corresponds to understandings of the Victorian empire and of the English "nation" during the nineteenth century, a time that marks the epitome of the British empire. The "other places" in which we increasingly encounter Victorian women are significant markers of the intersections between cultural definition and its exclusionist counterpart, cultural nonexistence, since they serve as the means by which problematic national subjects may be eliminated. The colonies can be imagined and specifically represented as places that are not-England but that nonetheless are defined by Victorian culture and politics in relation to British national culture and its interests at home and abroad.

The one persistent correspondence between the three situations of the emigrant women—at home, in relation to the colonies as cultural exports, and in their journey to the Elsewhere—is the question of safety and the "dangers" that surface repeatedly in the emigration discourse. Appearing in different contexts and signifying differently each time, the issue of dangers posed to emigrant women becomes a metaphor for women's hegemonic place within and without the confines of the nation and serves to comment on their relation to the dominant ideologies. Therefore, this concept is traced throughout my discussion.[4] This process of travel coexists with contrasting descriptions of the colonies as morally unsafe spaces in general and projections of women as potential rescuers of the race abroad. To complicate matters further, England itself often is represented as unsafe for women, with some arguments for female emigration making explicit connections between the detrimental effects of women's "excess" sexual value at home as opposed to the possibility of a more sufficient and beneficial sexual status in the colonies.

In recent scholarship more has been written about Victorian women's established presence in the "Elsewhere" as privileged colonists or as "travelers" than about the particulars of their removal there, permanently and en masse. Feminist studies on travel writing, for one, are both useful to my study of women's emigration and inadequate for it. It is not my intention to conduct a critique of Victorian women's travel narratives here, since this would be beyond the scope of my study, and also since other scholars have already accomplished much of this.[5] Likewise, studies of woman-authored travel narratives, Victorian female travel, and privileged women colonists have proliferated in the past several years, rendering them well-documented phenomena and concrete discursive areas to investigate. Rather, the discussion that follows explores the unmarried female emigrant's relation to the imperial agenda and to the nation, and presents her as distinct from the woman "traveler" who has managed somehow to intersect all the categorical definitions of Victorian women abroad and literally to float about in regard to her symbolic and critical significance. Historian and critic Margaret Strobel contends in *European Women and the Second British Empire* that, "[i]n comparison with accounts by Victorian men, women's travel narratives incline less toward domination and more toward discovery" (36). The emigrant woman is also in some ways a "traveler" in relation to her destination, and the politics of travel and observation still apply, as do the ensuing politics of texts produced as part of that process.

Even with the very exciting current work on empire and gender, not enough attention has been devoted to disenfranchised working women and virtually none to unmarried emigrant Victorian women of either class. Most recently five feminist studies—by Sara Mills, Laura Donaldson, Mary Louise Pratt, Jenny Sharpe, and Deirdre David—explore the problematic subjectivity of women within the imperial context. These studies reveal conflicts in cultural identity as in cultural and symbolic function, and analyze intricately complex (albeit often repressed) ideological strife. Thus far many

studies on gender's relation to the imperialist project and colonization have limited the agency of the category to expressions of sexuality by concentrating on the ways it served the imperial project.
Rightly, they have concentrated on authorized British imperial
males (and thus on the gender identities of empire builders) and on
gender relations as they were constituted between colonizer and colonized in the colonial context.

Questions also have arisen, although not always explicitly, concerning women's role in the imperial effort, with concessions made
to their alterity and relative cultural disempowerment. Compelling
feminist studies of Victorian colonialism have examined the role of
women and the category of gender in the colonial project; they col-
lectively propose that gender prescriptions were instrumentally instituted in the colonies to "acculturate" native peoples and places. It
has been reluctantly allowed that, often, colonial women were complicitous in the imperial endeavor, although they were "ambiguously
placed" in the colonization process (McClintock 6). Specifically in
relation to the gendering of the colonial project, postcolonial critic
Anne McClintock and other scholars interested in demystifying imperial oppression make compelling arguments for an apparent "masculinity" to the imperial endeavor. In *Imperial Leather: Race, Gender
and Sexuality in the Colonial Contest* she notes that colonial women
"experienced the process of colonialism very differently from colonial men" and that Victorian women appear to have held a different
relationship to imperialism from men, mainly by virtue of their positioning in the domestic ideology of gender (6). Concentrating on
the ways colonized places were "domesticated" in an English fashion
by employing Victorian gender ideology, McClintock also notes that
"colonialism took shape around the Victorian invention of domesticity and the idea of the home" (36). Her study is especially important because it exposes the complicity between domestic trends in
commodification and their service to the imperial project. Her thesis, that imperialism relied on both intra- and extracultural commodification, is most useful in thinking about the reciprocal
relationship between foreign cultures and England, the "Elsewhere"
and the material and symbolic transformations its appropriation
elicited within the England; that is, the colonies made their way into
conceptions of the "domestic" space, both geographically and ideologically. Hence, it has been established that the imperial project was
assisted by a cultural agenda that persistently relied on a strictly cir-

cumscribed gender ideology of domesticity, and that transgressions against it culminated in woman's expulsion into a No-Place. This is played out and is most clearly evident in novels such as *Cranford, Vilette,* and *No Name,* which are discussed in the later chapters. However, narratives rarely explicate sentiments toward the colonies and their indigenous peoples in terms that assume a progression of unmuddled thinking, nor do they explicate individuals' sentiments toward England's imperialist project. Rather, as Victorian scholar Patrick Brantlinger goes to some trouble to illustrate repeatedly, one may simply move from an espousal of imperialism and colonialism to its opposition and back again, often holding a number of competing and contradictory positions at once.[6] Furthermore, one's position on the issue of colonialism is not terribly significant, because Victorians held contradictory and even mutually exclusive attitudes toward it. Such positions are mediated by the categories of class, gender, and the problem of knowability, and manifest themselves in these simultaneous obsessions: An interest in imports, the state of the British economy, grandiose gestures and sentiments toward civilizing the world are all uniformly espoused for different ends at any given moment.

The emigration of a mass of unmarried and mainly middle-class women to the colonies challenges those conclusions that situate the empire "Elsewhere" and domesticity internally. It does so mainly by questioning both the gender identity *and* the imperial value of emigrant women, thus by extension implicating their symbolic and transcultural place in the colonization process. In thinking more specifically of women as social and national subjects, we may do better than to deliberate the extent of women's complicity in the imperial effort. By the same token, "exonerating" colonial women may not be the most productive tactic, since such approaches also work ultimately to negate the possibility of their agency. The better question to address, rather, is "What is the relationship . . . between any single text or person . . . to the discourse or discourses that frame it?" (Buzzard 447). Our questioning needs also to incorporate sociopolitical practice, so that "discourses" do not become a catch-all in our attempt to appreciate the complexity of women's actual place in the imperial project, especially given the broad ramifications of the practice of colonial emigration. Scott's claim that power politics and sociopolitical positioning are central to historical analysis cautions against overprivileging the dominant cultural positions, as is often the case in histories that are "written as if these normative positions were the product of social consensus rather than of conflict" (43). Rather, her cautionary approach asks that analyses of "the discourses that frame" specific texts and subjects also accounts for the instrumentality of power differentials without, however, neglecting the important "notion of politics and reference to social institutions and organizations"—which she posits as "the third aspect of gender relationships" (43). That is to say, the ideological (and hence more elusive) components of the category of gender also are constituted socially and materially, and women of various classes participate in the maintenance of those structures.

Emigrant Victorian women force us to rethink traditional binary oppositions and to investigate, instead, the space between England and other places. This study asks that we examine the women's roles in the context of the nation and their location in places that are not-England and also their relation to the broader cultural economy that is inclusive of the exchanges between England and the colonies. Victorian emigrant spinsters are most uniquely neither colonizer nor colonized, even as they may be said to be both. Insofar as they constitute the manifestation of the nation's perpetually expanding cultural boundaries, they figure as national subjects who are simultaneously not integral or legitimated parts of the empire. Given the ideological double standard exposed by Victorian female emigration, gender prescriptions of the time need to be viewed very differently now to account for those that were devised specifically for colonial uses. Postcolonial critic Franz Fanon's definitions of the "colonized" apply quite succinctly to the emigrant women, who, as with "every colonized people," "find [themselves] face to face with the language of the civilizing nation" and neither oppose nor submit to it (18). The emigrant woman is both "of" and outside the nation, both a constituent and an exile in relation to the empire. If we are to understand how unmarried women were revalued and commodified into appropriate items of exchange with the colonies (into commodities commensurate with cultural privilege and material goods), and then to contrive a meaning of that commodification, we must note "the characters that stamp product as commodities, and whose establishment is a necessary preliminary to the circulation of commodities" (Marx 87).[7] We also must allow for the possibility that emigrant unmarried women were in fact "traded" or "circulated" within the arena of the domestic ideal, first at home and then abroad.

As agents of cultural production, emigrant spinsters are arguably
"commodified"—that is, distorted in their relation to their material
lives and places in the hegemony; how do we analyze that process
and the final "value" rendered to them by that commodification?
How do we analyze the commodity as cultural subject? What relationship does this value bear to the economy and to other social
"values" on a national level? As chapter 5 elaborates, emigrant
women, especially middle-class unmarried women, constitute a particular kind of "excess" in the imperial context and in the Victorian
cultural economy. In thinking about the possibility that unmarried
emigrant women were traded between the empire and its colonies,
we are assisted by the well-known essay by feminist anthropologist
Gayle Rubin, "The Traffic in Women: Notes on the Political Economy of Sex," which incorporates considerations of gender into the
analysis of cultural commodification.

According to Rubin, there are some essential characteristics to
the practices of marriage and courtship as practiced in most patriarchal systems. As she discovered through reading Sigmund Freud and
Claude Levi-Strauss, the pattern of women's exchange is persistent
enough to qualify as "a systematic social apparatus that takes up females as raw materials and fashions domesticated women as products" (75). Therefore, while my study suggests that women are
conduits for a series of political and cultural imperial transactions
with the colonies, it is also likely that they themselves are the value,
or "raw material," being exchanged. Rubin posits that the implications of this ongoing, systematic exchange of women among men
(whether materially or symbolically) are great: "If it is women who
are being transacted, then it is not difficult to deduce from such
transactions that in most cases women's rights are more residual than
men's. Kinship systems do not merely exchange women. They exchange sexual access . . . in concrete systems of social relationships"
(85). The passivity of women that is suggested and required by a system that exchanges them among men is one that also guarantees the
prerogative of male activity in claiming access to women's sexuality.
Therefore, this double imperative (that women should be available to
men and that they should merely not interfere with the processes of
transaction) renders women politically disengaged from agency of
any significant kind, other than that of fulfilling the role of being
available. As the French feminist Luce Irigaray adds in her essay
"Women on the Market," women are objectified in a process that is

mainly not about them at all but in which they must nonetheless participate, since the exchange that takes place between men, "*The economy of exchange—of desire—is man's business.* For two reasons: The exchange takes place between masculine subjects, and it requires a *plus-value* added to the body of the commodity, a supplement which gives it a valuable form" (*This Sex* 177). While this dynamic is operative in the cases examined in this study of unmarried women's emigration, great difficulty arises when we try to locate the source of operative, systematic agency regarding emigrant women. One reason for this is that women's cause is taken up by both the government's agents and philanthropic civilians who professed to have only personal and altruistic motives. In fact, every facet of the middle-class female emigration project revolved around the issue of marketability (for marriage and other cultural uses) and of utility. Hence, the process of exchanging women's cultural contexts and trading women for other political and cultural values within the empire revolves around key ideological concepts—mainly valorizing womanhood—which frame the entire process.

≥≈

A final consideration, at the outset, is that what we term "the post-colonial" is perhaps a grand conjecture, and we must tread carefully in charting its course. This precaution is best justified by G. F. Plant's study of the past and future of England's imperial mission. *Oversea Settlement: Migration from the United Kingdom to the Dominions* outlines the colonial interests of England and reiterates the empire's concerns and goals. Among several examples of its persisting interests in colonial emigration, Plant notes the issue of "the white population of the British Commonwealth; [being] badly distributed" as a parallel concern to the fact that England is "densely populated" both are posed as pressing problems that emigration may rectify (2). Noting that his study is meant to formulate a "policy for the future," Plant brings to light what has been a subtle undercurrent in the emigration and colonization discourse. As he notes unambiguously, "One thing is clear, namely, that if the desired results are to be obtained, it is necessary to envisage a definite continuity of effort over a considerable period" (8). Such a continuity exists historically and continues to this day, so that—while it must not be thought that imperialism always has developed linearly and incrementally—Victorian colonialism's trajectory extends to the present day in a "continuous" manner that is not accidental. In fact it may be, as Plant's work suggests, administratively enacted.

The conditions and practices explored in this study persisted well into the twentieth century, with emigration figures reaching their peak in the 1920s at rates higher than even the 1880s.[8] Plant's text testifies to a consistency between the Victorian period and the modern; the pro-emigration arguments that surface in the latter were very little altered by time or perspective. Most startling are his observations concerning sex inequities within England and the measures that might be taken to restore a precolonial balance in the population:

> On the proportion of women to men in the population of Great Britain, the Commission [on Population] states that . . . "the 'normal' relation has been for at least a hundred years a small excess of men. Yet throughout this period there has in fact been an excess of women, and indeed until the last few years a considerable excess. . . . This was due, in the period before 1914, to emigration, which removed more men than women from the population" and to the heavy casualties . . . in the First World War. (11)

Responding to the commission's findings, Plant proceeds to chart the sex imbalance in England and to consider that in the 1930s, the number of women emigrating far exceeded that of men. His preoccupation with emigration as a balancing force for England's inequities of various kinds concludes with an observation on the disparity between demographic studies that were presumably scientific and the extent to which other cultural agendas and subjective interpretations have mediated the process of emigration. He states unequivocally that "whilst the Commission's conclusions are largely based on definite facts, they must to some extent be regarded as matters of opinion or of intellectual anticipation" (12). Readers are always translating existing interpretations in analyzing "definite acts" like emigration. As Said has emphasized,

> When the basic theme of imperialism is stated . . . it gathers to it by affiliation a vast number of assenting, yet at the same time more interesting, cultural versions, each within its own inflections, pleasures, formal characteristics.
>   The problem for the contemporary critic is how to bring them together meaningfully. It is certainly true . . . that an active consciousness of

imperialism, of an aggressive, self-aware imperial mission, does not become inescapable—often accepted, referred to, actively concurred in—for European writers until the second part of the nineteenth century. (*Culture and Imperialism* 128)

The issue of imperial emigration and the contested boundaries of the English nation gain contemporary currency beside studies such as Plant's, which strongly suggest that emigration politics and its attendant concerns are not exclusively Victorian, and in light of the problems with immigration and emigration that England continues to confront today. Nineteenth-century imperialism is revisiting England, and accountability for past actions is called for as the residents of its colonies come back to haunt it; strife is also evident by severe domestic racism centered on West Indian and Pakistani residents in England. It is also in view of these developments that neither the subject nor the scope of my study cannot be understood as "postcolonial."

Finally, the terms "colonizer" and "colonized" are themselves problematic in terms of the space I wish to explore, because they dichotomize the very tense and complex relationships involving subjects that are situated very differently in terms of power. Fanon reminds us of two very important properties of imperialism and colonialism: first, that the family is a microcosm for the nation (141), and second, that contrary to the processes of colonialism, "to understand something new requires that we make ourselves ready for it, that we prepare ourselves for it; it entails the shaping of a new form" (95). This kind of interpretive approach to England's domestic conditions as being contingent on colonial economies might serve as the "new form" of imperial hegemony that may be scrutinized in the present moment. Also, the "new form" is represented within the colonizing discourse by women who are no longer subsumed by the English "nation" because they have left their home country permanently. Our critical resituating of emigrant women in the imperial context also produces such a new cultural "form," including their "understandings" of their "new" cultures and homes. New material forms also are produced as migrant women find and occupy their new "places" and thus enact a number of distinctly material engagements, since their adjustment and "preparation" is both symbolic and experiential.

Conceptions of "Elsewhere" and of the Victorian establishment of symbolic national boundaries are also evident in domestic ethnographies and in similar practices within the geographic boundaries of England itself. The function of such apportioning of the home-land must necessarily be seen to inform similar practices abroad, in the claimed territories and cultures of the colonies and dominions. Therefore, we can best appreciate the emigration of women to the colonies and dominions as an extension of a national practice at home, one that also relegated women to the margins of legitimated "culture" and British citizenry. Making this argument helps us to understand, in part, the ease with which female emigration was effected and also complicates any assumptions concerning Victorian unmarried women's relation to the dominant cultural and national ideologies. Chapter 3 indicates that groups of English subjects had long been remanded to an "Elsewhere" that was at once domestic—that is, within the English isles—and also Not-Here, not part of the national and cultural hegemony. My reason for pursuing this point is that while female emigration poses distinct theoretical and hegemonic questions, I do not wish to present either the emigration or the nationality of emigrant women as essentially different from that of other disenfranchised subjects, such as the British laboring classes. The precedent existed for situating British subjects somewhere in between "Here" and "Elsewhere," situating them in ways that rendered them British subjects and at the same time not a national concern. The mapping of the subnation in sociological studies by both novelists and prose writers reveals that the "Elsewhere" is utilized within England although it is not fully constructed and is inadequately and awkwardly assimilated into the Victorian hegemony. Women were not unique in marking the place between Here and Not-Here, then, and this fact is symptomatic of how the British national culture worked to both disenfranchise and appropriate cultural subjects as it saw fit to do so at distinct moments in Victorian history.

The chapters that follow explore some of the problems introduced thus far and illustrate some of their occurrences in the Victorian context. Specifically, they demonstrate the impasse we encounter when we analyze subjects as both material and cultural products. Using concepts such as "surplus value" and the implicating processes by which commodities are invested with value, a construction that informs the entire study in many critical ways, these chapters examine the paradox of the cultural redefinition of middle-class women from cherished and sheltered subjects to ones representing a particular kind of cultural excess. Chapter 5, in particular, undertakes an investigation along the same lines by scrutinizing Victorian sexual politics and notions of sexual value. The earlier chapters primarily use Victorian nonfiction prose that appeared in general-access newspapers and periodicals, charting the terrain of imperialist initiatives and female emigration rhetoric and plotting the necessary ground for the analyses presented later. Chapters 3 and 4 investigate this transformation and also consider the politics and processes of revisioning the colonies so that the women justifiably could be seen as traveling to a better place. Chapters 3, 4, and 5 address the category of the literary and examine the dynamic of how "superfluous" women are seen to permeate the symbolic economies of literary texts. They pose questions concerning her inability to transcend geographic, ideological, and textual boundaries. Exploring further the relations between the social and the literary, chapters 4 and 5 also examine the ways structures and practices of imperialism, gender ideologies, and notions of domestic (as opposed to foreign) places permeate some texts that thus far have not been read this way. Working to delineate the dialectic and material superfluity or excess, the main argument in these chapters is that the literary and textual substance of various texts is, in fact, dominated and structured by the issues that surface within them only as marginal concerns.

1

THE POLITICS OF "SUPERFLUITY"

ટ૾

Empire, Class, Emigration, and the Single Woman

—"Do you know that there are half a million more women than men in this happy country of ours?"
—"Half a million!"
—"Something like that, they say. So many odd women—no making a pair with them. The pessimists call them useless, lost, futile lives. I, naturally—being one of them myself—take another view. I look upon them as a great reserve. When one woman vanishes in matrimony, the reserve offers a substitute for the world's work. True, they are not all trained yet—far from it. I want to help in that—to train the reserve."

—George Gissing, The Odd Women

During the Victorian period, thousands of women left England to seek work and new lives in the colonies and the dominions. In the four years between 1832 and 1836, nearly 3,000 women left England for Australia alone, a trend that did not subside well beyond the turn of the century.[1] However, we hear more about the colonial emigration of families and single men than about women who emigrated alone. This omission is especially pronounced in the case of unmarried middle-class emigrant women, the population generally called "genteel spinsters." A. James Hammerton's *Emigrant Gentlewomen*, the most comprehensive historical study on the subject of Victorian female emigration to date, reveals that

Victorian women's emigration was extensive. Among the most popular destinations for female and other emigrants, the United States
ranked first on a list comprised mainly of colonies with large and
well-established European populations.[2]

A significant number of the women who emigrated to England's
colonies and dominions were unmarried and hence were problematic within the context of Victorian culture, both in terms of politics and in broadly social terms. In their study on British emigration
to South Africa, Jean Jacques Van Helten and Keith Williams identify
two stages to assisted female emigration. They locate the turning
point in emigration patterns in the formation of the Female Middle
Class Emigration Society in 1862, when "the attention shifted from
domestic labour to the emigration of 'distressed gentlewomen'—the
daughters or widows of impoverished clergymen, officers and other
professional men. From the 1860's onward it was these 'superior
women' whom emigration advocates worked to send overseas" (20).[3]
This observation notes the increased visibility of "distressed" women
and also highlights the class-specific agendas of the post-1860s emigration assisters. Here I take issue with these two phenomena: The
problematic population of women for whom England had no place,
the spinsters, and the distinct kinds of assistance by which they were
transported away from England.

Throughout the nineteenth century, the social and cultural positioning of unmarried women was such that their broader national
"utility" or usefulness came into question. They were encouraged to
ask themselves: "Where am I likely to be of most use in the world?"
with the implication that they were to look outside England and to
the "world," a world that presumably offered options home did not.[4]
The female emigration discourse consistently contains very little
ambiguity about single women's hegemonic status as "undesirables"
and as overly problematic subjects. Hence, in relation to Victorian
gender and national ideologies, the standard argument made in favor
of female emigration, that "The question is how to balance the account [numerical discrepancy in sexes], how to transfer them from
the place where they are not wanted . . . to the place where they will
be valued as they deserve," always also poses questions concerning
cultural value (Rye, "Female Emigration Impartially Considered"
73). Rhetoric like this strategically places women's potential ideal
function, as well as their problematics, outside of England and locates
their meaning both within and outside England. The subject of

women's emigration calls for an analysis of colonialism in its relation to gender as an analytical category that resists the traditional insularity of analyses of the empire. Such an approach is especially necessary since, during the Victorian period, vast numbers of women fled, or were sent, to other places, to England's colonies and dominions. Studying female emigration asks that we question and unsettle the standard polarizations of nationhood and nonnationhood, of colonizer and colonized, as the only two possible conditions of national being. Traditional analyses of ethnicity and culture are often singular; they polarize notions of identity by situating constructed identities mainly in a negative relation to places that are not the empire and of gender as a problematic imperial and transcultural category. In this chapter I work to expand such analyses and to examine the status of emigration and the spinster in the imperial context, to produce an approximation of what Said calls "the *economy*" that makes imperialism "a coherent subject matter," including non-teleological and contradictory positions (*Orientalism* 202).

To gain a general and broad view of the high incidence of Victorian female emigration to the colonies and dominions, we need to consider both the prevalence of the "trend" of emigration and the numbers involved. As becomes clear, however, none of these figures is conclusive. The extension of England's national boundaries intensified during the Victorian period, beginning with the New Colonial Policy of 1839, which facilitated the emigration from the British Isles of dramatically increasing numbers of people: Whereas 130,000 had emigrated in 1842, by 1847 250,000 had emigrated, a remarkable contrast to 1829, when there were only 30,000 emigrants. Significantly, the population in England doubled between 1801 and 1851, a fact that suggests that there was probably a large-scale trade in national subjects and labor forces throughout the Victorian period (Thompson 94). Emigration historian Charlotte Macdonald's figures suggest that enormous numbers of women emigrated. In her account, which considers only one destination, a total of nearly 108,000 women were shipped to New Zealand between the years 1853 and 1880 (21). James Hammerton also notes that between 1899 and 1911, 156,606 women were sent to the colonies from England (177). Women emigrated to the colonies and dominions from the 1830s on to the 1890s, and far into the twentieth century. At mid-century, most female emigrants went to the United States, Australia, Canada, New Zealand, and the Cape of Good Hope, in that order

(Craig, "Emigrant Ship Matrons" 25). In this respect they mirrored the emigration patterns of males of the same period. Historian C. E. Carrington has noted that the popularity of destinations such as the United States, as well as the specific patterns of emigration, generally was motivated by monetary concerns. He points to the years 1884–1885, 1894, and 1908, when emigration rates were low, noting that these "pronounced dips . . . [were] related to financial crises in the United States. The high peak of 1883 was a time of depression in England but of prosperity in the United States" (503). In the year 1858, nearly 40 percent of all emigrants to the most prevalent destinations were women (Craig, "Emigrant Ship Matrons" 25). South Africa became a popular destination only after 1900, but then proved quite desirable also, since within four years of the 1902 establishment of the South African Colonial Society nearly 3,000 women were sent there (Paton 94).

What was the impetus for such great numbers of Victorians leaving their familiar places? Male *and* female assisted emigration formally dates back to the 1834 Poor Law Amendment Act, which instigated the first systematic efforts to "export" English subjects to the colonies. As historian Stephen Constantine notes in his introduction to the collection *Emigrants and Empire,* the incremental changes in the emigration numbers were dramatic. Whereas by 1860 only 26,000 had emigrated, the Colonial Land and Emigration Commissioners appears to have made possible the emigration of over 370,000 English citizens by 1869 (2–3). Likewise, Thompson notes that "Between 1853 and 1880 Britain sent out some 2,466,000 emigrants to destinations including the colonies and dominions, of whom an unknown but probably small proportion returned" (163–64). However, historian Dudley Baines estimates that this number constituted "only seven *per cent* of all emigrants at that time" (36), while "about a quarter of the emigrants were helped by friends or relatives and only some ten *per cent* were officially assisted" (50). Given these figures, it would seem that, as historian Eric Hobsbawm has observed, indeed, one of the "commonest non-governmental responses [to national economic depressions was] mass emigration" (*Industry and Empire,* 36–37). In its most basic essentials, the general male and female emigration figures suggest that the boundaries between England and its colonized spaces were indeed negotiable, if not altogether fluid. Apart from providing numerical details of general emigration, these trends also suggest a national condition and a state of mind, to the extent that "imperialism encouraged the masses, and especially the potentially discontented, to identify themselves with the imperial state and nation" (ibid., 70). Therefore, we are compelled to view emigration to the colonies and dominions as something more than a series of isolated acts and events, since all available information indicates that it likely was a national trend suggestive of a predominant quest for an alternative mode of "Englishness." It is also possible to consider the ways in which Victorian emigration might be perceived as a system and even as a national institution not unlike the traditions of vocational apprenticeship, marriage, and education. In fact, as I suggest in the following chapters, emigration from England to the colonies and dominions permeates many facets of the Victorian social arena and ultimately pervades its symbolic economy. At the same time, the whole concept of emigration takes on a different hegemonic significance as an imperial tool, since it becomes clear that England kept and took on numbers of new citizens as it simultaneously expelled others.[5] Furthermore, it may be, as C. E. Carrington has speculated, that the bulk of England's national subjects occupied some geographic place other than the British Isles by the end of the period of peak emigration rates, the 100 years between 1839 and 1939. According to his estimates, close to 10 million people emigrated; if they procreated at predictable rates, by 1939 they would exceed 75 million in the United States alone (506). If that were the case, it becomes difficult to maintain divisions between the "within" and the "without" of England, as it is to do with England's constituents.

SUPERFLUITY

Contradictory explanations for women's emigration pose a problem that is not entirely understandable in terms of social tension, material conditions, and even power inequities. It must be accounted for in the context of all these factors since what is constantly being renegotiated is woman's cultural subjectivity and function in consistently "excessive" negotiations of gender signification. For instance, it is not at all clear that emigration was designed to rectify the problem of "superfluous" women, as was commonly argued, since the women most in demand for colonization were between the ages of 20 and 30; it was believed that "beyond that age the possibility of natural and pleasant assimilation overseas diminishes" (Carrothers 275). The emigration advocate Mrs. William Grey argues that "forty would be near . . . the mark" at which a woman is viewed an old maid, a generous estimate that reflects Mrs. Grey's own agenda more than the reality, which rendered women "old" much earlier (6). As many as 200 single women under age 30 were exported each month for Queensland via government-sponsored free passage (Ross "Emigration for Women" 315).

If the object of emigration was to "save [England's] daughters from loneliness, from poverty, and from despair," as Adelaide Ross argued, then it could not prove an adequate solution, since the majority of spinsters were undesirable as colonial exports due to their age (314). The function of female emigration in relation to unmarried women remains a matter of speculation, despite the abundant emigration rhetoric, which grants that "It is true that there are all kinds of incongruities in colonial life, but how preferable such a life, to the homeless condition of nine governesses out of ten in this country" (Rye "Female Emigration Impartially Considered" 11). The issues relevant to the emigration of women during the Victorian period, both in its barest details and in the contemporary and current discourse pertaining to it, ask that we examine how both that knowledge and its implications are conceptualized and framed. The "Elsewhere" in Victorian culture is a symbolic space that is precisely *neither* the colonies nor England, and it incorporates the issue of emigration into a reexamination of how the politics of Victorian colonialism have been perceived and understood thus far. In attempting to map this negatively termed terrain of assisted emigration to the colonies, which exist in the Victorian cultural imagination mainly as a "Not-Here," one relies on the only known, the currently legitimated social discourse, to provide a foundation from which to begin to address the fact of Victorian women's absence, invisibility, and dislocation. One also makes reference mainly to Victorian conceptions of the "here" and the "now."

The "Here" of Victorian England's imagining of itself in relation to the globe is always and perpetually also the *now*, as historian David K. Van Keuren has observed. The "Here and now" is both a topical *and* a temporal proposition, as is illustrated in the narratives constructed by Victorian anthropological and ethnological collections in Van Keuren's discussion: "The end result of development was contemporary Victorian civilization, the beginning a rudimentary level of social organization far more primitive than could be found amongst contemporary savages" (31). Hence, in examining the "place" of problematic Victorian women, it is not only women's figurative and symbolic absence from the dominant culture that we address, as is generally the case in feminist examinations of the lives and works of Victorian women, but also their literal absence, since emigrant women are written *out* of much of recorded English culture just as they were eliminated from England, the physical place. As a result, questions concerning Victorian women's emigration are materialist in many ways; they also necessitate a theoretical exploration of the margins of dominant cultures, of the phenomenon of cultural invisibility and absence, and of the uses to which that absence has been put historically in analyses of colonialist arguments. If the geographic presence of a subnation and a subpopulation in England could be negated at will, as the literature of the age suggests is possible, then the lower classes of England occupy both a place and a nonplace. Unmarried Victorian women by and large belong to the lower classes, at least economically. Their place in society and culture is also problematic, since they did not adhere to any existing status category. Much like their situation within England, single women's removal to the "Elsewhere" may be construed as a nonevent because their destinations remain vague in the discourse. Except for the relevance of emigration to the empire's interests, emigrant spinsters simply stop being "Here." It is in this respect, and in the course of this exchange, that emigrant women gain a secondary visibility and a new cultural significance, especially since "the migration of women has always constituted a serious problem" not only for us now theoretically but also for the Victorians (Carrothers 274). The high incidence of female emigration suggests that England "exported" women, in a broad sense and to various ends. The possibility that it exported them as *gendered* cultural commodities is supported by the discourse assisting female emigration efforts, which persisted throughout the century, despite considerable domestic difficulties and shifting colonial needs. However, the government also was not quite willing to undertake the emigration of single middle-class women in an official capacity. As emigration historian Patricia Clarke notes, "Middle-class women generally were considered to be outside the scope of government-assisted migration, unless they were prepared to swallow pride and describe themselves as servants" (5).

Clearly, then, the mass exodus of Victorian women has extensive ideological and political implications for how we might think about the Victorian cultural economy as a whole. The extent to which this issue speaks mainly of the gender economy is evident in the paradox that women's emigration reached its peak during the same period when the largest number of people entered England from other countries. Therefore, the standard Victorian arguments advocating emigration as a solution to the country's rising unemployment and depleted resources must be seen as dubious at best, especially when considering the numbers involved. Thompson notes that emigration efforts were necessitated by overwhelming population figures and sees it as an extension of "the overflowing of [England's] surplus into the uncolonized territories of the world" (222). Such descriptions of the general patterns of emigration present it as a natural consequence of overpopulation and, by extension, naturalizes the processes of colonization. We must challenge the presumed accuracy or applicability of the terms "superfluous" or "surplus" and of concepts such as "overflowing" populations, which are often assigned to the Victorian emigrant population. We also would do well to be leery of historical accounts that accept unconditionally the notion that certain people are numerically excessive. We must ask, instead, in what sense are British subjects excessive or "surplus" except in that the nation defines them as such? Finally, "surplus" Victorian subjects may be so ideologically, materially, or both, so that their removal is not always a simple matter of adjusting figures in the expenditures and incomes columns of the national economy. This point is supported by Hobsbawm's observation that in the years between 1871 and 1911, "more people came into England than to any other country in Europe," and fixes the number of immigrants into the country at 10.4 million (*Age of Empire*, 344). This chronology is concurrent with the highest numbers of "genteel" women's assisted emigration in its most sophisticated and highly organized phase, since as Una Monk notes, "fully protected emigration was not developed until the 1880s" (44). However, the total number of female emigrants was never so large, as Patricia Clarke and others have observed. It is remarkably puzzling that the 1880s should have been the time of greatest effort on the part of female emigration assisters, since "by 1880 the field of opportunity for the governesses was becoming narrower in all the Colonies," suggesting that the main market for middle-class emigrant women was being depleted (Monk

42).[6] Perhaps these facts concur with and explain the increased efforts on the part of the emigration assisters, and the more impassioned rhetoric later on in the century. As long as middle-class spinsters could be put to work (which, as Victorian feminists were arguing, would remedy the problem), the fact that they were not is symptomatic of the ramifications of gender prejudice.[7]

Available statistics suggest that women were in fact not materially or practically excessive in relation to England's capacity to accommodate workers but also that, as exports, they were an imperial imposition upon the colonists, who insisted they had no need for middle-class female emigrants. It follows that if women were being "exported" by England, they were being exported not as English citizens but as problematic gendered subjects, since their nation was also "importing" a foreign male labor force. Thus, they were not being exported as labor or merely because they occupied England, but because they occupied a specific place in the cultural economy. If we accept that, as Van-Helten and Williams observe, "the so-called female 'surplus' was a deeply ideological notion," then emigrant women's cultural valuation becomes a central factor in gauging their function as "exports" to the colonies and dominions and their symbolic function in the Victorian cultural hegemony (21). If certain types of women were being exported, along with them went specific values and cultural features of Victorian England. Especially because of emigrant women's ambiguous cultural status within England, unmarried middle-class women's cultural "place" merits special consideration.

One other significant consideration in this issue is that emigrating women received enormous support from societies formed to facilitate their journeys and to secure their employment abroad. The emigration assisters' writings and activity, which comprise the major portion of the literature available on this subject, served to promote general interest in the "problem" of the unmarried Victorian woman. Between 1862 and 1886 the Female Middle Class Emigration Society (later, the British Women's Emigration Society and ultimately replaced by the Colonial Emigration Society) reigned as the leader in the female emigration movement. But other philanthropic organizations, such as the Girl's Friendly Society, the Salvation Army, the Traveller's Aid Society, and the YWCA, helped women to emigrate and further facilitated their emigration with introductions to colonists and with loans. Thus, the assisted emigration of Victorian women also calls to account the movements that facilitated such emigration and considers their social and political agendas in relation to the Victorian hegemony in general and to the imperialist and feminist movements in particular. The ideological complicity in the incorporation of emigrant women into the larger imperial project, exhibited by the societies formed to assist emigration in particular, needs to be scrutinized in order to appreciate the societies' political agendas and the implications of their activities for the colonialist and patriarchal status quo. The women's emigration agenda and patterns problematize the activities of progressive social organizations and call into question what we understand "progressive" politics to signify in the context of Victorian culture and society. They pose the question: In what sense could these philanthropic societies be said to be serving the needs or interests of women? Although distinctions were made between them and the detached, fair ladies who did good deeds out of a marginal sense of social duty, the emigrant assisters were perceived to be entrenched in their work and totally immersed in their experiences.[8]

To be sure, the emigration of "genteel" women was especially difficult and required much careful negotiation between public prudery and practical need. When it came to emigration, the societies more or less shared the agenda of the British Ladies' Emigration Society, which listed as its objectives:

1. Establishing colonial training homes in England;
2. Improving and overseeing the safety of ports for women;
3. Establishing a system by which matrons would accompany single women emigrants during the months-long journey to the colonies; and
4. Making efforts to ensure the women's safety upon arrival to the colonies, often by establishing "reception homes" for them. (Craig, "Emigrant Ship Matrons" 31)

As these goals suggest, the emigration assisters appreciated that they would need to provide for all stages of the emigration process, including the departure, the journey, and the destinations. Insofar as they undertook to transport and to protect the emigrant women, emigration assisters quite effectively "took charge" of this population of Victorian England's unwanted. This daunting task left the societies open to scrutiny and attack on moral grounds, a fact that may help to explain the overly patriotic and solicitous tone of much of their rhetoric. Emigration assisters were always having to defend their actions to the public, and the most prominent female emigration leader, Maria Rye, moved on to emigrating children following a series of difficult experiences with female emigration.

The emigrating women's relationship to the emigration assisters is problematic in many ways. Unlike the privileged colonial wives (the memsahibs) who immediately assumed a place of cultural authority and social privilege in the colonies, emigrant women pose additional challenges for analysis because they encompass problematic gender and class politics, as does the involvement of women's emancipation and philanthropic groups in facilitating their removal from England. Another early female emigration organizer, Caroline Chisholm, was a colonial wife who saw herself as an imperialist, a position she maintained until the very end, making clear that her philanthropy toward emigrant women was a service to the empire and that "her duty lay in promoting colonization."[9] However, that such sympathetic women should put so much effort and energy into sending women abroad rather than providing for them at home, at a time when feminists also were insisting on domestic legislative reforms, is significant and even may be construed as reactionary. Furthermore, claims that various branches of feminist activism stemmed from the spinster problem and in response to spinsters' specific needs is questionable. It makes more sense to trace the evolution of Victorian feminism over many decades and in response to many different inequitable conditions. The project of the emigration assisters stands in stark contrast to the feminists who were very active at home—and their agendas. Even if the emigration assisters were to succeed, the qualitative and political impact of that success, for British women, remained problematic. In 1862 Bessie Parkes, editor of the feminist *The Englishwoman's Journal,* posed a necessary question concerning the motives of emigration assisters. Speaking as one of many women invested in improving conditions for all women within England, she asked, "[A]re we trying to tide the female population over a time of difficulty, or are we seeking to develop a new state of social life?"[10]

This understanding of the women's emigration facilitators is reinforced by the emigration societies' requirements for the perfect recruits, requirements that, as has been observed, rendered them relatively ineffectual in their professed efforts to assist women out of their immediate and pressing dilemmas. By December 1879, only

215 women had been effectively colonized under the auspices of the Female Middle Class Emigration Society (FMCES), the longest-lived and most prominent of the emigration societies (Clarke 107).[11] Among the guidelines published in widely circulated leaflets, are the following limitations:

1. The Society confines its assistance entirely to educated women—no applicants being accepted who are not sufficiently educated to undertake the duties of a nursery governess.
2. Every applicant is examined as far as possible, with regard to her knowledge of cooking, baking, washing, needlework, and housework, and is required to be willing to assist in these departments of labour, should it be necessary.[12]

In addition to clearly illustrating the exclusionary nature of the FMCES's mission, these two categories also prove virtually mutually exclusive, since they describe two very distinct classes of women. Middle-class women, who were for the most part educated as per the first requirement, were not likely to possess the skills described in the second. Similarly, working-class women would be more likely to qualify as domestics but would lack the requisite educational background; hence, Clarke notes in an understatement that, in practical terms, "Some of these rules were unrealistic" (12). What is most interesting about this set of requirements, apart from their apparent disregard for existing class realities, is that they seek to construct a new class and gender category, one that would satisfy the expressed needs of the colonists while attempting to rescue distressed gentlewomen at home. Among the many justifications for female emigration, two that surface repeatedly are that it is single women's savior, and—for feminists—that the women themselves want it.

By all accounts, the majority of Victorian female emigrants were working class. However, as I have suggested, their symbolic significance ends there, since members of the working classes were by no means to serve as emblems or as representatives of the empire and also since they were not seen as being contained or protected by the ideology of domesticity, as were middle-class women. The disparity between the empire's omnipotence and the disempowerment and virtual cultural inconsequence of the working classes did not encourage their emigration to be identified with the empire's goals of omnipotence. The emigration of the working classes must be seen as a much simpler process of England's dumping *select* populations out of the country, based mainly on material/economic considerations. The studies by Hammerton, Clarke, and Vicinus suggest that the problem of women's emigration mainly concerns middle-class women. This seems to be the case, and is so possibly because the working classes had been emigrating for a much longer time. Also, where the working classes were concerned, issues of propriety and cultural expectations did not figure significantly in the process of their emigration, despite the observation that "the tone of [emigrant women's] letters . . . suggest[s] a level of gentility rarely encountered among the lower-middle or working class" (Hammerton 135). The term "emigrant spinsters" must refer to women of the established middle class, insofar as that is practical, since these women were displaced, socially, economically, and culturally or symbolically. In turn, the term "distressed" pertains to the fact that these women were just a step above the most menial working classes and often, in fact, may have occupied a place below those classes in some respects. In the emigration discourse, middle-class spinsters are likened to working-class emigrant women as often as they are distinguished from them. They are described as "more often helplessly placed so far as pecuniary matters are concerned than most household servants," whether from "circumstances, misfortunes, and losses" (Hammerton 236). Nonetheless, I am reluctant to follow Hammerton's—and the emigration societies'—example in classifying all society-assisted emigrants as "genteel," simply because they do not qualify as such in any substantial way when emigration becomes a serious consideration and a last resort for them.

The hegemonic contradictions concerning gender's relation to class are more pronounced in the case of middle-class women's emigration to the colonies, since the "genteel spinster" falls somewhere beyond the traditional class divisions, as suggested by her intricate relationship to Victorian gender ideology. According to the concerned Victorian Charles Hamley, the virtuous and most commendable spinster is the polar opposite to the domesticated middle-class female; the self-sufficient spinster is "the woman who has shown herself equal to the charge of her self" (99). The unmarried Victorian woman must perforce take on working-class characteristics, since only in this way is the prevailing order of things maintained against categorical challenge. By virtue of their numbers, middle-class emigrant women stand as bold challenges to pretensions relevant to class distinctions, as they constituted a *"mass"* population. Josephine Butler notes in "The Education and Employment of Women" that so many women should be "working for their own subsistence . . . is not an accident, it is a new order of things," an order that threatened the very boundaries of the already insecure middle class.

In their most practical instances, prevalent notions of "superfluity" and "redundancy" are also exclusively applicable to middle-class women, since working-class women had long held an established place in the cultural and material Victorian economy. Working-class women's cultural and social positioning did not fluctuate as often or as drastically as the cultural identity of the middle-class woman, whose very essence relied most heavily on her identity as wife and mother and on her place in society. Whether working-class women married was not as pressing a concern for Victorian society since it did not in any way dramatically affect their status as cheap labor. Thus, although both middle-class and working-class women were "exported" to the colonies, it is middle-class women who are encountered in the discourse of the "superfluous" woman and also those who are deemed "unsuitable" for colonization. This symbolic fluidity reasserts itself in the colonial context, where both the unauthorized *and* authorized presence of English women appears to serve a number of functions simultaneously. Furthermore, given the cultural invisibility of working-class women, it is middle-class women's presence in the "Elsewhere" that gets problematized in the discourse, although numerically, it was mainly working-class women who emigrated to the colonies. In "Old Maids, A Lecture," an 1875 pamphlet, the education-reforms activist Mrs. William Grey distinctly points to class and morality stereotypes that conflate women and "according to which the single woman who is rich and independent is also honourable and honoured, notwithstanding the absence of the magic wedding ring which raises the wearer to unquestioned pre-eminence . . . while she who is poor and lives in threadbare independence . . . becomes a laughing-stock as the disagreeable and ridiculous old maid" (12).

Discussions of gender and class are masked by questions of morality and virtue, as might be expected where women are being discussed. This double-standard inequity and fall from social grace, based solely on financial status more than on class affiliation called for the "rescue" of "genteel" women and stirred the sympathies of so many Victorian philanthropists as well as women's rights advocates. While the issue of class is terribly problematic and central to the issue of female emigration, analysis of the discourse reveals an even stronger gender component. Insofar as women are culturally invested—even on a mainly ideological and idealistic level—with an essential goodness and purity in their projected essential *difference* from men, speculations concerning middle-class women's suitability to the colonies encompass a gender ideology that extends to non–middle-class women as well, and that is complicated both by the societies' missions and by the limitations imposed by the host countries' own needs. The essence of the problem here is that the societies sought to export what was basically an undesirable object of exchange—middle-class unmarried women: "If it were distinctly known that there was no assisted emigration for any but servants, and that there was a body of women ready to emigrate, as willing and as able to work in other spheres of action as their sisters and servants, surely the hand of charity, of sympathy, and of support would not be wanting or denied by English ladies to start, arrange, and uphold so admirable an institution" (Craig, "On Assisted Emigration" 236). The colonies asked for women who would be willing to perform various tasks, including the most menial household chores, whereas the "superfluous" woman had no such training or experience.

The implications of these philanthropists' classist selection of suitable emigrant subjects are most instructive in their relation both to the women themselves and to the colonists and colonies to which they were sent. Maria Rye cites a letter from Bishop and Mrs. Baker of Sydney: "The colonies ought to assist largely in [the protection and employment of women], but you know the many difficulties and evil influences that have to be encountered here; and how we have suffered from swarms of ignorant women, who are a misery to any place. But if responsible, well-taught persons could be introduced in any numbers they would, as you say, be of incalculable benefit to the colony" (*Emigration of Educated Women* 10). The whole question of women's emigration scrutinizes women on moral grounds, when the biases of the established colonies are considered, and "ignorant" women are conceived as a problem to the colonies that were already seen to be in danger, morally. Thus, a mutually obligatory relationship is established between colonialism and emigration, and it is formulated as a mutually binding one. Furthermore, the class identity of emigrant women becomes more and more paradoxical and disingenuous because it transcends all known (British) parameters of social stratification, experience, and ideological categorization. Hence, while emigration societies such as the FMCES professed to exist to serve the needs of English women at home, their colonial agenda did not take into account the prevalent gender ideologies that dictated and limited Victorian women's range of experience. In this respect, the agenda of the emigrant assisters can be viewed as either naive or disinterested in the gender dynamics of their age, as their colonizing agenda does not incorporate the specific circumstances affecting women as gendered national subjects. The desired ends of female emigration reflect changes at home and in domestic gender and other social relations. As many apologists for women's emigration were to argue, socioeconomic status was a determining factor in formulations concerning woman's cultural value. Middle-class women merited special consideration because "female servants do not constitute any part . . . of the problem," since "they are attached to others and are connected with other existences, which they embellish, facilitate, and serve. In a word, they fulfill both essentials of woman's being" (Greg 1862, 451).

Even if the "essentials of woman's being" vary from her usefulness to others and her place in the hegemony as "servant" to others, her contingent cultural value does not. It remains a static characteristic and serves to present Victorian women's projected place in the proper cultural context. This specific point concerning utility is relevant to what W. R. Greg sees as the main problem with the status and social position of "superfluous" women: Women's value has fluctuated much too drastically, and they no longer occupy their proper places. This shift in value has far-reaching ramifications, since one of its consequences is that men no longer know their own places in gender relations and presume to exploit morally women who are culturally compromised. The formula Greg presents as a solution to this complex set of problems is amusing in its practicality: "As an immediate result of the removal of 500,000 women from the mother-country, where they are redundant . . . all who remain at home will rise in value . . ." (Greg 1862; 460, 459). Solutions such as this were quite widespread among imperialists in general and invited much harsh criticism from Victorian feminists. Nonetheless, they do make clear that the "problem" as such is that Victorian culture has "undervalued" women who are otherwise represented as cherished cultural emblems. According to this reasoning, sending *numerically* "superfluous" women out of the country results in their increased cultural and/or ideological value within it. This dialectic of women as physical objects for political exchange and as numbers is increasingly presented as an analogue to the more theoretical and vague category of "the cultural condition" of England. The exchange between women as objects and the complex "condition" of the nation both authorizes women as cultural agents and also renders them dispensable market goods upon whom is contingent the well-being and revitalization of Victorian culture. As a purely materialistic consideration, this formula ought to provide the needed solution to the problem of "superfluous" women. However, the problem was an intricate and complex web of material and ideological concerns, and hence its difficulty, for many of the emigration assisters. The colonies and emigration enter the picture of women's problematic status mainly in helping to balance the scales of women's falling cultural and social value.

The way formulations of gender crossing cultural lines are framed is most telling; in them the gender ideology embodies class conflict at its very core at the same time that it attempts to override it. In some respects women's emigration rhetoric is culturally transgressive, although it seeks to take an inoffensive middle ground from which it might best be able to "help" women. In one among many instances of the double mission of women's emigration rhetoric, Hammerton notes that "In encouraging educated women to become colonial servants, the emigration societies had to tread carefully to avoid offending the sensitivities of both colonial employers and the women themselves" (155). These kinds of negotiations, between the perceived practicality and necessity of women's emigration and the production of subjects appropriate for emigration, culminate in a fantastic narrative that, not surprisingly, implicates and informs the very identity of "Elsewhere" as well.

IMPERIAL MISSIONS

The ways in which women have been situated in formulations of Victorian culture and in the imperial discourse suggest that we need to investigate the margins or boundaries between England and its corollaries, both its subordinate female subjects and its colonies and dominions. We need to explore the discordant discursive space that exists between England in its identity as a nation and its parallel relations to the subjects it subverts by situating them in ways that are subordinate to itself. The issue of emigration gains significance in itself, since, as Thompson has observed, "much of Britain's weight in the world was felt not through her export of manufactured goods but through her export of men [*sic*] and capital" (163). Therefore, while it makes sense to examine England's investment in foreign commodities and objects of trade as a distinct practice, women and human subjects in general also fall into the category of imperial commodities and may even be considered alongside the trade of inanimate commodity "goods." Part of this task is facilitated by the knowledge that the most urgent "race for the colonies" began in the 1870s, when the economic *and* political conditions in England were the worst (Thompson 203). The process of colonization, then, can be seen to have responded both to material and to generally "cultural" conditions. This analysis of women's emigration implicates colonialism's relation to gender and scrutinizes Victorian ideologies of homogeneity and difference as they were disrupted by the crisis of unmarried, "superfluous" women—of whom it has been said that "at best, [theirs] was a 'life of obscure gentility'" (Trollope 63). "Obscure gentility" and "superfluity" became meaningful terms in accounting for middle-class women's problematic status within the Victorian hegemony. They also suggest how middle-class unmarried women came to be commodified as colonial exports. Throughout the century, it never ceased to be the case that, as Greg noted, "even in our own complicated civilization, marriage, the union of one man with one woman, is unmistakably indicated as the despotic law of life. This is *the* rule" (1862, 438).

Women's leaving England reflected on Victorian society's shortcomings. The rhetoric advocating their emigration produces recurring visions of Victorian culture as an unsafe space for women in characterizations that suggest England was a place from which one had good reason to wish to escape. In diagnosing the condition of both unmarried women and England as being analogous, Greg extends his argument by figuring English society and culture as diseased and "unwholesome." Greg's essay is representative of a body of literature that most explicitly makes the connection between women's status and the condition of England as the nation that encompasses them and the kind of problem they represent: "[T]here is an enormous and increasing number of single women in the nation, a number quite disproportionate and quite *abnormal;* a number which, positively and relatively, is indicative of an *unwholesome* social state, and is both productive and prognostic of much wretchedness and wrong" (436). This argument, according to which married women are indicators of England's "wholesomeness," endorses a reciprocity among women, the institution of marriage, and national well-being that surfaces repeatedly in the female emigration discourse. In this respect, women become indirectly significant in serving as *signs* that are of national importance. This argument is also most notable for the rather clever ways in which it establishes an essential link between woman and the state of the nation, although it does so in a rather traditional sense of treating woman as a "problem" or a "burden" to the state. Moreover, according to Greg, the number of "excess" or "superfluous" women both produces and predicts a cultural degeneration, so that the women themselves might be seen as a threat to the national and cultural well-being of England. This kind of analogy between the condition of the nation and the status of women appears repeatedly as the basic premise of emigration advocacy and is refigured in telling ways. Emigration arguments that represent England as unsafe or as undesirable are especially instrumental in establishing a symbiotic relationship between the national "condition" as it is seen to impact Victorian women's cultural value and their social status itself. The main critical contribution of such arguments is that they establish women as an emblematic segment of the Victorian national and cultural economy.

One Victorian examination of the problem of "superfluous" women offers a description of women's status that is strikingly similar to the much earlier one by novelist Margaret Oliphant from 1858 and serves to justify women's emigration. Its author, Mrs. William Grey, suggests that spinsters were socially ostracized already, long before they began to be sent abroad. According to Grey, unmarried women are considered "social failures" in England; she scans the different appellations for the single woman, concentrating on one categorization in particular, that as "social superfluity" (9). In this analysis, the problem of "old maids" is caused by women's limited options, both socially and professionally, since Victorian women were at the mercy of male-interested institutions. Like other apologists for "superfluous women," Grey implicates and problematizes domestic issues such as marriage and women's place in the professions, issues that become central to discussions of female emigration. She states: "[T]he only honours in which a lady can graduate are those of a bride. The only profession open to her is that of marriage. Very often it is their only chance of independence, their only escape from the thraldom of a pupilage, easy and natural at the age of pupilage, wearisome and intolerable in later years. Is not ambition 'the last infirmity of noble minds'? Why should it be ridiculous only in the genteel spinster?" (8). Grey emphasizes the cultural censure against women who have "ambitions" toward self-determination and exhibits a critical awareness of the extent to which the future of women was contingent on male activities. Suggesting a connection between England's class and gender "undesirables," Grey notes a correlation between woman's social valuation and the exclusive "male uses" for which women are deemed suited: Women are culturally valuable only insofar as they are useful to patriarchal purpose, the article concludes, since "any use [women's] lives might be to themselves was evidently not thought of" (9). In this way women are culturally significant only in their relation to their contexts and in terms of the existing structures they mediate; they do not exhibit any cultural autonomy or distinctness of purpose and essence. The status of Victorian women within their own domestic cultural economy is central to appreciating even the import of their cultural displacement. As Grey did not fail to recognize, considerations of women's emigration consistently problematize their general cultural status, applicable either to "Elsewhere" or "here": "[O]ur business is not with the modes of disposing of the superfluous women, but to enquire *whether they are* superfluous. Let us look around us for the answer. And to go no further than our own country and this century and names familiar to us all" (10, emphasis added). Citing important women such as Jane Austen, Maria Edgeworth, Harriet Martineau, and Frances Power Cobbe as examples of unmarried women who were all the same accomplished and not "superfluous," Grey constructs a social history that is inclusive of problematic women and argues for their necessity in the present moment and place.

England's own condition comes under scrutiny again, as the morally laden question of woman's virtue is at issue. According to many emigration advocates, the uses or functions women are asked to serve within the context of Victorian culture are illicit and immoral. Hence, women's surplus numbers within England weigh against them and any possibility of their attaining substantial cultural value; the ramifications of this imbalance are mainly moral and, specifically, sexual. It is suggested that in the absence of drastic change, the status of women is expected to continue to degenerate. The formula for restoring women's value is framed even more grossly as Greg discusses the practicability and necessity of female emigration as a solution to degeneration of gender relations within England: "When female emigration has done its work, and drained away the excess and the special *obviousness* of the redundance; when women have thus become far fewer in proportion, men will have to bid higher for the possession of them, and will find it necessary to make them wives instead of mistresses" (1862, 452). This formula reveals most clearly the pertinence of considerations of sexuality to the issue of female "redundancy" or "superfluity." For, this logic goes, if the problem confronting women and Victorian society is that too many women remain unmarried, then manipulating and elevating their status as objects of sexual desire ought to restore their former place of social importance and facilitate a less explicit relation to matters concerning sexuality. The unmarried woman's value in relation to the middle-class gender and sexual economies is problematic mainly in that she is "superfluous" in a most pragmatic way; the adjustment that would remedy this is to make her desirable once again by making her scarce. It is also significant, then, that although arguments for women's emigration often are contrived to center on colonial abundance and on the perpetuation of imperial initiatives, a closer look reveals that gender and sexual economies are the main ingredients in the rhetoric. In fact, this is the case in some very telling ways, as Grey's article indicates.

Given the intricacies of female emigration as a gender-centered project, it is significant that rhetoric often complied with general emigration justifications, in urging women to "[go] from places where they [were] not doing very well to places where they [had] a vague hope of doing better" (Ross 1882, 312). Emigration offers at least a dual benefit, as Isa Craig observed. It "opens a wide door of hope and of escape from crime, while it benefits those who remain behind; relieving the labour market at home and creating fresh markets abroad." But it also "benefits the working class by strengthening their attachment to the country" by sending them away ("On

Assisted Emigration" 239). Several paradoxes are encapsulated in this formula for improving the nation. They rely on the sentimental notion that distance makes the heart grow fonder, that better national subjects are produced outside the nation, and finally that England cares enough about its subjects to send them away. However, despite the complex contradictions encompassed these propositions, they are accepted unanimously and are promoted as solutions by the emigration advocates.

G. F. Plant makes the same simple point in his study, *Oversea Settlement*, observing that among "the elements in the success of a colonization scheme, . . . the colonists should be doing better than they were at home" (51). He also attaches a broader significance to women's emigration, but on different grounds. Suggesting a reciprocal relationship between Victorian emigration in general and women's emigration, his study reveals that the "Colonial Land and Emigration Commissions in 1873 had pointed to the excess of females over males in the United Kingdom and had blamed emigration for part of the excess since in unassisted emigration the flow of men . . . was always in excess of the flow of women" (48). The assisted emigration of women, then, was instituted partly in order to supplant the specific consequences and gender ramifications of the longer-standing emigration of men, much as the condition of "surplus" or "superfluous" women is commonly and unquestioningly attributed to general emigration patterns. Thus, in keeping with general patterns in the history of women, circumstances affecting the lives of Victorian emigrant women were prompted by those pertaining to the lives of men and may even be said to have come about in *reaction* to policies initiated on behalf of men. In a similar fashion, the systematic institutionalization of women's emigration reflects back on England's colonialist project, in that it served to eclipse crucial inequities in the nation's cultural economy. (This is especially the case in literary representations such as those by Charles Dickens and Elizabeth Gaskell, which I consider in later chapters.)

Although literary representations suggest that removing oneself to Elsewhere could only be beneficial, nonliterary discourse makes a different argument. Here the emphasis appears to be on the difficulty, if not the impossibility, of escape, especially given social structures limiting women's mobility. Critic Martha Vicinus outlines this particular problem in an early study, *Independent Women*, which accounts for the condition of Victorian women outside the institution of marriage, and thus outside the very periphery of cultural recognizability. As Vicinus observes, the difficulty of her project lies in the ambiguous ways in which spinsters sought to "eke out an existence . . . on the edge of respectable social circles" (23), and also in that "reformers saw work as the key to the single woman's liberation" (24). More interestingly, Vicinus illustrates that those women who could not leave England or who were fortunate enough to stay on at home formed female communities to sustain them during the difficult decades. Such communities emphasized traditional gender roles and accomplishments considered appropriate to women at the same time that they defensively created an insular and classist seclusion for themselves. An interesting example of how self-preservation metamorphosed into vehement conservatism, the agendas of these unmarried women were only tentatively radical; their significance lies in the women having asserted themselves as "independent women," a categorization also supported by historian Joan Perkin's study on the subject.

Based on the remarkable number of writings concerning single women, it appears that unmarried women constituted, for the Victorians, a special class and a special concern. This population of "independent" women was, in fact, a major preoccupation for socially minded Victorians, as the literature of the age testifies. While such women are repeatedly alluded to as a problem and a shared worry, both sympathetic and derogatory addresses to the issue suggest that spinsters must not be allowed to remain "independent" and uncircumscribed entities. Outside marriage, woman's life and her future prospects were nothing short of a gender anomaly. At the same time she was also an open-ended narrative, a story whose ending could be neither predicted nor projected, but whose possibilities had to be predetermined. Moreover, insofar as she had no determined "place" in the Victorian hegemony, the unmarried middle-class woman is a nonentity at the same time that she is a nuisance.[13] She is invisible because she constitutes a challenge to the edicts on bourgeois sexual and moral privilege. These two main features of the Victorian period, female emigration and the rhetoric on spinsters, were not at all coincidental but combined to form a cultural imperative.

The status of the spinster as a woman who exists outside marriage and its many rituals is thus analogous to the polymorphic and perpetual "unknown" that was the colonies. The institution of marriage carried as much weight as it did not only because of its practical usefulness in circumscribing the development of women's lives but also in its perceived centrality to the global importance of Victorian culture. In a defense of unmarried women entitled "Old Maids," Charles Hamley makes a concession to popular opinion, that "to be married is, with perhaps the majority of women, *the entrance into life,* the point they assume for carrying out their ideas and aims" (95). Conceding that "we do not give up our respect for those martyrs to station who keep themselves single for an idea," Hamley identifies the "highest type of old maid" as one who "has made no sacrifice, nor is she in any sense a victim, for marriage as a state is not necessary to her idea of happiness . . ." (97). As "independent" agents, middle-class unmarried women can be viewed as having initiated the deliberate foundation of a subnation within England.

While the construction of "Elsewhere" is considered at length in the next chapter, here I want to concentrate further on the emigration of women as a social movement with serious implications for the national cultural economy and in its relation both to material conditions for women and to gender ideologies prohibiting their extended presence outside of England's geographical boundaries. When Victorian culture could not provide a vast number of women with a place in society, it did away with them by depositing them in a vaguely construed "Elsewhere." As Margaret Oliphant argues, the terms in which "superfluous" women are discussed in Victorian discourse are very telling. In her analysis, the "problem" with unmarried women was not in they themselves but in their treatment by the many who held opinions on the matter. This treatment established for women an alternative "economy" and a distinct and different set of cultural values and "morals." In the Social Darwinistic hierarchy they occupy a distinct place, one that is different from all other women and all other suitable national subjects. As a result, they are treated as something distinct from England and Englishness itself and also as something other than what England recognizes as "foreign" subjects—at times women almost surface as not being exactly human: "[W]riters on the subject invariably treat this half of humankind as a distinct creation rather than as a portion of a general race—not as human creatures primarily, and women in the second place, but as women, and nothing but women—a distinct sphere of being, a separate globe of existence, to which different rules, different motives, an altogether distinct economy, belong" (144). Women also are perceived as the locus of the problems surrounding gender roles late in the period, and a distinct one at that. In one example, unmarried women are posited not only as social problems but as "injurious" to "those around them" and "a curse rather than a blessing"; their significance lies not only in their being social anomalies but also in their potentially harmful effects—they are admittedly culturally significant in a contextual way and in their relation to the nation and to the Victorian hegemony (Rye, "Female Emigration Impartially Considered" 73). So long as this was the prevailing view, the mere removal of single women outside of England could be posited as an automatic and instantaneous solution. Whether the "general race" to which Oliphant makes reference is limited in its constituency to the English, or whether she would extend the category to include the empire's colonial subjects, is not at all clear. But even if it is not all-inclusive, the place of women in the national hegemony clearly is seen to be contingent and marginal. Oliphant's objection to the excessive problematization (or blaming) of women highlights the rupture in Victorian domestic and gender ideologies—that is, those that do not acknowledge that they have failed and that do not know what to do with their failed systems. However, this is a class-specific distinction, since the inherent goodness of upper-class women, specifically regarding their cultural and social influence, is promoted as a tenet of British elevated (High) culture (albeit one that was under threat of extinction, as Greg concluded). These distinctions comprise an important segment of emigration rhetoric.

IMPERIAL EXCHANGES

Accounting for why so many women left England during the nineteenth century would be greatly facilitated by primary accounts of this phenomenon. In probing the political and cultural meaning of this mass exodus, assessing the emigrant women's own writings might prove definitive as a means of exploring specifics, such as how they perceived themselves as British subjects and whether their self-conceptions underwent notable change as a result of their emigration. In addition to benefiting from the efforts of emigration societies and the creation of alternative spaces for existence, such as the colonies and dominions, emigrant women also could be treated as a natural resource of sorts, by both England and the societies. In a less explicitly practical manner, emigrant women also were potentially useful because they were in a position to provide experiential, first-person narratives on the nonauthoritative colonial experience, letters that, as the emigration facilitators' correspondence indicates, were in demand.[14] The existing correspondence about the need for emigrant women's letters constitutes the bulk of letters on the subject of female emigration, so these metatexts override and subsume their stated subjects. As texts, emigrant letters must be seen to differ from the travel diaries of privileged women and the shipboard diaries written by emigrants on their way to the colonies. Whereas those diaries were narratives of the journey written for the benefit of both the writer and relatives or friends back home, letters written by emigrant women specifically for the emigration societies must be read in light of the fact that they were ruled by several constraints. They had as their audience the very people to whom the emigrants had to prove they were a good investment and by whom they had been (and continued to be, albeit less effectively) morally scrutinized; on a less personal level, they were authored to satisfy a contractual agreement between the emigrant and the societies, and were also meant to satisfy an institutional need for information about the colonies. The emigrant women assisted by the societies constitute a kind of investment the product of which would be knowledge; their correspondence served the same purpose.

The reasons for the desirability of emigrant narratives are many, but one possibility implicates the women's cultural value to the societies and to domestic affairs in England in particular. That is, emigrant letters bridge the gap between the "Elsewhere" as an unknown and the necessity of transforming that unknown into a natural outcropping of the nation, an extension of England. Such narratives would provide practical information but also would serve as evidence that survival and success in the colonies and dominions were, in fact, possible. Furthermore, they could serve as windows into unfamiliar worlds very far away. As theorist James Clifford writes, the emigrant women's documented experiences are potentially useful as particular kinds of texts, those invested with a truthfulness and authority they do not (and cannot) necessarily possess: "Precisely because it is hard to pin down, 'experience' has served as an effective guarantee of ethnographic authority. . . . [But] experience evokes participatory presence, a sensitive contact

with the world to be understood, a rapport with its people, a con-
creteness of perception. . . . It is worth nothing, however, that this
'world,' when conceived as an experiential creation, is subjective,
not dialogical or intersubjective" (37). It is significant, given the
societies' pressure on the women to produce and provide such
texts, that although the "world" they received in them was a "sub-
jectively" construed one, this feature did not diminish the text's
desirability or value in the eyes of the emigration assisters. The presumption behind this could well be that future women emigrants
would come to occupy the very same space as the original authors:
the private, domestic, insularly subjective sphere in the colonies as
at home. In this case, the letters written by emigrant women might
prove "authoritative" enough, despite Clifford's astute point, since
the question of authority does not carry the same significance here
that it did in the mainstream culture and discourse. Maria Rye relied very strongly on such correspondence from emigrants to the
colonies to support her in her efforts. She used the emigrant letters as persuasive tools quite extensively whenever her work came
under attack.[15] In fact, the emigration assisters were not alone in
privileging the polemic uses of personal narratives concerning the
colonial experience. Margaret Strobel observes that "published letters and novels formed a significant source of information about
India for a popular audience in the first half of the nineteenth century" (36). As early as in the 1840s, Caroline Chisholm tried to
rally support for her work on female emigration by publishing
them in *The Herald* and other newspapers (Roberts 118). Sidney
Herbert confirms the authorizing uses of personal letters when he
notes that "a single letter from a successful emigrant in a quiet
country town stimulates voluntary emigration more than a volume
of eloquent anonymous essays, or the removal of a ship-load of isolated Londoners."[16] Also, the appendix to Samuel Sidney's pamphlet on female emigration reforms offers a series of emigrant
letters in full, letters that are cited as the final authority on emigrants' issues and the main substantiation of his claims. Such evidence suggests that emigrant letters are important not only as a
knowledge-producing medium but as rhetorical ploys in fortifying
arguments for emigration with irrefutable evidence. As Maria Rye
would state, such letters were invested with much power in providing "authentic information on the subject of emigration [that
is] exceedingly valuable" ("On Assisted Emigration" 240).

The potentially ideal primary texts for a study on female emigration, letters written by emigrant women to the emigration societies assisting their emigration, are not very helpful. Although they are abundant in number, they can best be described as "resisting" texts that do not lend themselves to extensive analysis. They are mainly short, obligatory notes attending to practical matters and yield very little by way of personal information despite the societies' repeated efforts to turn emigrant women into a source of information on conditions pertaining to women's status in the colonies: "From the very beginning help was sought from the settlers themselves. They were encouraged to write a frank account of their experiences and to pass on any information which could be useful to those who followed them" (Monk 5). Even though they were obligated to provide the societies with information as per their tacit agreement, all too often emigrant women failed to do so in any significant way. Patricia Clarke, whose study of emigrant women's letters is the most comprehensive, acknowledges that the middle-class women assisted by emigration societies offer the fewest letters. She notes that although by the Female Middle Class Emigration Society sponsored 302 emigrants, there are only 113 letters on file, a number of which would qualify more as brief notes than as letters (107). These particular letters do not conform to the long and successful tradition of emigrant letter-writing meant to prepare and persuade friends and family to emigrate. According to Dudley Baines, personal-narrative texts were viewed as bearing such a close relationship to experience that "potential emigrants seem to have obtained their information . . . through letters from emigrants who already had gone" (37). The bulk of emigrant correspondents resist rendering elaborate narratives of their colonial lives, as if suspicious toward the uses to which this correspondence would be put. In the terms outlined by Clifford concerning the relationship between intercultural experience and its textualization, the writings of the emigrant women ought to be construed as relatively and potentially more valuable extensions of their experiences abroad. They are the main means by which their experience could be appropriated by those who did not share in that experience but sought to learn and benefit by it, as would be true of the emigration assisters. The letters would, in fact, have effectively commodified and appropriated these women's cultural experiences: "*The text, unlike discourse, can travel.* If much ethnographic writing is produced in the field, actual composition of an ethnography is done elsewhere. Data constituted in discursive, dialogical conditions are appropriated only in textualized forms. Research events encounters become field notes. Experiences become narratives, meaningful occurrences, or examples" (Clifford 39, emphasis added). As Hammerton has observed, the extant letters by emigrant women to the societies do seem to express varying degrees of culture shock and dissatisfaction (135). One emigrant woman writes, "My ideal of New Zealand life has been spoiled: and although it is undoubtedly the paradise of servants, I am afraid the paradise for governesses has yet to be discovered" (Monk 41). Letters like this one exhibit a kind of authority and initiative in putting to rest those fantasies of "Elsewhere" that would have it accommodate an infinite variety of Others. Baines documents the popular appeal of emigrant letters as sources of information important to would-be emigrants and supports the claims of the emigration societies concerning the practical usefulness of the letters (37).[17] However, Edward Said offers a necessary broader critical perspective when he notes that in the imperial context, as in the case of the imperial archive, "experience and testimony [were] converted from a purely personal document into the enabling codes of Orientalism science," thus becoming a formalized body of acquired and appropriated knowledge (*Orientalism* 157). Considering the status of personal observation, experience and testimony in the context of the imperial project casts suspicion on claims that emigrant letters were simply immediately "useful" by positing that they were put to characteristic imperial uses.

Unlike the correspondence of emigrant women, letters written by established colonists prove more useful in that they project visions of a different future for the emigrant women. Such letters offer a reenvisioning of emigrant women's lives as subordinate English subjects within the colonial context. In doing so, they also note the differences between women "imported" from England as a labor force and established women colonists. Some such explanations indicate that new positions were created to make full use of the contributions that emigrant women could make to the colonial experience:

> The colonial girl is rarely a lady-help: she is either a servant proper, or else she earns her living at a trade or in the teaching profession. The lady-help is only possible in well-established countries, where class distinctions are

a reality in the colonies, where society is in a delightful state of topsy-turveydom, and a landed aristocracy unknown. But having been accepted as a factor in the labour world, she is becoming as popular as she is in England, and every year sees a larger number of refined, educated independent women emigrating to the lands beyond the ocean. ("What Women May Do")

This correspondence indicates that the colonists looked favorably upon the emigration of refined and educated women on a cultural if not a material level (since emigrants' abilities to adapt and to find suitable places in society were questioned), as long as the emigrants accepted an assigned function in the colonies and recognized that it was distinct from what they might have expected in England. There is also a suggestion that colonists sought to capitalize on the emigrant women's dilemmas and falls in status and sought to utilize them as an acculturating influence. This was true to such an extent that special positions—namely as lady-helps—were created specifically for them. One emigrant woman writes from Sydney, Australia, in 1865 that although she does not look forward to "mak[ing] acquaintance with a new class of people—'the nouveaux riches'" [sic] she "may now consider [herself] 'colonized' so it will be only viewing a new phase of life" (quoted in Clarke 87). Such resolution and acceptance of their circumstances on the part of emigrant women suggests more that they were ready for any change than that they embraced change. For the most part, however, the answers to the question of how emigrant women perceived themselves in relation to England may lie outside of those women themselves, since one of the main functions of their emigration was to satisfy the persistent complaint among Victorians on the lack of "reliable" and useful information about the colonies. Furthermore, emigrant women's role is complicated by the pivotal role played by gender in the emigration rhetoric.

The relationship between women and the personal (as opposed to the category of the *national*) was inscribed from without first. Most significantly, this relationship was forged by the emigration societies themselves. Accounts suggest that the societies first guaranteed the women's private status and then sought to capitalize on it. Personal references were one means by which the candidate's elusive "character" could be vouched: "The servant will be carefully selected in England according to the Rules of the Association, her references being taken up for her service capacity, her moral character, and physical capability. A most careful scrutiny is exercised as to the reliability of the testimonials" (South African Sub-Committee). Equating the "moral character" of the potential emigrant servant to her physical well-being and her level of practical experience best sums up the significance attached by the emigration societies to the "character" of the women it worked to expatriate. Emigration societies like the South Africa Committee had very clear and strict moral requirements for women; the requirements were concerned mainly with the their souls, their characters, and their inner selves before tentatively touching on their abilities as workers. In conjunction with the practical, labor-specific requirements, which were informed by the stated needs of the established colonists, the qualifications for female emigration called for women whose attributes were so widely diverse that they probably did not exist in Victorian England or at least constituted a negligible minority among women wishing to emigrate.

As I elaborate later, the trajectory of the emigrant women as spectacle and as commodity is far reaching. The "safety" or assurance of that commodity's value is fixed as inconsequential and culturally inoperative, a point made most rigorously in narratives about women out of context. Repeated allusions to the vulnerability of such commodities makes reference to the collapsing of sexual codes and class divisions. Notions of shipboard privacy may have been intended mainly for the safety and security of the emigrant women themselves, since they had already, as a class, come under considerable scrutiny and ridicule by the public, as Oliphant argued. Testimonials from emigrant women themselves suggest that in addition to sparing the emigration societies embarrassment, private introductions also assured their safety abroad. In a letter published in *Gentlewoman* (1893), an emigrant woman laments, "if it had not been for the people I had introductions to I should have found myself homeless with a fortnight's salary in my pocket."[18] It would seem, then, that the privatization of the assisted emigration process was not rooted in the ideology of domesticity but is more likely an instance of the intersection of specific material circumstances with practical dangers. Both at home and abroad, the emigrating women are envisioned as being "surrounded by the most overpowering and insidious temptations," temptations that remain unnamed because they were so sinister but that have moral undertones (Greg 1862, 436).

These dangers were so prevalent as to mobilize the assisters to secure the women's safety by providing them with chaperones and information as well as warnings.

An important function of the emigration societies was to see that the women actually reached their destinations safely. The perceived danger was not only in the colonies or on board the emigrant ship, but within England as well. Hence the Travellers Aid Society (TAS), whose aim was to "strain every nerve to keep their sisters out of danger" and thus "do what they can to help secure the whole standard of womanhood," issued thousands of handbills to train conductors and travel officials (72). In these leaflets the TAS cites instances of very young girls who set out to find employment and who are endangered by those who would want to corrupt them morally. Conductors are asked to question young women who travel alone, and to offer them help with accommodations and information. Ultimately, they are to alert a TAS worker, who would come to the young woman's rescue. When young women "willfully go into danger," the conductors are asked to "befriend and persuade" them to see the local TAS worker (Travellers Aid Society Report, 68). In facilitating emigrant women's transition between England and the colonies, the assisters take on the role of surrogate guardians.

It becomes increasingly obvious, as we consider this extensive preoccupation with emigrant women's safety and the dangers that threaten it, that in addition to England no longer being a suitable space for women's existence, there was no safe space for them *between* England and the colonies, in the most practical terms. Additionally, where moral temptation and corruption were the perceived threats, the emigrant women as exports were not likely to be maintained as "pure" or as moral emblems of England's "best, brightest . . . purest," as Adelaide Ross described them (317), since the very act and process of transportation from one context to another was likely to cause them irreparable damage. Conceptually, then, the emigration process itself was likely to render these women "changed," socially and culturally, during the voyage from "Here" to "Elsewhere." Elusive references to dangers away from home are in accord with gender prescriptions that render women a precious commodity symbolic of purity, in danger of corruption. Colonial and domestic dangers are imagined quite vividly yet are alluded to obliquely and most discreetly as distinct from those girls "who . . . willfully [go] into danger" (ibid., 31). Women's emigration can be said to represent an absence or a lack, a gap in the emigration and colonial rhetoric that necessitates an examination of its contexts, just as "Elsewhere" gains definition in relation to the imperial problems it masks. The incriminating perception of problematic women by the public— their public identity and physical vulnerability, in conjunction with their subordinate status in a culture that did not value or know how to accommodate gender paradoxes—would account for why so many women found themselves outside England. Despite their very different constitutions, "Elsewhere" and emigrant or "redundant" women share a common symbolic function in the Victorian cultural economy, one that is characterized by an overproduction of con- flicting meanings comprising their cultural significance. In "Queen Victoria, Empire, and Excess," Adrienne Auslander Munich notes ex- cessive representations of Victoria as a ruler and suggests that this ex- cessiveness serves to mask the ideological incompatibility of the roles of wife, mother, and ruler in the cultural imagination: "To counter- act the lack that is signified by no linguistic marker, the age responds with superfluity, or excess of representation, as if cultural production were filling the gap left by a missing term, a concept, a figure" (266). Such excess is represented in overt efforts to promote national fer- vor, not only by the Great Exhibition of 1851, but also by the 1887 and 1897 Queen's Jubilees and the mass-produced images of the queen as triumphant head of the empire. Hence, such grand occa- sions have been described as "gigantic advertisements for the new Empire," highlighting the fact that "two generations of material progress and commercial expansion were now suitably summarized in these romantic pageants" (Thompson 172).

It becomes increasingly apparent as we examine women's emi- gration patterns and rhetoric that women's emigration measures were effected not only in response to real social needs, since the issue is complicated by emigration's objectives, which failed to per- tain to most culturally eligible women. If the main justification for assisted emigration was that these women would be better off in the colonies, women's *effective* colonization is based on an imperial fan- tasy that Victorian literary texts invariably serve to perpetuate. How- ever, this was the case only conditionally for women emigrants, who often struggled in crossing class lines to join the ranks of the servant or the working classes. In several instances, historical accounts sug- gest that they become indentured servants, insofar as they were ob- ligated to work for periods of time to repay the cost of their passage.

While this change in class status was an improvement over their previous status as "redundant women," they might have managed likewise in England, where the service industry experienced a growth
late in the century, at approximately the time women's emigration
reached its peak.[19] Although Hobsbawm argues that, materially, it
was not possible for unmarried women to remain dependent on
their families and therefore both female independence and emigration can be seen as inevitable (*Age of Empire* 202), this material cause
need not preclude considerations of ideology's instrumentality in the
coercion effected through much of the female emigration propaganda. That is, although female emigration may have been materially
and economically inevitable, the argument still had to be made for
exporting women, and possibilities at home were forfeited for more
imaginative ones abroad. Hence, the population figures alone do not
suffice to explain the persistent efforts and propaganda for female
emigration during the period, because emigration also served to
solve the problem presented by the ideological division of labor on
the basis of gender. More broadly, women's emigration was a response to the economic conditions and trade practices that ultimately situated England's wealth and finances in that "Elsewhere."[20]

On a more personal level, women's decision to leave England for
the colonies and dominions was contingent on their ability to envi-
sion themselves existing outside the nation, and under very different
circumstances. The women who left for explicitly imperialist reasons
(that is, for the express purpose of serving the empire rather than
their own individual needs) were situated very differently from the
emigrant women, within England, outside it, and in relation to it
from abroad. Historian Pat Barr's classic study of their placement in
the colonies is instructive in suggesting that a different aspect of
England as a nation was exported with the introduction of the memsahib. Margaret Strobel concurs that the memsahib helped enact
"elaborate social rituals [which] maintained the social distance between Europeans and indigenous peoples and reinforced social hierarchy" (9). While they were clearly utilized as vehicles for the
empire's exportation of "culture," unlike the emigrant women, the
memsahibs—or, to use Strobel's term, the "incorporated wives"—
left "home" only to find it awkwardly reconstructed for their benefit in the colonies, as evidenced by the physical appearances of places
they occupied: "In the rows of mansions at Chowringhee, Calcutta's
richest quarter, no expense was spared to re-create for them the am-

biance of luxurious western-style comfort" (12). Given these details, it is puzzling that emigration assisters should use the terms "colonization" and "emigration" interchangeably. In terms of their self-conceptions and their social status abroad, both the memsahib and the colonist women had a claim to cultural authority that emigrant women did not. Examples of the particular kind of cultural positioning and authority enjoyed by the memsahib are offered in letters that best illustrate the relative mobility and leverage granted to the married colonial woman but not her single and disenfranchised counterpart.

In her *Letters from India,* the memsahib Lady Wilson suggests that the colonialist woman had a concrete place in cross-cultural economic exchanges, in two ways: First, she was used as a bargaining chip and as a marker for the power struggle between the colonizers and the colonized. In that exchange, woman signifies the extent to which the colonizer engages in a trust polemic with the colonized and also the politics of gender are put to use in communicating the terms of this relationship. The male colonists' "argument is that until an Indian gentleman will allow them to meet his wife, they will not allow him to meet an English lady" (34). A symbolic social incident is cited by Lady Wilson, in which an "Indian gentleman" assumes the cultural prerogative of denying colonists access to his women; the colonist retaliates in kind by withholding from their interactions the symbolic presence of the British lady. In this example, woman is used as a means of tipping the scales, culturally and symbolically; the British female colonist serves a significant role in the antagonistic relationship between colonizer and colonized, and becomes an emblem of power and its negotiation. Second, the female colonist sees herself as having a certain authority and agency over the colonized and a cultural-political agenda of her own. Lady Wilson comments, "Jim takes me with him when he visits the dispensaries in the towns, or examines the boys in the schools. Our greatest ambition is to establish a school for girls, as well as an Indian woman doctor in each of the four towns before we leave the district" (35). These two instances illustrate the complicity between gender prescriptions and imperialist objectives, as much in the "our" and "we" that she pronounces with confidence, as in the colonizer's appropriation of the Indian custom of sheltering wives from public exposure.

Lady Wilson's physical presence in this context endorses her symbolic significance from a distance: In India, she is a tangible object of cultural meaning and value, the source of an immediate confrontation between the two cultures in conflict. By virtue of her high social visibility, the memsahib becomes an emblem of that confrontation and of British prowess, as Barr's depiction illustrates: "the constant burden of complaint [for the memsahib was] the numbers of strangers she had to entertain, while those whose company she most desired were either thousands of miles away or surrounded, as she was, by the undesired" (125). In herself, however, and in terms of her gender subjectivity, the memsahib continued to exist as symbol of excess, a signifier of cultural value out of context. Like emigrant women, she linked colonial confrontations with absence or lack. The memsahib's cultural substance, then, consists of abundance, excessiveness, and utility. Contrary to analyses that polarize the memsahib from the working-class colonial, and much as the emigration societies sought to emphasize the women's class differences, this example of the memsahib's cultural and transcultural significance can be utilized as a model for conceptualizing the emigrant women's *practical* significance in the context of the colonies in contrast to their problematic ideological status within England.

This issue is deliberated by critic Jenny Sharpe, who examines, in her chapter entitled "The Rise of the Memsahib in an Age of Empire," the ways in which fiction of the Indian Mutiny enhances anticolonial insurgency latent in historical accounts of those events. Interesting as is this analysis of the English woman's role in imperialist and colonialist discourse in general, I want to concentrate on Sharpe's formulations on the memsahib's relation to domestic ideology as exported to India; that is, the transportation or exportation of Victorian domestic ideology to the colonies to accompany the transplanted women. Sharpe considers how the authorized colonial English woman, the memsahib, reconciles her liberated goals with the imperialist initiative and how the English woman's contested identity becomes aligned with colonialist goals. In an example from Flora Annie Steele's novel, *On the Face of Waters,* Sharpe looks at the ways a New Woman is pitted against racial and cultural conflict only to come out of it a relative victor in terms of gender, albeit at the very high cost of the Indian woman's cultural identity. The memsahib can challenge the normative domestic ideology constraints that bind her in an unpleasant and overly restrictive place abroad, but she must do so by upholding a level of oppressive racial and intercultural relations that compromises her identification with Indian women and distorts her understanding of the latter's subjectivity. Sharpe's view of the relationship between gender and race, and its implications for thinking about Victorian women's fluctuating position in relation to imperial power, is most astute: "The contradictions to white femininity are more evident in a colonial context where the middle-class English woman, oscillating between a dominant position of race and a subordinate one of gender, has a restricted access to colonial authority" (12). This observation emphasizes the relative inauthority granted to unmarried women especially, so that she is twice subordinated to the gender and race status afforded married colonial women. Hence, Sharpe's point concerning the memsahib's relation to the established order of gender and racial relations is important for thinking about emigrant women, but not directly or positively so. It helps us think about the dynamic embodied in the single emigrant woman, specifically insofar as she lacks a direct relationship to the domestic ideology ideal, as did affluent middle-class and married women. To use a term recently elucidated by Margaret Strobel, single women differ considerably from married women in the colonies and abroad in general mainly because they cannot be said to be "incorporated" in any sense of the word: not in terms of gender, class, or society, but also not in terms of the symbolic or meaningful status of women out of England and in the colonial context.

Another important point concerning single women in the colonial context is that "Anglo-Indian women were not permitted the same liberties as their English sisters who came over as social reformers" (Sharpe 95). Specifically in their difference from the memsahibs, the social reformers parallel the unmarried women in question, in the sense that they too are found in the colonial context outside of the boundaries of the home and beyond the strict mandates of the ideology of domesticity. But they were still more "authorized" as the nation's cultural agents than were unmarried women emigrants. In one example of a more progressive organization, the Ladies' Association for the Promotion of Female Education Among the Heathen the single women asked to fulfill the missions of the organization are instruments of the memsahibs, much as the former are agents for the nation-state:

> even the Indian missions that had previously discouraged single women
> from joining began to recruit women missionaries for educating secluded

> upper-caste/class zenana women. The infrastructure established during the
> post-Mutiny period made India safe for single women. Missionary work
> now had a greater appeal for British women, who considered teaching
> zenana women more prestigious than working with poor and low-caste
> native converts (which missionary wives continued to do as before). The
> unmarried, middle-class women who were hired as governesses, zenana,
> and missionary school teachers generally found the higher wages and pro-
> fessional status overseas preferable to employment in England. (Sharpe
> 94–95)

It appears that unmarried missionary women worked in the service
not of the empire or the nation per se, but of the memsahibs who
had a limited sphere of agency and activity, and also of themselves,
in securing more status and higher wages than they could back
home. Their motivation for filling this "vacancy" in missionary
work, that of working most closely with native women, was not an
extension so much of the colonial agenda, although it did function
as such ultimately, but in furthering their own individual and personal aims. Missionary work, for unmarried women, was first and
foremost labor, and only second an ideological or propagandistic
tool for satisfying the goals and ends of the empire. This detail ac-
centuates once again the very pivotal differences between the memsahibs and unmarried women in relation to the nation and regarding
their cultural and social (indeed, their gendered) mission in the
colonies.

It is useful to see how in an analysis that concentrates on one
central historical event, the Indian Mutiny of 1857, and with a population with fairly assured status, negotiations of status and gender
identity implicate racial inequity and imperialist initiatives. What is
important is that these kinds of negotiations needed to happen at all
and that gender liberation always implicates race relations. This is the
case with single women in the colonies not so much in terms of
whether they were "racist" or pro-empire but in how and where
they fit with the whole scheme of colonization in the interests of the
empire as opposed to the interests of their own survival. As Sharpe
illustrates, the domestic ideology ideal is invested with a great degree
of national importance:

> The stereotype of the memsahib is not simply a false representation of real
> women but also a sign of the domestic lives they lived. The Anglo-Indian
> version of the domestic ideal resembles its English counterpart inasmuch

as the restriction of middle-class women to the home is the sign of national virtue and moral superiority. But it is also different in the sense that the domestic sphere is a space of racial purity that the colonial housewife guards against contamination from the outside. (92)

And, she continues, "the 'innocent space' of the home ceases to be innocent once racial segregation is considered part of domestic work" (92). In this sense, the domestic sphere serves no greater or lesser function in the colonial context than it does in the domestic one: All that is contained within it is sacred and ultra-valuable, all that is excluded from it circumspect and problematic. Given their endemic symbolic importance, what might it mean that a large number of women, once protected under the auspices of middle-class gentility, were now on the fringes, the periphery of that nationally guarded space? Who are the women who are made to stand outside the invaluable space of the national, cultural, and social ideal, the home of one's own, the space to which one belongs and which one invests with meaning and importance? Like the working-class women, unmarried middle-class emigrant women had a choice in either becoming indirectly "domesticated" as servants or hiring themselves "out" of that sphere by taking on public employment. Thus, they had some limited access to domesticity.

The exploration of such questions suggests that women were put to several imperial uses, and that they were, in fact, useful to the empire in practical ways. Furthermore, the "other places" to which "superfluous women" were sent are significant as markers of the intersection between cultural definition and its exclusionist counterpart, cultural nonexistence. Feminized, the colonies are represented as places that are specifically not-England and yet perpetually submissive and receptive. They are also typically defined by Victorian culture and politics in relation to British national culture and the empire's activities at home and abroad. Therefore, the characterization that emerges of the colonies is one that undergoes persistent revision and proves conducive to a series of appropriations. I turn to this matter in the next chapter.

Figure 2.1: Visions of Colonial Abundance. Courtesy of the Prints and Photographs Division, Library of Congress.

2

PREPARATIONS FOR TRAVEL

&

Colonial Exports for Ideal Destinations

So great is the scarcity of women's labour that the demand is practically without limit, and a yearly emigration of some thousand women is needed to supply the deficiency. Good Servants are scarce everywhere, and will of course command the highest wages; but even the untrained girl, who in England has no chance of obtaining any but the roughest places, and receiving no training whatever, is welcomed, if of blameless character, by the Canadian mistress, has good wages given her, and is placed in a position permanently to improve her own prospects.

—Advertisement, British Women's Emigration Society,
"Proposed Emigration of Young Women to Canada"

This chapter explores the paradox of matching up to very problematic materiality of Victorian women the ambiguous identity of the colonies and the projection of both as analogous, compatible concrete entities. Both women and the colonies figure as parallel entities of "relative value" in Victorian discourse. Both are cultural commodities whose value lies not in their materiality but in their potential for effective trade or exchange between material contexts, between the nation and the colonies. The colonies and emigrant women acquire a symbolic and hegemonic significance from midcentury on; they are commodified in the search for an appropriate authenticator of the national and imperial Victorian identity. An examination of women as colonial exports and of the constructed identity of the colonies reveals an interdependence between the two. Women come to serve as indicators of how the colonies and the nation are constituted in the Victorian imagination in terms that both use and challenge normative gender ideologies.

Women's emigration and their relation to the imperialist project point back to Victorian gender ideologies that persistently place women within the home. They also point to colonialism's more general problematic relationship to gender. As chapter 1 proposes, women's value is recognized as being contingent on the interests of the dominant culture and gains importance as such in the emigration discourse. Proponents of women's emigration were astute in emphasizing the degree to which women are dependent on the activities of men, thus acknowledging the influence of the Victorian imperial context. This chapter expands upon this contingent cultural valuation of women and the concept of women's having been put to "male uses." Given my thesis that women's emigration served several cultural functions and was instituted in response to compelling ideological and material needs on the home front, its significance takes on a broader meaning. Mrs. Grey's observation that "any use [women's] lives were to themselves was evidently not thought of" also extends to women's projected place in the colonies (9). The "male uses" to which emigrant women are compulsively put are also patriarchal and colonial "uses," since women were to have a prescribed mission and function there; in the colonies, as at home, what was asked of them was "self-denial." Similarities and differences in the male and female emigration process, especially in the arguments for families emigrating and the importance of women's accompanying their men abroad to make transition easier, are evidenced in the literature. As an Australian government-sponsored pamphlet maintains, "A man in a new land needs his family to cheer him. A woman's duty is not to fear for herself, but to try to make a home happy anywhere. Her self-denial may save a man from despair or drink, and children from poverty and care."[1]

The imposed dichotomy between woman's own best interests and her required servitude is illustrated in dominant discourse characterizing England as Mother in the most intimate and personal terms and calling for women's service to both the "Mother country," the "vigorous . . . fatherland," and "those great daughter nations," the colonies and dominions. Such discourses sometimes lament the loss of the United States—"our most vigorous offspring"—as a colony (54).[2] Women also are seen as potentially capable of acculturating and civilizing the spaces of the colonies, where "vast natural wealth [lies] unused" and where their contributions will be to areas other than "mere material prosperity."[3] Women were viewed as being potentially capable of assisting in the imperial project, then, and were asked to do so in a most predictable manner, within the institutions of the family and marriage within the ideology of domesticity. The ability of women to assist in the colonization process is viewed as contingent on their participation in those institutional functions and on their respect for boundaries. At the same time that imperial rhetoric maintained woman's cherished place in these social and ideological systems through cultural valuations of female passivity and motherhood, unmarried women were encouraged to seek their fortunes or at least to escape misery in little-known lands—and unaccompanied at that, although often guarded by emigration assisters. These two movements, the one toward coerced domestication, the other toward necessitated exile, mark the important disjuncture in Victorian national and gender ideologies, so that the emigration of unmarried women highlights the paradox lying in between rhetoric and practice. In the appropriative processes of the imperialist project, women's function is both interesting and complex, especially as the nation consistently imposed censure and prescriptions on both women and the colonies.[4]

Working to chart the subject-positioning of the emigrant spinster in her relation to the nation and to the colonies, we must concern ourselves with the "dominating frameworks" that both "contain and represent" the imperial effort (Said, *Orientalism* 40). In terms of its gender prescriptions in relation to the imperial project, the Victorian period encapsulates problems which ask that we explore the boundaries between England and its corollaries. Toward this end, we must examine the spaces that are "not-England" but extensions of England and of Victorian culture. The symbolism of the space between England and the colonies is manifested in its preoccupation with the process, function, and ensuing implications of emigration and in the ideological process of England's subsuming and encompassing non-English lands, peoples, and cultures. In contemporary arguments, both emigration and imperialism are represented as serving England, ensuring its cultural and economic well-being. The class of people generally recommended for emigration is seen as having a distinct purpose and place in the imperial project: For every English subject there is a function in the "Elsewhere" of the colonies but also a parallel socioeconomic problem that his or her removal would remedy at home. However, as Hobsbawm holds, such justifications for emigration may have held more value as propaganda than as practical solutions, since "there is no good evidence that colonial conquest as such had much bearing on the employment or real incomes of most workers in the metropolitan countries" (*Industry and Empire* 69).

Discrepancies between rhetoric and material practicability like this highlight the disjunction between the material and the ideological import of colonialism and emigration. Such a disjunction is illustrated in an 1886 article entitled "The Colonial and Indian Exhibition," in which the author's reassurances concerning the vast economic imperial contributions of the colonies contextually conflict with descriptions of the colonies' desires toward national independence, made possible by their economic growth. The colonies are seen as "growing with the force and rapidity of youthful giants" in some instances; nevertheless, much of the discourse recommends that such material progress be kept under imperial control. Hence, an article on the display of colonial material goods is transformed into a political treatise concerning colonial administration and British domestic disputes ("The Colonial and Indian Exhibition," 50–51). Such preoccupations concerning the relation of nationalism to exploitative materialism bespeak more of the national and domestic political condition of the "mother" country than of its administered relations with the colonies and their subjects. As Robert Colls and Philip Dodd also argue, the importance of colonial nationalism "lay not in any appraisal of geopolitical affairs . . . but in the only way Empire really mattered to Britain—at home, in the political culture" (49).[5] Inasmuch as Victorian imperialism may be said to concern mainly the mother nation's preoccupation with itself, Colls and Dodd are right to emphasize that the main impact of the imperial project was that it "relocated the relationships between State and people" (49). Chapter 3 works to illustrate this point. To the extent that women's emigration advocacy resituates women's relation to the nation, their exportation is significant to England not only because the women themselves are an issue but because they constitute a significantly problematic segment of the English nation and conceptions of English nationality. Their removal to the colonies necessarily implicates the cultural fissures they exposed within the Victorian social context.

The processes through which women are assigned a value in Victorian domestic culture and in relation to the imperialist project are complicated by the fact that Victorian women are not a problem only in the domestic culture; they also are not entirely desirable as colonial exports. As W. W. Carrothers and as James Hammerton have documented, middle-class women posed serious conflicts in the emigration rhetoric, conflicts that had not been created in references to respectable and consequential British subjects. In one instance, both historians note the difficulty that the emigration societies encountered in promoting the transport of educated women. Amid repeated references to the "difficulty" of helping middle-class women to emigrate, Carrothers notes in his retrospective evaluation that "the voluntary emigration of women can scarcely be said to have been an unqualified success" because of "the unsuitability of many of those migrating" (274).[6] It is interesting that women were deemed unsuitable for emigration on many grounds. Mainly, they were viewed as having poor preparation as colonial workers thanks to their limited work opportunities at home, a technical difficulty compounded by the fact that their sex also posed conceptual and moral problems for colonists.

Emigrant women were mainly hired as domestics in the colonies. Their emigration provided the colonies with thousands of domestic workers, and thus it served England's more practical colonial needs and interests. Women who wanted to emigrate to gain economic independence were forced to make the great transition into a working-class social identity. This was not such a difficult proposition since the change in identity would be effected out of context. But given the changes she embraced, the "genteel" emigrant woman challenges categories of class and gender and class-based gender prescriptions, such as the refinement that would preclude her performing domestic chores. Middle-class emigrant women occupy a place in between such categorical distinctions, as Isa Craig illustrates in her plea on their behalf: "Why should not a class of women, superior even to those so occupied [as needlewomen on estates] in England, work for their living in this way in the pleasant homesteads in New Wales and New Zealand? . . . Such a life . . . must be preferable to the lonely care-worn life with its incessant toil and inadequate payment in an over-labour-stocked market like this" (237). Likewise, attempts to create the appropriate middle-class female emigrant required her to become a servant since, as Craig put it repeatedly in 1859, the state of affairs regarding female emigration pertained most directly to issues of class and class identity. She noted, "*There is no free and no assisted passage to any colony, for any description of woman except household servants"* (235). This disparity highlights the significance of middle-class female emigration, in that its process changed drastically when a class other than the working class was being transported. This new class factor reverberated in the new aims of philanthropy and in the new class identity of the female emigrant. Middle-class female emigration became an elaborate industry, in the technical sense of the term. Emigration societies worked to produce the appropriate middle-class female emigrant by establishing the modes of her production. As mentioned earlier, one source of this process was the training house, where distressed middle-class women were prepared for colonial life and domestic servitude. Such measures institutionalized most formally the less codified reeducation of emigrant spinsters in their new colonial identities and roles. In no uncertain terms, the women were informed of the skills and abilities they had to acquire and the personal changes they had to undergo.

As chapter 1 suggests, many precautions were taken to morally screen women who wished to emigrate, suggesting a concern over the quality of "exports" to the colonies. Also, the women's ability to adjust to new circumstances was a predominant worry. Female emigrants' "unsuitability" is an even more complex proposition, since it makes reference to the projected and actual needs of the colonies and dominions. The concept of single and middle-class women's "unsuitability" also makes reference to Victorian culture's inability to incorporate successfully into its hegemony a symbolically valuable cultural commodity: woman. In the same self-reflexive gestures of the imperial interest mentioned earlier, woman's "suitability" for colonial emigration calls into question the extent of her "suitability" in any context that is seen to be mutable, including her place within England. That Victorian England chose nonetheless to rid itself of its problematic women by way of the established emigration methods and justifications, and that it encountered considerable difficulties in this process, reveals something of its own internal contradictions with respect to the domestic gender politics and to its imperial agenda.

THE COLONIES

The issues subsumed by middle-class women's emigration advocacy, then, consist of simultaneous and conflicting objectives: the desire, on the part of England, to rid itself of its "superfluous" or excessively problematic women; its desire to supply the colonies and dominions with an acculturation they were not deemed capable of producing for themselves; and a simultaneous reluctance to have women serve that function, a reluctance informed by Victorian gender prescriptions. These issues also concern the colonies' and dominions' assertions of their own constructed cultural and material identities and distinctly detached national characters that could not be adequately prescribed from across the oceans and from beyond their cultural boundaries. In these instances, the "daughter nations"—the dominions—assert an independence from the empire that permeates colonial rhetoric and is seen as problematic. Because of such acts of autonomy, a distinction is imposed between the available women wishing to emigrate and the stated preferences of the colonies.

If the colonies' and dominions' stated needs and preferences were to determine the character of the female emigrant, at least in part, they were not at all comfortable with dispossessed, middle-class unmarried women embarking on their shores. The dominions saw ample use for working-class female emigrants but did not know what to do with "genteel spinsters" who might not know their places, even if such existed for them abroad. As an advice columnist wrote, "I cannot think 'Energy' would do well to emigrate, seeing that her abilities, as she expressly states, are 'more intellectual than domestic.' These are precisely the gifts that are best utilized in the complex life of the old world" ("Answers"). In turn, middle-class unmarried women were far too "complex" to be fitted easily into the social structures of the colonies and dominions. If women were "unsuitable" for emigration, then, they were so in a number of interesting ways, among them in their relationship to culture and refinement. While they were ideologically suitable for inculcating the colonies with both, seemingly the message could be appreciated better if it were delivered by a different messenger. Unmarried middle-class emigrant women were deemed unsuitable by the dominions not only in practical terms as problematic subjects that they could not be assimilated easily; they were also undesirable as emblems of the empire and as signifiers of the British imperial industry.

The problematic positioning of the emigrant middle-class unmarried woman as a cultural and national commodity necessitated an actuation of the existing dynamics between the colonies and England, a

receptivity on the part of the former that would complement the negotiation of middle-class English women's status as domestic "undesirables." In justifying depositing its female undesirables (who were
also at once its cherished domestic symbols) at the doorstep of the
colonies, England would need to negotiate a series of paradoxes.
Hence, we see in the emigration rhetoric a forced reciprocity between
the colonies and England, an interdependence prescribed from without the colonies themselves—a definition of colonial practical conditions and cultural assessments established by Victorian England, one
that concerns questions of femininity and the value of gender ideology. Prominent female emigration activist Maria Rye writes on
middle-class women's undesirability by the colonies in 1861: "[T]he
only method by which this difficulty can be overcome must be by securing the co-operation of the colonists, and by convincing the heads
of the different governments that *the introduction of such as class of
women will not only be a relief to England, but an actual benefit to the
colonies themselves—an alleviation of morals being the inevitable result* of the
mere presence in the colony of a number of high class women" (9).

The equation established in this argument entails the effective
colonization of women as a class-specific process that would, once
the women were socialized and stratified into the existing and projected structures of the colonies, yield an intrinsically moral change
in both. The nearly extinct and paradoxical figure of totally domesticated virtuous Victorian womanhood is employed in a different
context. Woman's presumed superior morality would be rendered
useful once again, and the colonies themselves would be "moral-
ized" by her influence, thus supplementing their singular "want"
that administrative means alone could not successfully ameliorate.
However, this formula requires a significant amount of coercion for
its success, since established colonists themselves provide little indication that morality was, in fact, wanted, despite numerous accounts
from new and socially refined emigrants that the colonies are undesirable, morally as well as socially. In fact, the opposite seems most
likely. As noted in chapter 1, letters from both female emigrants and
established colonists suggest that the women's moral safety abroad
could not be ensured and that several emigrant women either fell
out of sight or were otherwise "lost" after arrival in the colonies.[7]
The metaphor of being "absorbed" backfires as a double-edged
metaphor, rendering the colonies a kind of black-hole nonspace
where geography cannot be charted. Furthermore, the suggestion of

appropriately fitting middle-class spinsters into the colonies and thus restoring them to an earlier and better social status serves to render the colonies a kind of magical non-place, a territory that defies categorization. Therefore, emigrant women's "place" in the colonies could not be assured from a distance, since that geographic destination was not yet effectively incorporated into the Victorian imaginary. In short, it was still immaterial, purely a product of the ideology of imperialism.

Defining the "needs" of the colonies from without so as to accommodate the excessively fragmented status of the middle-class Victorian spinster establishes her function in and benefit to the colonies must be a "cultural" one, since the category of "culture" is at once rigid and subject to ongoing revision in the colonial context. The above passage from Maria Rye illustrates most clearly the two-pronged approach of the female emigration assisters and their accommodation of the problem of the colonists' resisting outside interference. If colonists themselves could be convinced of their need for "higher-class" women, the problem of women's "redundancy" would be taken care of, as would be the female emigrant's reception and cultural placement in the colonies. There is an assured efficacy to this process, apparently, since in Rye's argument, women emigrants need merely to *exist* in the colonies in order to be beneficial to them, an argument that eliminates more problematic details of the women's actual function in the new setting. Ideally, according to Rye's proposal, colonists would welcome the middle-class women into their midst and unconditionally accept the beneficence of such a gesture of inclusiveness. The formula that would make this exchange possible relies quite extensively on the tenuous and contingent identity of the colonies, constituted both in terms of an excessiveness and ambivalence of their materiality and according to their symbolic usefulness. Homi Bhabha comments on precisely this way of conceptualizing the colonies and "Others," aptly describing it as a "process of ambivalence" that is "central to the stereotype" produced concerning other places and cultures. In this analysis, an ongoing revision of the signification of the colonies would effectively ensure their practicability and their cultural utility, regardless of changes in their material relation to the empire: "*[T]his process of ambivalence, central to the stereotype, . . . gives the colonial stereotype its currency: ensures its repeatability in changing historical and discursive conjectures; informs its strategies of individuation and marginalization; produces the effect of probabilistic truth and predictability which, for the stereotype, must always be in excess of what can be empirically proved or logically construed"* (*Location of Culture* 66). This "ambivalence" or systematic intangibility of stereotypes, and their transhistorical manipulation, illustrates the extent to which the colonies' empirical identities, if not their uses, may in themselves be viewed as excessive, much like the women who were sent to them. Furthermore, this is a deliberate ambivalence. The two main components in the equation of women as imperial exports and the colonies as unconditional, appropriate receptacles have as their foundation the central function of the immaterial and the inconclusive, the "ambivalent" function of the symbolic, signifying excess. Furthermore, Bhabha's chapter on mimicry, much like the one on stereotypes, suggests that while the colonies may be likened to England and fashioned after the national fantasies it creates for itself, the colonies must always, in fact, "be like us," but not "exactly so" (1990, 86). They must approximate the appearance of the empire only enough to suggest the compromising connection between them, to reaffirm their status as extensions of the empire; the discernible differences between the colonies and England always must contain the signs by which they are marked as appropriated spaces, as claimed property.

This relationship is suggested in a pamphlet issued by the Australian Emigration Agency in London, "To Intending Emigrants," which confronts every conceivable reluctance toward emigration. Among the many "difficulties" or obstacles to emigration that the writers attempt to appease is the primary attachment to "old England," countered by the assurance that "Queensland is only England over the water, with English people, customs, and religion. It has fewer rates, but more work; less competition, and greater freedom; cheaper food, and higher wages." To those who are reluctant to be "strangers in a strange land," there is the assurance that "colonists are always kind to newcomers. In one sense, it is quite true that the colonies in question were very English. In Canada, "one characteristic was more singular and striking than all the rest: [T]his was their absolute conservatism, their utter disregard for all change or progress, their cheerful contentment with their ancestors' culture" (Lemon and Pollock 90). In going to Australia or Canada, one went to a place where an ideology of nationalistic excess prevailed, a place where the mother country was more omnipotent than it had ever actually been. Australia also was distinguished by a "social environment of overwhelming

Britishness, rural mystique, nationalism and xenophobic—even racist—attitudes" (ibid., 194). The fierce homogenization among colonists owed much of its force to the systematic eradication of native populations, and so emigrants were also on space that had for the most part been "cleared" of foreign elements.[8] However, the emigrant who is now envisioned as making the decision to leave one England for another must qualify as a pioneer of sorts; he is extolled to "Think seriously, decide promptly, and carry out your resolution boldly" ("To Intending Emigrants").

In conjunction with their tenuous definition as distinct entities, the colonies are asked to serve a number of functions in relation to the needs of the empire and specifically of the emigrant women's facilitators. The colonies are represented as amorphous, as yet unstructured along the lines of class and social utility and position. They are a kind of organic haven, insofar as some argue that the colonies represent an early stage in the social and evolutionary process. As other letters quoted earlier in this study suggest, the colonies undergo various and conflicting characterizations. Because they are used alternately as sources of fantasy fulfillment and as dumping grounds, the possibilities for imagining the colonies are endless: "If we look to the resources of our colonies, to their untold wealth and powers yet to be expanded, the rapid stride they are making towards refinement, and in the elegances of life—surely we may take courage and hope, that there, amidst the many homesteads of our wonderful colonial possessions, some, at least, of our worthy, industrious, poor, young countrywomen may be safely transplanted" (Rye, *Emigration of Educated Women* 14). The gap in the development of the nation is a feminine one. Women may, in the fantasied "natural" course of progress, arrive at the moment when their nation-building skills are required. In such organicist and Darwinian models of cultural development and class formation, the colonies and the women become bound together in an interdependent relation regarding the mother country. In regard to female emigration, the colonies are alternately envisioned as hostile environments or as havens, just as "redundant" women are imagined either as conduits of purity and goodness or as perniciously withholding their goodness and as morally suspect or misdirected. Once again the function of the colonies in relation to the empire is to accept its excesses, specifically those that become problematic at home.[9]

In conceptualizing the colonies as gendered spaces, specifically as underdeveloped female spaces, and as receptacles for subjects and values that England experienced as undesirable or excessively problematic, it may be possible to formulate an understanding of the uses to which "Others" often are put—in this case, both women and the colonies qualify as such Others. By the same token, the colonies are represented as being in an infantile state of development, a place whose identity has not yet been determined, a kind of "nowhere" and "nothing" in reference to class systems and cultural formations. This much also has been observed by David Spurr in *The Rhetoric of Empire: Colonial Discourse in Journalism, Travel Writing, and Imperial Administration,* who notes that the ways colonies are conceptually approached and represented by the imperial powers can be classified as falling into several categories, among them "negation and affirmation" (146). Spurr remarks that the main feature of these ways of perceiving and representing the colonies and Others is the extent to which many of them are mutually exclusive or at least contain some inherent contradictions. Preparing the colonies to receive the women emigrants entails the colonies' "insubstantialization" and "naturalization," their two most prevalent characterizations. Mary Louise Pratt also lists "the systematization of nature" as one of the key strategies in imperializing practices (36). Spurr's main interpretation of the "insubstantialization" of the colonies, which centers on imaginings that render them "exotic," facilitates the "inner exploration of the boundaries of consciousness"; this "insubstantialization" of the colonies also may be viewed as perpetual and in perpetual service to the empire's material interests (146). The main "ambivalence" lies in the simultaneous extension of the empire into the colonies and the elimination of England as an appropriate context in regard to labor and as a market for its own domestic resources. However, the reverse relationship seems to describe more accurately the instrumentality of the colonies in British domestic functionings. Colonial ambivalence is eradicated in this way, as Pratt elaborates: "The systematizing of nature carries this image of accumulation to a totalized extreme, and at the same time models the extractive, transformative character of industrial capitalism" (36).

Such translations of the colonies are significant, specifically as they are asked to extend a practical service to emigrant women. They correspond to the semiotic transformations sustained by the emigrant women, who are themselves multiple and contradictory.

As feminist critic Catherine Clement has observed, culturally women always have embodied contradictions like those exhibited in characterizations of the colonies:

> More than any others, women bizarrely embody . . . anomalies showing the cracks in an overall system. Or rather, women, who are elsewhere bearers of the greatest norm, that of reproduction, embody *also* the anomaly. . . . They are allied with what is regular . . . and allied as well with those natural disturbances . . . which are the epitome of paradox, order and disorder.
>
> Thus women are all decked-out in unrealizable compromises, imaginary transitions, incompatible syntheses. (Cixous and Clement 8)

In similar ways, the colonies always must contradict their very essence. In conjunction with their tenuous definition as distinct entities, they are asked to serve a number of functions in relation to the needs of the Empire and specifically of the emigrant women's facilitators. The occasion of female emigration serves as a conduit for the ongoing quarrel between England and the colonies, one that, as its operative terminology suggests, is predicated on issues of independence and "rebellion." Not only are spinsters undesirable at home, they also are scrutinized and negotiated in the process of transport, since neither the colonies nor England seems to want them. If unmarried Victorian women arguably can be seen as "refuse" rather than as valuable export commodities in their social and historical contexts, they are transformed into apt raw materials for export when they are being marketed for the colonies. According to David Thompson, the colonies' significance lies in the multiplicity of their potential uses: "The colonies came to be valued both as manifestations of national greatness and as sources of raw materials and markets for manufacturers" (203). Their figurative, symbolic uses prevail in the popular discourse attendant to female emigration, masking the second and more practical significance.

There is no doubt that the empire's ability to control the emigrant populations of the colonies was a central national concern, as becomes clear when we examine the imperial and emigration rhetoric. Such concerns and priorities are borne out by imperial practice as well. For example, it took only four years for 3,000 emigrants to be planted in South Africa following the establishment of a colonization society there in 1902 (Paton 94).[10] When it became clear by 1860 that the majority of emigrants were choosing the

United States and not a British colony as their most favored destination, concern arose over the potential losses of national resources—embodied in the British citizen—to another nation, one
with which England was already economically competitive. By 1894
The Standard printed an overt articulation of such concerns, which
accounts for England's "interest" in the emigration process and with
representations in the imperial rhetoric of desirable destinations:

> [O]ur colonies are losing some of the best settlers who leave our shores for
> a fresh start in life. . . . Not only the United States and South America, but
> other parts of the world, have long been vying with each other and with
> our Colonies to attract high-class settlers from our land to theirs, and no
> adequate means are adopted by our government or our Colonies to pre-
> vent it. . . .
>
> [T]he overcrowded condition of our professional and commercial cir-
> cles at home is driving many men and families abroad every month, who
> accept the alluring overtures made from foreign countries, and who are
> lost forever to Britain and to British colonies. (*The Standard*)

In the end, England's "surplus" population is transformed into a most
desirable one in the global context. The material reality, however, is
pressing indeed, and one that is not physically escapable through the
aid of rhetoric alone, although it would prove symbolically negotiable: "Only the nightmare shadow of bankruptcy or debts sometimes lay over their [middle-classes'] lives . . .: the trust in an
unreliable partner, the commercial crisis, the loss of middle-class
comfort, the women-folk reduced to genteel penury, perhaps even
emigration to that dustbin of the unwanted and the unsuccessful, the
colonies" (Hobsbawm, *Industry and Empire* 84).

Conceptualizing the transcultural relationship between England
and the colonies and dominions in this manner is apt not only because
it takes into account the symbolic function of the colonies as a repos-
itory of England's many "excesses" but also because, in the case of unmarried women, the colonies are invested with the power to answer
any domestic predicament. Having the colonies fulfill such a function
is not a simple matter, however, and surfaces as a contentious area in
the emigration and colonial discourse. Articulating the common
politicized dissatisfaction of colonists with England, one Australian advocate of female middle-class emigration illustrates a plaintive appreciation of the relation of the "mother nation" to the colonies:

> The colonists . . . sometimes think that England looks upon her colonies
> as pieces of waste land upon which rubbish may be shot at *ad libitum*. . . .
> [W]e think ourselves old enough and important enough to have our tastes
> and habits consulted. . . . If our good mother will kindly remember this
> and take the trouble to examine into our different requirements, and suit
> her gifts to our wants, instead of rebelling against them we shall accept
> them gratefully and turn them to good account. ("Emigration, Impartially
> Considered" 74)

This observation of the empire's relation to the colonies is something more than a figurative or symbolic concern, since the
colonists also saw the cultural and political ramifications of the
function the colonies were asked to serve. Despite such astute
awarenesses and observations of the power relations between the
colonies and the empire, however, colonial "ambivalence" continues
to find expression in the interests and functions of the colonial
stereotype, much of it produced by established colonists for the
benefit of intended emigrants. The tension between England and
the colonies over who would control the quality and flow of emigrants culminated, as historian Suzann Buckley has observed, in
England's ceasing to support emigration schemes, leaving much of
that work to private societies (20).

Colonial "ambivalence" also finds expression in the interests
and functions of the colonial stereotype, as illustrated in Lady
Wilson's characterization of India. I invoke her again as the voice of
the authorized colonist. The more remarkable feature of Lady Wilson's letters is the extent to which they note and comment upon
the details of the culture over which she assumes superiority. Lady
Wilson poses a crucial question concerning the valuation of difference but does so theoretically, moving from the very concrete to
the abstract: "I wonder," she asks, "if a language is richer or poorer
than others if it possesses a hundred names for one thing, each name
accentuating a slight difference in the object?" (41). Reasserting her
husband's theory that there are practical uses and mandates for such
multiplicity, Lady Wilson rejects that interpretation and entertains
the possibility of others. This gesture would seem to support the assertions of critics who note that female colonial subjects do not
seem to mind multiplicity and ambiguity. Lady Wilson extends her
method of observation to the landscape itself and describes the very

physical setting in figurative terms suggestive of the relationship she wishes to establish between it and herself. In that relationship, as in that of the empire to the colonies, the reciprocity is coerced and the colonies "insubstantiated." Lady Wilson sees the Indian landscape as "so much more becoming to everybody than the crowds in which they are more or less swamped in England. It is as if a picture were to be transferred from its row to an easel, or a lion from its cage to a desert" (104).

This observation, and its reference to England as the *known,* imposes an order about the setting, which allows the observer to maintain an impressionistic distance. It is at this juncture that the observer-subject's cultural positioning contradicts critics' readings of ambiguity as neutrality in imperial women. The observation itself is finally displaced when, more practically, it is followed by the conclusion that, "put any young Briton in a country that has to be governed, and he takes to it all, like a duck to water" (104). Lady Wilson's attraction to the landscape is resolved by an end to her thinking about her new country and by a sharper focus on its culture than either its physical features or its practical politics. Exercising authority over the more familiar matters of "culture" rather than politics, she comments more confidently on the aesthetic features of this foreign and new—to her—place. This immediate acculturation of India serves as the necessary precursor to her exposition on the empire: Having established her place within the imperial symbolic economy, she speaks as its legitimated and authorized subject. Deliberations and fanciful wanderings culminate in a vaguely construed colony and a politicized observer-subject in herself. She no longer suspends judgment, nor is she initiating an alternative understanding of India. Lady Wilson is now fully immersed in her singular identity as authorized English subject, whose exclusive allegiance is with the empire and the imperial project: "[O]ne feels faint traces of the primeval Aryan blood in one's veins, and a strange fascination in some of the odds and ends of philosophic booklets which one comes across. They are such an extraordinary medley of profound speculation and sudden collapses into impossibilities" (160–61). In the case of an observation that is immersed in the subject it investigates, then, Lady Wilson demonstrates the tendency to abstract and to gesticulate toward one's self and one's lineage, which—when pursued to its logical conclusion—represents the colonies as a tabula rasa and the observer as a transported and ethereal being, albeit one that is also well connected to practical reality. In the face of imperial assurance, the colony becomes either insubstantial or chaotic.

The symptomatic manipulation of the symbolic significance of the colonies illustrates the cumulative effects of stereotyping and communal significance of conceived institutions in relation to both the material and the imagined, projected needs of the cultural present. This dynamic encapsulates the answer to attempts to frame the construction of the colonies as an institutionalized and normalized variable upon which is based the imaginary's relation to the material. Moreover, the perpetuation of the colonies in this convenient guise is coerced, since it is not a tangible position for England to maintain in relation to its material subordinates and resources. Several articles that seek to advertise the beneficial aspects of the colonies set up a reciprocal relationship between the two, suggesting that the colonies are opulent precisely in reverse relation to England's insufficiencies: "England has become too small to provide a subsistence for her ever-increasing population, and, therefore, it is necessary that some should leave and establish themselves in other countries where land is to be had at a cheap rate, and *labour* is needed *instead of being a drug in the market, as it now is here*" ("Letter to Emigrants," emphasis added). Much like the emigrant spinster whose cultural significance remains continuously ambivalent and problematic, labor generally is considered a raw material and a resource; it also is seen as one that has outgrown its usefulness in the geographic confines of domestic England. Hence, the insubstantiation of the colonies often is complemented by an exaggerated sense of their lush materiality, their very *real* existence, which is juxtaposed against a negative overabundance in England itself.

Despite the indeterminacy that arises when "redundant" women's presence in the colonies is imagined, and despite the ambiguity of the colonies both as actual places and as symbolic receptacles for these women, Adelaide Ross postulates that sending women to the colonies would adequately address this poorly defined problem: "whether it be to lands not yet Christianized, or to the colonies where *temptations to a material view of life assail the emigrant on every side,* let us send . . . those who, though they may be struggling with the difficulties at home, are yet our best, our brightest, our purest . . ." (317). Such propositions attempt to position women *universally* while maintaining the primacy of their containment in the Victorian domestic ideology. In the final analysis, woman's relation both to the construction of "Elsewhere" *and* to the empire's interests is mediated by her desired albeit forced identification with the nation, the home, the "here" as opposed to the "Elsewhere." Along with her tenuous identification with the nation, these contradictions and double standards work to situate woman within the cultural ideology of the empire and suggest that "the significance of the single woman should be sought not in social statistics but in the space where she had suddenly become defined as a problem—the space of ideology."[11] Indeed, women become emblems for the condition of Victorian society, a culture that needed a variable signifier to qualify its shortcomings and predicaments, and utilized women in that capacity. Women are used as a figurative tool for England's establishing tenuously meaningful relationships with the colonies, intricate relationships not easily effected through administrative means. Therefore, the variable of women's presence or absence is specifically reflected in the Victorian cultural, national, and gender economies. Women's emigration parallels the analogous creation of an alternative space where they might exist more peacefully and comfortably than they were able to in England. Having been rendered "redundant" within capitalist patriarchy, single women were allocated to the colonies. Simultaneously, characterizations of the colonies shift, rendering them spaces better suited for female occupation.

It is instructive to consider how the colonies underwent redefinition in order to stratify and negate their problematic relation to both the nation and the women they were asked to accommodate. The suitability of single women's transportation to the colonies requires an analysis of Victorian social and cultural systems that serve to marginalize the identities of the colonies and dominions and their perception by the English. A redefinition of the colonies is instrumental to their contrived constitution as spaces that would parallel the formulation of women as apt raw material:

> [W]hen a young Society is increasing in size and number, its special characteristics will be more marked. As it grows larger the individuals that compose it tend to become grouped into different classes, each class having its own work to do. Or to reverse the statement, the whole work that has to be done in the community becomes subdivided, and each kind of

work becomes the special function of a group of persons, and ceases to be
the general duty of all. (Hatton 152)

This construction produces specific possibilities of a new colonial
community, a new land, and leaves much room for women to claim
a place for themselves. The imagined organicity of the colonies as
still being in an infantile stage of development also invites outside
mediation and intrusion toward its development to a cultural matu-
rity. Also, since this kind of community is amorphous and thereby
not prescriptive or prohibitive in any way, the promise that "each individual is able to do a little of everything" (152) entails the seemingly natural and inevitable process of the division of labor—the
emergent class system would place middle-class emigrant women in
their appropriate roles within it. In a correspondence that exempli-
fies how the colonies are infantilized so as to facilitate the argument
of their capabilities for growth, Maria Rye applauds a letter from
Mr. Colborne, of Natal, which interestingly resembles travel-tourism
advertisements. In one portion of this letter, Colborne enthusiasti-
cally "describes" the kind of promise the colonies hold of a progress
that is depleted in Victorian material culture: "The colony is very fast
improving in every way; the climate is exceedingly salubrious. I have
no doubt but that people of the class named by you would find it a
very beautiful change, as there is every opportunity of such people
finding comfortable homes and engagements." The colonies are productive imaginative spaces and embody the promise of rapid, effort-
less, and inevitable progress.

Even when the virtues of the colonies are, in fact, imaginable, as
is the case with climate, one's imagination is asked to expand further
to approach unimaginable irreconcilables:—"THE CLIMATE IS
HOT—But it is a healthier heat than other lands. Englishmen work
there all year round. The death rate is not near so bad as here. For
nine months the climate is almost perfect, and that cannot be said for
English weather, with rheumatism and consumptions so common"
("To Intending Emigrants"). Like the women themselves, the
colonies are perpetually reimagined to meet the needs of the present
cultural moment. Other representations, in which the colonies are
precious because they are new and little known, suggest that their
value ultimately may lie in their adaptability and their indeterminacy. As one account has it, "there is no comparison between a 41-
acre farm in an old country and one in a new colony. The former

has all the elements of diminution; every child is a fresh charge; the latter, all the elements of increase; every child is a source of strength" (Herbert 18). While the very material features of the colonies are called forth as an inducement for emigration and argue for their desirability, ultimately their ethereal and mystical qualities make the strongest appeal. Therefore, even though material profit lay at the core of both Victorian emigration and imperialism, this materialism is always fluctuating in its proscribed role in the imperial project. However, what remains constant is that the *core* formula for appropriation and entitlement relies on the production and exchange of commodities; "the new imperialism adopted the idea that there was a direct correlation between commodity production and territorial expansion" (Richards, *The Commodity Culture of Victorian England* 130). It may not matter, in the end, whether the production of commodities occurs within England since Victorian commodification involves the transformation of national subjects into imperial commodities. Abroad, the commodification of imperial possessions could always satisfy imperialist objectives.

WOMEN AND THE NATION

The affinities established between middle-class, unmarried emigrant women and the colonies are suggestive of the socially contrived marriages between Victorian men and women. As an institution, by the 1880s marriage was no longer an effective means of pairing loose ends and ensuring social stratification or obeisance, as New Women were stressing.[12] In keeping with her ambivalent and multifarious function, the unmarried middle-class woman appears also to be the perfect complement of England posing as the locus of the world empire. She is also the ideological and conceptual mate for the requirements of the process of cultural and national expansionism. Making the argument that colonists are preferable to colonizers, one female-emigration advocate repeats this marriage metaphor most explicitly: "marry the land to the frugal labourer, and he will be able, and glad to pay the passage of his wife, and his son's wife" (Sidney 19). In light of Homi Bhabha's contention that the "nation" is compelled to harmonize its discordant features, and if we accept that "the nation emerges as a powerful historical idea in the west[,] an idea whose cultural compulsion lies in the impossible unity of the nation as symbolic force," the construction of the unmarried woman as the keeper of morality and as the nation's self-negating and sacrificing "sister" can be seen as an important ingredient in that forced and compulsive harmonization (*Nation and Narration,* 1). The unmarried emigrant woman is an undesirable cultural impediment to national symbolic unity in her status as mainly a domestic discontent and a visible local embarrassment. She is, however, inducted in the ongoing mission of enforced unity of national purpose. In this appropriation, woman's incorporation into the ranks of the nation potentially benefits not only the nation but also the unmarried woman herself. Hence her symbolic complicity in the colonial project, even at the very outset and prior to her emigration.

Ross stated in her own deliberations on redundant women's emigration that if the pressing question was "What are women doing with their culture and their energy?" then an answer was forthcoming: "They can be put to use Elsewhere." This "Elsewhere" is indeed suitable to the purpose, since its definition could be controlled and infinitely contrived (314). The "excessive," "superfluous" energy and culture embodied in "superfluous" women (as per Ross) can be discarded elsewhere. As one geography teacher noted, the situation for women might be remedied yet, but it would require a conceptual revision of the women: "Elsewhere" ought to be seen as "part of ourselves," neutralizing what she describes as "the dread of emigration which is doing such terrible mischief to English women" (quoted in Ross 314–15). The colonial project theoretically could accommodate England's women, as it did its many "undesirable" under- and unemployed men, by offering a seemingly boundless figurative space for them: "As the system develops more largely, women will learn to look upon colonial life in the same way in which their brothers do—not only as an inevitable necessity to be encountered bravely and cheerfully—but as an opening for ability and perseverance, and escape from a constant ill-rewarded struggle to *the space, the plenty, the generous abundance, of a new country*" (Ross 316, emphasis added). In the Victorian national imagination, the colonies are spaces defined although not confined or circumscribed by the empire. In this way they are perpetually and unconditionally useful. The colony is automatically a desirable space by virtue of its antithetical difference to the "constant ill-rewarded struggle" emigrants knew to be their lot in their home country. Thus, a "new country" is defined by the old as a "generous abundance" of "space" and as a place of "plenty." If

English subjects could be persuaded to see the colonies as a source of such endless potential, then the colonies would indeed become unconditionally desirable. Much effort was put into rhetorically guaranteeing the success of woman's transport and the suitability of her new place. After the spinster herself undergoes redefinition and after the colonies are redefined, the space between the "Here" and the "Elsewhere" is invested with transformative powers: "There is a magical transformation effected in both male and female character by the constant activity and daily diligence of a thinly-peopled colony, which it is difficult for those to realize who have been dependent all their lives on servants and shops for the supply of their wants. But it will be both just and prudent that the women applying for free passages should clearly understand that they are to expect no town life, but the rude plenty of a semi-solitude" (Herbert 5).

The power to define other places as not-England is revealed in England's enacted self-conception as the center of the globe, and thereby as the focus of *culture* as a legitimated, and exclusive, category. In the case of women it wanted to export, culture went with them as a positive accompaniment. However, the problems posed by gender to the fantasy of homogeneity have not yet been delineated. While these are useful ways in which to conceptualize England and its relation to the colonies, it is not as feasible to argue that the process of female emigration meets the descriptions of "nationhood" that make expansionism possible. Despite its ambivalent relation to the nation, the rhetoric of Victorian women's emigration demonstrates a persistent reliance upon notions of "organicity" and "homogeneity," even when criticizing the culture they sought to escape. Furthermore, any rhetoric concerning cultural or communal homogeneity that surfaces in the emigration discourse serves to argue for the incorporation of women into the former. Therefore, the process of women's emigration and incorporation into the figurative and material spaces of the colonies, and arguments concerning their relationship to the imperialist imperative, is mainly intracultural and only second cross-cultural. Perhaps this is necessarily the case, since women's problematic symbolic value and presence *within* England creates a considerable fissure in the "organicity" of the Victorian and the colonial communities and cultures, and because the "consensual transmission of . . . tradition" is not endorsed by the subjects in question (5). In this respect, as in perhaps no other, middle-class emigrant women resemble most closely the colonized rather than colonizers.

Ross's fervent arguments redefine emigration philosophies and conceptions so as to make emigration suitable for women, a revision informed by gender in opposition to the previous efforts and justifications for mass emigration by class: "The chief defect in the history of past emigration has been this—it has been looked at from the wrong point of view, as the last resource of the unlucky and the ne'er-do-weel, not as the legitimate outlet for energy and the strength of the teeming multitudes" (312–13). Such a redefinition of emigration, and a new understanding of its function, effectively constitutes English subjects as worthwhile exports, but also changes the definition of those suitable for export so that it may include middle-class women as well. The many allusions to the untold "temptations" confronting women are specific to England's inability to protect and accommodate its unmarried women. Reading the concern over emigrant women's safety on another level suggests that England itself is to be seen as morally dangerous and even perhaps as a place from which there is need to escape. Based on Ross's evidence, it would seem that within England, women's sexuality has become culturally threatening in its very excess. Ross quotes from Dr. Livingstone's *Life and Letters:* "The state of society, which precludes so many [women] from occupying the position which Englishwomen are so well calculated to adorn, gives rise to enormous evils in the opposite sex—evils and wrongs which we dare not even name, and national colonization is almost the only remedy" (313). The middle-class woman's formal ornamental role, her role as object, is contested in redefinitions that are prompted by the proposition of the emigrant woman who has been rendered invisible in the cultural and social domain. Making the same point as Mrs. Greg concerning the evils of women's lives stemming from men's misuse Ross designates the colonies as the most appropriate site for depositing women in search of refuge and safety. In the same stroke she designates the colonies as sites for depositing social elements and behaviors that are unmanageable within England and are unacceptable within its cultural context. Clearly, one of the "contradictions," to which I have made allusions, surfaces in this rhetoric. For instance, it is interesting that Ross should describe South Africa in terms that are idealizing and fantastic but in the process makes the point that the reason it is such a wonderful place is really the beauty and abundance that exists *naturally,* "to be found wherever the hand of the husbandman has not appeared to turn them into the garden of the Lord" (315). In proceeding then to advocate the presence of "men" and the husbandry of the colonial land as desirable, Ross proposes that the purity of colonial lands can contain the contradiction intrinsic in peopling them with England's undesirables.

The reiterated analogies between the colonies and the emigrant women also serve as an apt metaphor for the compromises exacted from both in order to facilitate this transaction. Both women and the figure of the colonies are made to submit to the nation's requirements, and both are posited as its subordinates. It is within these parameters that the colonies are described by emigration facilitators, as in the pamphlet of the Oversea Department, "Britain's Call from Overseas." The colonies are solely material resources, an attribute nonetheless leveled by their abject cultural status. They are to be viewed as possessing ample natural resources at the same time that they are also seen as lacking in nonmaterial resources such as "culture." The colonies are in need of "strength that is greater and *more lasting* than mere material prosperity," and thus a hierarchy of value is established. The power differential is extended as English people are extolled to "hear the call of the younger countries are making to those of us who live in the home land. They want, some consciously, others perhaps unconsciously, to be strong as Britain at her best is strong . . ." (2). The privilege of translating the colonies' "perhaps unconscious" desire and need for the right kind of "strength" falls to the emigration facilitators. The possibilities toward that interpretation abound and are effected in conjunction with the material problems confronting England, currently *not* "at her best." The needs of the colonies are interpreted as being "for those things which make up the spiritual side of a nation—literature, art, religion" (ibid., 2). If the colonies were providing England with material goods, then England could be seen to reciprocate by providing them with its nonmaterial wealth, values that are indeed "excessive" in the imperial context and in relation to the fetishistic fascination of the Victorian British with "things." Historian Lori Anne Loeb's recent work suggests that advertisements as intrusive images served to showcase the overabundance of goods over which England claimed proud ownership and persistently to make the argument that England owned excess.[13] In fact, the empire seems to have prided itself on its excesses, its superfluous and unnecessary possessions; it flaunted its excesses, its surplus goods: "Advertisements for all sorts of products meant to be enjoyed at home . . . increasingly forwarded variety, selection, even superfluity as a commercial ideal" (Loeb 26). Such gestures serve to disempower the colonies by depriving them of self-representation and in conceiving of them as devoid of agency, a method of appropriation that is very similar to the chatter about "old maids," which treated them as a problem to be solved by qualified others.

Defining woman's universal mission as concerning culture rather than practical and material needs, one arbitrator between women and the colonies, The Women's Branch of the Oversea Department proscribes the colonial nonmaterial needs that emigrant women would satisfy, as if discussion of women's relation to materiality—whether "Here" or "Elsewhere"—were an unconscionable offense to Victorian sensibilities. The female emigration project reflects most closely the pervasive denial, within England, of unmarried women's problematic economic and social status. It is in this nonmaterial and broadly acculturating capacity that women are employed to serve the colonies; thus their significance is mainly a nonmaterial and noneconomic one. The "spiritual side of the nation" that England hopes to export to the colonies includes the spinsters, excessive women who represent a residue from past and present problems within England who, as middle-class poor, defy material categorization. Defining women in nonmaterial terms is a practical necessity since the colonies and dominions were making clear that they had very little use for middle-class, educated women; they preferred more menial laborers who would have fewer reservations about their subordinate "places" in the colonies' less rigid class structure. The argument had to be made, then, that the absence of "refined" women from the colonies left the "vast natural wealth in their lands lying unused" ("BCFO" 2). As long as women would be made to fit in any economy as educators and as consumers, their colonial roles were in accordance with the domestic ideology of gender, which did not, however, apply to the large number of the displaced and dispossessed middle-class spinsters within England. Out of this context, the emigrant woman might be reunited with the normative middle-class ideologies from which she had been disenfranchised at home. Therefore, while unmarried women were unprotected under the domestic ideology in England, they were reconnected to it rhetorically so that they might transmit it to the colonies in the series of appropriative exchanges established by the empire. Woman's status in this configuration is as conduit for the empire, but she is also her own means and ends of exchange. Suzann Buckley finds that the emigration scheme as a whole failed to effect any material, practical change in the lives of women: "[W]ere it not for the fact that some unemployed British women were aided in finding positions, . . . the whole business . . . could be judged, at best, a ridiculous chimera, at worst, a contemptible view of the role of women in the empire. This aspect modifies it to a very expensive placement service and matrimonial bureau" (37). Emigration schemes were, however, by and large significant in establishing a dialectical link among the empire, the colonies, and "superfluous" women.

The precedent for these negotiations of women's cultural functions outside of England's borders was already in existence in domestic gender ideology discourse, as set in Victorian cultural critic John Ruskin's argument in "Of Queens' Gardens." In this well-known and much-analyzed essay Ruskin posits that women are in a position to influence the world and, in the same stroke, eliminates that possibility. Ruskin asks, "What is [woman's] queenly office with respect to the state?" and concludes, paradoxically, that "[w]hat the woman is to be within her gates, as the center of order, the balm of distress, and the mirror of beauty, that she is also to be without her gates, where order is more difficult, distress more imminent, loveliness more rare" (38). Posing the "stereotype" of women in contrast to that of the colonies, woman is omnipresent as a symbol of beauty and goodness, seems to possess these qualities innately and to possess the capability of instilling them in others and in the "Elsewhere," in other contexts.[14] That innate goodness is a simultaneous impossibility in the absence of her "garden walls," the national and cultural boundaries that inscribe her function. Insofar as "a woman has a personal work or duty, relating to her own home, and a public work or duty, which is also the expansion of that," according to Ruskin, woman can be held accountable for circumstances and actions that reach beyond her domestic sphere, since they must in some way bear a relation to it (132). Hence, when responsibility is assigned for actions outside woman's immediate frame of influence, the category of the female must bear much of it. As Ruskin's accusation concludes, women are to be held liable for a wide array of national, international, and cross-cultural evils: "There is not one war in the world, no, nor an injustice, but you women are answerable for it" (136). In a similar vein that universalizes woman's function, female emigration poses a general and elusive problem: "[M]uch remains to be done; there is something in this world amiss, and it is a hard matter to unravel it" (317). Both the problem and its solution are unspecified, until women are haphazardly introduced as a parallel problem and a potential use.

There are some important distinctions in the different propositions of situating women at once within and beyond England, as there are in endorsements of the domestic ideology. Arguments made on behalf of unmarried women and others that align women with the institutions of the home and marriage must be viewed as spurious since Victorian women's relationship to marriage is highly problematic—especially from the 1860s on, when the rhetoric concerning "superfluous" women suggests an acknowledgment that the institution of marriage could not serve the social needs of Victorian society and its women. Therefore, propositions that "women [are] the conservators of order" in Charles Hamley's defense of spinsters (95) and that marriage is "the ordinance which keeps all the world in its place" (94) can best be seen as arguments that, in endorsing the ideology of domesticity, also are asking that it practice what it preaches. They become exacting reminders, in short, that this is a guarantee to all morally worthy women. However, since that appeal clearly failed to produce any concrete results, extending woman's "use" to the colonies predominates as the rhetorical alternative of choice.

The point surfacing repeatedly—that middle-class, "genteel" women of education and culture were not suitable to meeting the colonies' needs for domestic servants—was quite problematic when it was these very women who sought a new and different social and cultural place for themselves, having been displaced in England. Socioeconomic class, in fact, proved to be the one negotiable factor for emigrant women who had little else to negotiate in terms of their colonial placement. As one emigrant spinster put it, the colonies are desirable as lands where "it is not considered to be beneath one's dignity to turn your hand to anything"; she found that she gained some important choices: "The salary is not up to much, only ten dollars a month; but I hardly think a lady help will get more; a servant would get twenty, but one has to pay for being treated as a lady. . . . I think I shall like it, and shall at least stay over the winter, then I shall see if I cannot get a larger salary . . . The work is certainly hard, but everyone works even the wealthiest people. . . . "[15] While, as I mention earlier, a considerable number of emigrant women were most willing to cross class lines and adopt this new role, their continued "redundancy" or threatened "excessiveness" even in their new contexts caused considerable worry. A typical newspaper article warned that "In Canada a girl whatever her birth and education, who cannot cook, superintend a household and make her own dresses, is looked on as ignorant."[16] If the colonies and dominions were the only "out" the assisters and others could imagine, then the women's disqualification from them would inevitably equal a deserved despair. The image that was to counter this despair and fear was of women who were placed successfully in situations "Elsewhere" and who were somehow magically, "immediately absorbed" by their new contexts:

> "It is really exceedingly easy for a young woman of her class to emigrate. The Queensland government has long been shipping them off in large numbers. They are sending now eight vessels a year thus freighted with domestic servants, who may be of any age from 12 to 35, and who have only to get a certificate of respectability from any magistrate or clergyman."
> "And what becomes of them?" was a question put yesterday . . .
> "They are all immediately absorbed," was the reply. ("Shipping Off Domestic Servants")

Narratives like this pronounce the imperial fantasy that the colonies "absorb" England's excesses and that they do so naturally. The question of how many emigrants the colonies can possibly "absorb" is rarely articulated by the imperialists, although it surfaces as a concern for the established colonists, as I have suggested. As one Australian columnist put it most crudely, "[A]re our spinsters already on hand to be neglected in favour of the imported article? It is a fallacy to suppose that our home market is so entirely bare as that we are compelled to depend upon foreign produce" ("Emigration, Impartially Considered" 81). When the colonists speak to the issue of being asked to "absorb" emigrant spinsters, the economy of the colonies surfaces as one that is rather similar to England's, although the latter is a "foreign" country. The colonists have their own spinsters to contend with. Thus, there are indications that emigrant women were not ideal exports to the colonies and that they were not effortlessly "absorbed."

Overly optimistic portrayals of the emigration process and experience clearly aimed at encouraging women to leave the country but did nothing to prepare them for the reception or difficulties they would encounter. Also, they did nothing to accommodate the conflicting characterization of the colonies as both welcoming receptacles and as places that are morally dangerous and chaotic, a kind of Hell to the fantasied Heaven within England, if only because the latter is *known* rather than imagined. The colonies' capacity to "absorb" emigrant spinsters is limited by the former having their own domestic cultures. Nonetheless, trusting that the colonies can in fact "absorb" excess subjects and objects produced by Victorian consumerism and commodification persists as a "demagogic fantasy" that serves to foster the illusion that "the emigration to the colonies would provide a safety valve" for England (Hobsbawm, *Industry and Empire* 69). Attesting to the fluidity of the colonies, Una Monk quotes a letter by Maria Rye sent from Australia in 1865, which is very telling in terms of its vision of England and the colonies. Whereas England represents the familiar, the comfortable, and the known, the colonies inadvertently are depicted as a kind of vacuum that poses the possibilities of self-definition, self-actualization, and autonomy. In contrast to these secondary virtues, which suggest that the colonies are excellent because nonintrusive, England's offerings of positive influence not to stray from the boundaries of respectability and "culture" are dubious at best. In the colonies, failed English people will

> work because they *must* and are virtuous because they are surrounded by scores of good homes and by inducements of every kind to go right—all this vanishes or very nearly vanishes here, and the Colonies, like the testing fire of the Apostle, tries every man's work and every man's character to the very core. It's very marvelous how alone people are here—women—men—families—it's all alike—they are here today and gone tomorrow. And the natural result is that individuality is very prominent—I don't object to that, neither will you—but you can easily see how that would tell in creatures, I beg their pardon, women, who have no individuality to bring out. (4)

It would appear, based on promises like this, that the colonial context offered something different from and more than the nation ever could. In the colonies, causality is returned to an earlier phase, one that does not teleologically produce an underclass and excessive albeit presumably valued cultural subjects. The colonies are an "out" from domestic and national accountability, then, and are called to serve such functions. Finally, they are also catalysts for fantastic personal change, the conduits of personal and national progress.

By the 1880s, when general economic conditions in England had deteriorated and general emigration figures reached a new peak, "redundant" women commanded the attention of philanthropists and came to be written about more overtly in literature. Questions concerning their status became more pointed, explicitly highlighting their indeterminacy in the wider cultural economy. Women's "energy" and cultural potential clearly had become "excessive" in themselves and in the domestic context. As Joanna Trollope notes, spinsters "were not only a nuisance because they did not fit in but also because they were an embarrassing, separate race that *could* not fit in" (63).[17]

Against this backdrop, saturated with hopelessness and misery and distinguished by an absence of options for mere survival, unmarried women surface as invested with an alternative kind of value and possibility: They become apt raw material especially well suited for export. They are invested with an inherent and presumably essential "plasticity" that endows them with an "adaptability" inherent in "the female nature" (Orr, "The Future of English Women" 1026, 1024). Even in nonmainstream arguments that seek to invest women with actual power and to reveal their undervalued and commodified condition, unmarried women surface as possessing qualities that are useful for the colonies but apparently are not of any practical use to England at the present moment, when all kinds of opportunities for employment and education are denied them. As one Victorian pointed out, the right kinds of "conditions" for women's usefulness simply "do not exist" (Orr, 1014). Such formulations produce specific possibilities of a new colonial hegemony and leave much room for women to claim a place and a role for themselves.

The argument had to be made most strongly at home specifically for *unmarried* middle-class women. A new valuation and cultural revision of the "old maid" or the "superfluous" woman surfaces continually in the discourse of the age. Here I want to look at one example of such arguments, made in 1884 in "The Future of Single Women," by Noel Hatton (actually the pseudonym of the feminist and marriage reforms activist Mona Caird). This passage highlights the relevance of her arguments to woman's perceived or projected place in the "Elsewhere," which is here represented as the "now" that makes change possible, as opposed to "then," a more traditionally bound place. It also features a redefinition of the very character and essence of the "old maid" as she was commonly imagined:

The mental life of a single woman is free and untrammelled by any limits except such as are to her own advantage. Her difficulties in the way of development are only such as are common to all human beings. Her physical life is healthy and active, and she retains her buoyancy and increases her nervous power if she knows how to take care of herself, and this lesson she is rapidly learning. The unmarried woman of to-day is a new, sturdy, and vigorous type. We find her neither the exalted ascetic nor the nerveless inactive creature of former days. She is intellectually trained and socially successful, her physique is as sound and vigorous as her mind. (158)

The new definition of the "old maid" is quite contingent to imaginings of the colonies and dominions. The state of things in England is shown to be one that is suitable for various kinds of species growth and improvement; however, the new and improved English female subject may have to seek her place somewhere else since she has, in a sense, outgrown the one place that had created her fallen state to begin with. The new female subject has, in fact, become better suited for the endless challenges and variability of the colonies than she is for a difficult and stagnant social existence in the homeland. The argument follows that since English women have in a sense evolved out of their previous dependency, they also have outgrown England. Following along these Social Darwinistic lines of reasoning (according to which social change is equated with organic progress), this portion of the population is considered not only ready but even best suited for exportation to a new place. Just as "new land" is naturally better than old land, the "new" unmarried woman type is representative of boundless potential and ability. She may very well, according to this new definition, qualify most specifically as England's "best and purest," although she is generally unacknowledged as such (Ross 317). The unmarried woman becomes the locus of endless possibility once again, the very embodiment or symbol of the adventurous and limitless frontier herself. At the same time, if she is not its conqueror, then she may be its mate: "*The world is before her in a freer, truer, and better sense than it is before any individual male or female*. . . . Whether it be in the direction of society, or art, or travel, or philanthropy, or public duty, or a combination of many of these, there is nothing to let or hinder her from following her own will, there are bonds by such as bear no yoke, no restrictions but those of her own conscience and right principle" (Hatton 158). Because she is not bound by the institutional conventions of marriage, the unmarried woman is free to roam and also free to offer herself to whomever or whatever may benefit from her abilities the most. Furthermore, given that "her own conscience" already has been asserted as "free and untrammelled by any limits," her goodness and usefulness are as boundless as is her interiority, her hidden and innate resources. The unmarried woman's main value, according to such formulations, may now be seen to lie in her unfaltering and innate goodness and the endless capabilities emanating from within her.

Hatton's vision of the unmarried woman matches Ruskin's vision of the domestic sphere extending to encompass the world, to the point that woman becomes, as George Eliot puts it, "the world's wife," whose task is "the preservation of society" (*Mill On the Floss* 620). It also challenges woman's traditional place in the domestic sphere as it extends Ruskin's coerced alignment of woman and the nation. In this new formulation, the unmarried woman "is fitted to fill a place which has always stood empty in the history of work," a place that has a use for her boundless and indefinable abilities that are nonetheless based on her being "tender and loving" in a womanly or feminine way (Hatton 159). She is in a position to "stand as [the] representative before the nation" of women and children and thus fulfills a duty to the nation, as assigned to her by Ruskin (Hatton 159). The argument made here, as well as in many other works, places all emphasis on the *national* or universal uses to which unmarried women can be put and may simply reflect an already existing, broader preoccupation with England's status as "nation." It may well be that relating women's value to national function and benefit is a segment of the equation in establishing women's national and cultural subjectivity. If this were the case, the women's emigration rhetoric and the movement toward general emigration can be seen as a natural extension of the reiterated projections of "nationhood" and "nationality" on the part of the Victorian English, irrespective of gender. It is important to note, all the same, that in the context of colonial emigration, the redefinition of women as cultural subjects is inextricably bound with their place in the configuration of the national identity of English culture. Thus, it makes sense that Hatton is compelled to incorporate a national mission into her redefinition of unmarried women as ostracized subjects. In terms of the issue of accountability, her argument also harks back to the promises made by patriarchy to Victorian women and exposes the failure of that institution.

THE TRADE

If England was exporting its men and women, it also sought to export with them some traditions and values. It is questionable that unauthorized emigrant subjects succeeded in filling their prospective places in the scheme of acculturation and domestication of other places, other social and cultural systems. In addition to confronting the difficult task of attempting to fill vaguely defined roles, the experience of emigrating also left middle-class female emigrants very vulnerable to public scrutiny, scrutiny that constituted an affront to their class and gender sensibilities. The repeated call from *all* the colonies for qualified and willing domestic servants made the classification of "domestic" rather a desirable tag for many women who were in a cultural and material limbo within England. Middle-class, "genteel" spinsters were in a reverse situation in some ways: They also were willing to cross class lines, to forge new social and class identities for themselves. They too were negotiating their "relative value" as cultural subjects and as national objects for exchange within the empire. However, they did so mainly by trying to insert themselves into the more economically promising position of working-class domestic servants. Whereas ideally crossing class lines might have rectified matters sufficiently, this was not an easy transition, nor was it without further complications, because genteel emigrant women threatened to collapse class distinctions in the process. As W. R. Greg asserted in no uncertain terms, unlike the middle-class unmarried women, "female servants . . . are in no sense redundant" (1862, 453).

Having been rendered problematic at home, middle-class emigrant women sought a new space and a new identity, and attempted to forge a concrete symbolic transition between England's gender and class prescriptions and the possibilities that might conceivably exist in the colonies. Imperialist initiatives were instrumental in effecting the women's emigration, while *gendered* emigration rhetoric challenged their efforts toward self-definition. Hence, the question of unmarried women's relation to the domestic ideologies of gender as well as their role in the domestication of the colonies is not a simple one. The main reason for this is that the status of middle-class unmarried women was complicated in several ways within England itself, which was not equipped to deal with their vast numbers nor with the implicit challenges they posed to the domestic ideology of gender. Middle-class emigrant women constitute a kind of excess in cultural terms, because they have outgrown their ideological places, having become symbolically and materially "redundant" in terms of their place in the broader scheme of gender relations. Given that England sought to alleviate some of its own domestic problems by depositing its "undesirables" Elsewhere, as the available evidence suggests was the case, it is significant that as English subjects middle-class emigrant women are invested with a "surplus" value that was not immediately useful in the colonies. As Greg did not fail to note, "the class of women who are redundant [in England] is not exactly the class that is wanted in the colonies" (52). Specifically as it may relate to ideologies of the nation, the symbolic power with which middle-class women traditionally were invested is especially questionable in the case of *unmarried* women.

From the very inception of organized emigration, arguments criticizing it mark the correspondence between England's material and cultural insufficiencies and variously construed imaginings of the colonies. Such opinions mainly criticize emigration as an escapist strategy used for evading the real and pressing needs of the nation, and unsettle basic assumptions concerning England's relation to the colonies. In "Emigration or Manufactures," Greg scrutinizes emigration in terms of its economic and national impact on the English domestic economy and social conditions. Claiming that the benefits of emigration to the English economy were exaggerated in the public discourse, he cleverly concludes that emigration raises the simple question of whether "to bring the food to [the people], or to send them to the food" (105). Greg shifts the focus back on the populations of manufacturing towns in England and away from the "Elsewhere" as the locus of the resolution to problems confronting England: "The first and most natural method of providing for our increasing population—viz., by the extension of manufacturing industry at home" (115). He continues: "Emigration is a natural and, at times, a beneficial operation. It is a suitable relief for the redundant numbers of a limited territory, and is the means destined by Providence for populating the wide earth with the hardier and more energetic races of men. But it should not be forced, and it should come in its natural order. It is the second, not the first, resource of an increasing population" (117). Even if it were the case that emigration is a natural and inevitable phenomenon, according to Greg, it must not be resorted to as a drastic measure for alleviating problems at home. However, it may be seen that Greg's thinking about emigration as a natural process does not apply to women, for what would their function be in other lands, since they are not suited to populating and presumably "energizing" the earth. It follows that the women's rights advocates sought to reinstate women's moral character and functions.

The unmarried woman's nationally proscribed identity and her potential function as a national subject would extend beyond the geographical boundaries of England, thus posing the question of how single women might be deemed most suitable for emigration. A change in her image and in her public perception entails a refiguring of her social and cultural function beyond the domestic domain in both the national and social sense. In her example of the governess, critic Mary Poovey suggests that for a Victorian woman to lose her middle-class status was also to lose the "natural morality" that was unquestioningly assigned to bourgeois women (14). Given the class shift experienced by most spinsters, it follows that women's advocates and feminists sought to reinstate their moral character and moral social functions. In fact, at a time of increased consumerism, spinsters lacked the accoutrements of middle-class gentility, which in practical terms left them unidentifiable as members of that class. Lacking the "paraphernalia of gentility," middle-class spinsters also could not figure as a tool of "status enhancement," which was the central function of other middle-class women (Loeb 28). Likewise, spinsters of limited means, who could not "pursue gentility through material acquisition," also had limited agency over the perception of their moral character (30).

It follows, then, that in the sympathetic rhetoric, the unmarried woman becomes figurative mother to the world and to the nation; she leaves the domain of the personal and the family, which have been oppressive and harmful to her, and joins the ranks of a much less concrete structure, a tenable place of authority over unknown entities and ideals:

> *"She has an extended sphere of public usefulness."* The causes of liberty, of purity, of temperance, education of the slaves in America, the reform of laws in England, the progress of Liberty in Europe. . . . *An unmarried woman is able to secure better conditions of life to a nation of children who are neglected or abandoned,* by devoting herself to public duties, to furthering their education, or to enlightening the public on the laws affecting them. Their

> happiness and welfare become hers, their improved condition is essentially
> the product of her life, as a mother a woman may benefit two or three, as
> a single woman she benefits thousands. (Hatton 161, emphasis added)

When she resurfaces as figurative mother to the world, the emigrant
spinster is constituted as the natural extension of England as empire
and as mother to the colonies. As described here, the single woman
fills a symbolic gap between woman's ideal role as mother in the domestic realm and extends her usefulness in the "Elsewhere" in the
role of nurturer, thus negating the spinster's predicament in being
childless. Undergoing constant redefinition, the spinster is a "relative
creature," as one Victorian named her, to an even greater degree than
her married counterparts.[18] Consequently, the spinster is understood
to be valuable precisely insofar as she is a malleable commodity;
lacking the generally prescribed boundaries of personhood, she may
take on other identities. Her place in the ideology of domesticity is
thus also always rhetorically guaranteed.

If "the thousands" at home should still be unsure as to how
woman may be of use to them, she may now find her place among
others, multiple and infinite "thousands" whom she is naturally prepared and suited to serve in traditionally envisioned and humanitar-
ian ways. When the emigrant woman takes on the guise of mother
to the world, slavery, democracy, poverty, temperance, and education,
among other fields, become her new domain in which to be useful.
As Greg observes in the next quotation, this definition of womanhood coexists with others, which fragment and misconstrue her
essence. In this respect, women come to resemble the colonies in
terms of the ways they are perceived by the English but mainly in
the methodology applied to constructing an identity for both.
Likening women to the colonies, and the treatment of women to
that of the colonies, Greg criticizes the nation for its inattention to
specific and material actuality; his criticism makes clear that women
are subject to the nation's shortsightedness that it also displays in its
relation to the rest of the world: "The British world—philanthropic
as well as political—takes up only one thing at a time; or, rather and
usually, only a fragment of a thing. It discovers an island, and proceeds to reason on it and deal with it as such; and it is long before it
learns that it is only the promontory of a vast continent. WOMAN
is the subject which for some time back our benevolence has been
disposed to take in hand, fitfully and piecemeal" ("Why Are Women

Redundant?" 435). Highlighting women's devaluation in the cultural context of England, Greg's analysis suggests that the many references encountered in the discourse to the untold "temptations" confronting women are specific to England's inability to protect, accommodate, or care for its unmarried (and hence unaccounted for) women. Most important, exporting women would enhance the value and desirability of the women who remain in England. Removing women from England would make it and them better places and subjects. The passage just cited also suggests that England has yet to discover or know its women, just as it is shortsighted about the colonies it discovers. Women and the colonies are thus juxtaposed as corollaries in their relation to England the nation, a risky dependency and contingency, since the nation also has the power either to ignore or to legitimate them as such. The colonies are aligned with other national "inferiors," definitions and patterns of signification being based on their contrast to the dominant culture.

Despite such observations, criticisms, and complaints and England's unfavorable comparison to "Elsewhere," its image as omnipotent nation remains intact and unscathed. It would appear that the nation, invested with infinite symbolic and figurative authority, is, in fact, generally capable of accommodating contradictions and neutralizing them. It may be a morally dangerous place for women and encourage emigration to "Elsewheres," but it is also capable of maintaining its omnipotence in strictly figurative ways. In imperialist discourse, the "culture" of Great Britain, the empire, is simultaneously legitimated politically and distinguished from places from which culture is seen to be missing. Based on this, it would seem that the cultural and signifying "excess" that constituted emigrant women as a class and as a social phenomenon was being deposited into a cultural vacuum. Paradoxically and quite "excessively," women also are seen as being deposited into endlessly various spaces. Both the women as transient subjects and their destinations, the colonies and dominions, are effectively transformed when they are construed as "knowable" and "known," when they are defined and identified by the national English culture. As nation, England identified and negated, in theoretical terms, the space that exists among itself as nation, its domestic subcultures, and the colonies as imagined spaces. This was accomplished conceptually, in the way Pratt describes: "that textual apartheid that separates landscape from people, accounts of inhabitants from accounts of their habitats, fulfills its logic. The European improving eye produces subsistence habitats as 'empty' landscapes, meaningful only in terms of a capitalist future and of their potential for producing a marketable surplus" (61). This formulation was proposed not only on the level of public discourse but also on the level of controlled and deliberate production of knowledge about the emigrant experience concerning the colonies; its production was self-motivated and not ideologically manufactured. The emigration societies, as I have suggested, fabricated alternative meanings and knowledge concerning the colonies through the writings of the women whose emigration they sponsored.

As Bhabha observes, knowledge-producing transactions like the ones just described are especially meaningful in the ways they expose England's systematic presumptions. The rhetoric of cultural difference relies on "statements of culture or on culture [which] differentiate, discriminate and authorize the production of fields of force, reference, applicability and capacity" (*Location of Culture* 34). However, this process of identification by way of "difference" is also prevalent within England itself, where we see ethnographic studies of the British underclass produced consistently from the 1840s to the 1870s. The kind of ethnography and anthropology effected within England and about the English themselves appears to problematize Bhabha's emphasis on definition by difference and the impact that this act has on parallel representations of Others. Most interesting about the passage is its point about the ways in which "culture" is subjectified and complicated or made complex, and perhaps the extent to which it can be said to do so in its own interests. This is relevant to "redundant" women serving as variable cultural commodities precisely in service to that mission. Second, it is an important reminder of the prevalence of notions of cultural difference in Victorian England not only in the nation's relation to the colonies and dominions but internally in the stratification and classification of English domestic subjects. This is one side of the emigration rhetoric, and one that qualifies its boldness by emphasizing woman's cultural influence toward refinement. The colonies themselves stood opposed to its ideology by stressing their own stated preference for women who were not quite so "refined" as to not be practically useful as domestic servants. This gap in interests between English gender ideology and the colonists' ambivalent relationship to it could be bridged only by some effective variable, namely a recharacterization

of the colonies themselves and a definition of colonial culture enacted in response to the interests of the mother country.

Although their historical existence may now be fragmented because they were predominantly encoded into formulations of a gendered nationhood, emigrant Victorian women serve to illustrate the
problem of the Other-once-removed but also of foreign Others'
spaces as they are repeatedly appropriated for the accommodation of
yet differently situated and displaced Others, those in dominant cultures. Mainly because their own domestic national culture did not
know how to place them within their original contexts, they also
were not immediately suitable for establishing relations with the
Elsewhere. Their incorporation into the "Elsewhere," into the
colonies and dominions, required an established determining and
determined origin or source, a kind of culturally symbolic point of
departure that was not necessarily determined, defined, or fixed, for
women leaving England as exiles of sorts and at the same time dou-
bling as colonial figures who are unauthorized by the nation and yet
are within the boundaries of national culture's self-representations.[19]
The indeterminacy of the concept of the nation is compounded for
women, and particularly for unmarried, culturally and socially displaced women because their relation to nationhood is complex.

The next chapter examines the "conceptual indeterminacy" of
middle-class women's relation to the Elsewhere as represented in
several such narratives. However, as this chapter argues, it will not
suffice to conceive of Victorian emigrant women merely as conduits
for the dominant culture's contradictions and excesses, despite their
elusive place in the material and cultural Victorian economies. Ultimately, it also would not be productive to perceive and represent
them as such, since there is evidence that some women resisted the
notion of making "Elsewhere" their home, while others seemed
most eager to leave the discrimination they encountered within the
confines of Victorian capitalist patriarchy. In all cases, emigrant
women's relationship to the colonies and the Elsewhere manifests an
encounter that is mediated and informed by gender ideologies and
by problematic women's status within the boundaries of the nation.

3

DOMESTIC MAPS

ॐ

Internal Migration, Gender, and
the Sociography of "Elsewhere"

"Say what you like, our Queen reigns over the greatest nation that ever existed."
"Which nation? . . . for she reigns over two. . . .
"Yes, . . . Two nations; between whom there is no intercourse and no sympa-
thy . . . ; who are as ignorant of each other's habits, thoughts, and feelings, as if
they were dwellers in different zones, or inhabitants of different planets; who . . .
are ordered by different manners, and are not governed by the same laws.
"THE RICH AND THE POOR."

—Benjamin Disraeli, *Sybil, Or the Two Nations*

Victorian middle-class emigrant women constituted a particularly distinct social class because they were economically
impoverished while they were also tangentially situated
within the middle class, which purported to protect them even as
it rejected them. Without doubt, these women were problematic
cultural subjects, materially and also symbolically. They were not
marketable as workers or as potential wives, while culturally they
remained only contingently valuable in the domestic gender ideology, their main sphere of significance. Hence, insofar as they
were not valuable in the broader ideological economy of gender
that privileges motherhood, middle-class spinsters were decidedly

"excessive." The previous chapters suggest that the problematic status of women in Victorian society is textualized on an ideological level so that emigration advocates and the spinsters' apologists can contrive a solution to their "excessiveness."[1]

This chapter foregrounds the precedents for depositing gender and class undesirables into spaces outside England, thereby displacing and dislocating them. It investigates the construction of the "Elsewhere" within the literary domain and locates the problematic significance of gender's relation to class and to England's cultural boundaries. These concerns are manifested in three very different yet congruent texts: Friedreich Engels's *Condition of the Working Class in England* (1845), Elizabeth Gaskell's *Mary Barton* (1848), and Charles Dickens's *Great Expectations* (1861). *Mary Barton* and *Condition* come out of the "hungry forties" to describe the social and cultural transformations characteristic of Victorian England and witness England's failure to provide for its subjects. They also represent a mapping the nation as a parallel effort to mapping the Not-Here; the two texts reveal the elaborate difficulty in these ethnographies and suggest that it stems from the conflicted composition of the nation. *Great Expectations* narrates a later stage in that development, at which responsibility for the underclasses is transferred from England to the colonies.

Questions concerning Victorian women's emigration from the Here to the Elsewhere suggest the necessity for examining the constituency of the Here in the specific cultural moment of the mid- and late Victorian period. The reason for this is that the Here is not only a place but also a time, as cultural theorist Caren Kaplan observes in her study of the role of travel in Modernism: "Within the structure of imperialist nostalgia . . . the Euro-American past is most clearly perceived or narrativized as another country or culture" (314). An examination of how the Here is construed exposes the ways in which it is problematic itself, especially in relation to how it was imagined that women might be placed Elsewhere. Motivated by concern and sympathy, Engels and Gaskell forge into the complex multitudes of the city of Manchester to make direct observations and to produce knowledge. The points Engels and Gaskell make concerning the Here of the nation as an Elsewhere and as encompassing the Elsewhere are interesting in terms of the gender dynamics they reveal and specifically regarding exclusionist prescriptions that align women with the masses. A location of *domestic* displacement appears as the colonies' analogue. That location is an Elsewhere comprised of the perpetual migration of the dispossessed classes. Eric Hobsbawm notes that because of the very questions imperialism posed concerning "the will to rule" and "survival of the fittest," the "empire . . . was . . . *more immediately vulnerable to erosion from within,"* and insinuates that "empire [led] to parasitism at the centre" (1968, 83 emphasis added). Hence, threats to the imperial imperative were seen to be posed not by outsiders but by the domestic dispossessed classes, the existence of whom could only cast doubt on the empire's proclamations of greatness. Opposition to the imperialist imperative, thus, could be effected most easily from within, since the empire's very virtue could be challenged by its poor.

This conception of the inner workings and domestic ramifications of Victorian empire-building helps us to understand the problematic national status of the underclasses, including "superfluous" women as a neglected population. Configurations of the Elsewhere inform the Victorian hegemony but also are utilized by it. The role of gender in this symbolic system is best exemplified by the texts by Engels and Gaskell. My discussion here explores the subtle and unacknowledged ways in which places that are not England figure in the constitution of the nation, specifically those produced by these two authors as self-conscious ethnographers of the Victorian domestic front. Therefore, "Not-England" as the antithesis of a unified and stable cultural front is a fabrication, a nationalist and imperialist fantasy. As many Victorian literary texts suggest, gender and the import of an Elsewhere are inextricably interconnected and the problems posed by one often are solved by the other. The constitution of both the Here and the Elsewhere acquire symbolic significance when women are asked to find their proper places outside of England.

In thinking about all that the nation contains we also encounter the *beyond* that is appropriated by it. The texts discussed here illustrate that colonial and gender relations are mediated by Victorian culture's incorporation of Elsewhere into its narrative economies. The agency of this Elsewhere is emphasized when it is a source of money and when it offers new possibilities for plot events that normally would be impossible within England. In the works analyzed, the main tension in the plot rests in the fact that women walk a very fine line between acceptability and propriety. The easiest escape from these impossible confines is a *fall into* distinction, a moral fall that exempts women from gendered societal strictures and frees them from the dictates of bourgeois morality. For these heroines freedom from the oppressiveness of convention is possible only through negative characterization or agency toward self-determination, rebellion, and deliberate immorality. Here too, as in much of the emigration discourse, England is represented as an unsafe place for those things or subjects that Victorian culture wished to cherish and preserve, namely women and certain moral values. This, in fact, is the crucial paradox.

The solution to domestic conflict that surfaces in literary texts is an "out" of sorts, a way of figuring foreign places as receptacles for English undesirables of any kind. This solution *creates* an alternative space for characters who are problematic either in terms of gender or class, or both. It is the "safety valve of the nation" (Begg 6). The Victorian period's social undesirables are also its literary undesirables, and both are removed to discrete spaces in novels. In examining the structures contained by the nation, a series of questions surfaces that probes the issue of how gender imperatives permeate the literary domain. Literary texts give us a way to understand the instrumentality of gender in national concerns and open up to analysis the realities that in both literary texts and social life, the expectations that women would marry was, in fact, an imperative. Thus, literary texts enable us to trace the "place" that the Victorian spinster may be said to occupy and the ways in which "female space" is conceptualized in those instances when the female falls outside the proper domains of the ideological domestic sphere. In some cases this space is best understood in its absence, when it is made clear that there is no appropriate hegemonic place for women existing outside the prescribed social arenas.[2] Considering this process of removal further, Victorian culture did, in fact, appropriate and utilize such alternative spaces not only beyond its own geographic borders but also within them.

Concentrating on the creation and sustainment of a subnation within England, it becomes clear that the need for Elsewhere was indeed great, both in material and imaginative terms. This fact is suggested by the many surveys of domestic England that reveal, in unequivocal terms, an impasse among ideology and practice, imperialist rhetoric, and domestic reality. Studies such as Victorian commentator Henry Mayhew's *London Labour and the London Poor* (1861–62) suggest that while such accounts were being written up in interesting ways, this project appealed to English middle-class subjects as much as the tales from foreign lands entertained and fascinated them. Such texts also testify to the extent to which they enabled the commodification of the poor, albeit not intentionally so. The social protest novel, along with surveys like these, functions to introduce by indirect, "aesthetic" means the working classes to the middle class—that is, from a safe distance, since it was a guaranteed function of class stratification that their paths would not normally cross. Ultimately, however, the message they reiterate is that the domestic is also foreign, that the Here may be quite as dangerous and unfathomable as the Elsewhere.

Henry Mayhew's mid-Victorian social survey of London workers in *London Labour,* based on research conducted in the late 1840s, instigated and reproduced a number of interviews with England's underrepresented, which featured the latter speaking of their own experience. This preoccupation with producing particular kinds of knowledge persisted to the end of the century, with Victorian writer Charles Booth's publication of *Labour and Life of the People in London* (1889), a series of investigative surveys on the lives of London's underrepresented. These two figures and their texts loom largely over the domestic landscape of Victorian England and are precursors of the travel writer, participant–observer, and social reformer fused into one polyphonic text comprised of multiple voices and multiple subjects. Discussions concerning the distinction between foreign and domestic cultures permeate Victorian culture's self-conceptions. In Gaskell, Mayhew, Booth, and Engels, the laboring poor figure as undiscovered territory, despite the fact that these authors' social and political agendas sought to emphasize the ways that invisibility and absence was systematically manufactured. Their writings reveal their awarenesses concerning the necessary progressive ends of inclusion in representation. By and large, however, women and the category of gender are not problematized in these works, although they are central to the functionings of the laboring class. Rather, the writers produce an interesting amalgamation of social "problems" that negate the agency of gender. Women, gender, and the underclass are collapsed so that "class" becomes the overriding characteristic in these works, obscuring the very presence and agency of gender that the narratives themselves expose.[3] In the case of *The Condition of the Working Class* and *Mary Barton,* women surface as the one problem that is not solvable within the context of England, and gender is offered as a consideration that serves further to complicate domestic narratives rather than to answer the problems posed in them.

NARRATIVE AUTHORITY: TEXTUALIZING THE UNSEEN, CONSTITUTING THE "ELSEWHERE"

The Victorian fantasy of a homogeneous and organic national culture is revealed to be precisely that: a projection of a fantasy. The "Nation" is a ruse in the ways it uses Elsewhere to project domestic predicaments into a distant past and locate their resolution there. Sojourns into the Elsewhere that is constitutive of the national past are invariably sentimental and voyeuristic, as is suggested by the works I discuss. Considering that Elsewhere is a cultural construct that develops in contrast to the known, it makes sense to consider how the subordinate classes and "superfluous" women (whether they are so morally, socially, or sexually and figuratively) are situated in relation to it. Our attention is drawn to the spaces they vacated for those they variously deemed as more desirable. Elsewhere is utilized to expand the boundaries of the nation; it appears both as an expansion of the Victorian domestic scene and is also constituted domestically, within England itself. James Clifford's *The Predicament of Culture* outlines the development of the field of ethnography over the last two centuries, commenting on the methods it developed for studying peoples and cultures.[4] Studying anthropology as an evolving science and a cultural practice, he notes a synchronic detachment *and* involvement in participant observation. Clifford isolates the nineteenth century as a turning point in these developments and analyzes participant observation as a means of both containing and amassing knowledge. His thinking about cultural observation and translation allows us to consider how the Elsewhere and its Others are constituted in relation to the observer. It also helps us to explore the issues of cultural translation and interactive textual production pertinent to Victorian female emigration, since Victorians' own ethnographic projects reveal their conceptions of proper British subjects in contrast to subordinate Others.[5]

The question of Victorian women's emigration, from the Here to the Elsewhere, forces an examination of the Here in the specific cultural moment of the mid-Victorian to the late-Victorian period. These questions are significant especially in relation to gender and

Victorian exclusionist prescriptions that align women with the masses.[6] Conceptions of the Here must be addressed before we can turn our attention to how it was thought or imagined that women might be placed Elsewhere. Considering that Elsewhere is a cultural construct that is developed in contrast to the known (that is, the domestic situation of women and the social classes' positionings within England), it is necessary to consider how the subordinate classes are figuratively and symbolically situated within the nation—the place they were vacating, in preference to places somehow deemed more desirable. The cultural and conceptual gaps textualized by Engels and Gaskell have a distinctly material analogue. They correspond directly to an economic gap in the national landscape, one created by what Hobsbawm, in *Industry and Empire* has called the vast "emigration of capital" (118). He notes that "by 1870 something like 100 million [pounds] were invested in foreign countries," a statistic and trend that was "merely one part of the remarkable flow of profits and savings in search of investment" (118). Therefore, the importance of Elsewhere always must be seen to lie in its economic profitability as well as in its symbolic usefulness.

ã€

How are undesirable "subjects," in all senses of the word, approached by authors of the period? How are they accounted for? More important, how are female undesirables configured into the Victorian economy of nationhood and national subjects? The obfuscation of the boundaries among the literary, the anthropological, and the social-scientific in domestic "ethnographies" of England's lower classes also extends to representations of spinsters. However, what gets textualized both renders visible and makes invisible the tangential institutionality of the population that is described. The final product of their efforts evidences that what becomes textualized in such special ethnographic efforts is testimony to how unmarried women are rendered invisible, even in the midst of efforts to rescue them. Clifford's working definition of "culture" helps us to conceptualize Victorian imperial culture, specifically insofar as it addresses its indeterminacy: "[A] 'culture' is, concretely, an open-ended, creative dialogue of subcultures, of insiders and outsiders, of diverse factions" (46). This understanding facilitates the study of Victorian spinsters' emigration in two ways: First, emigrant women were simultaneously constituted as

Others or as puzzles to be solved within England and also as Ourselves insofar as they were viewed as contributing to the country's national character; second, emigrant spinsters also posit England as the Elsewhere since they exist within it as displaced subjects. Understanding "culture" as fraught with contradiction helps in examining Victorian narrative accounts that feature a nation in part constituted by the Elsewhere, as Engels and Gaskell illustrate.[7]

Friedreich Engels and Elizabeth Gaskell take on the task of charting the location of the working classes in England, and in the process provide useful information about Victorian conceptions of class and gender in relation to physical boundaries and to the limits of understandings of nationhood. The working-class subject emerges as a national, domestic Other. Using the very imperialist terms to describe colonial native populations, Gaskell takes issue with "the agony which, from time to time, convulses this dumb people" (37–38) and gives them a voice, although she also appropriates voice in narrating regional working-class dialects.[8] The authority with which emigrant letters were invested as truth-revealing accounts, for example, supports the view that observation is an imperial activity and is acknowledged as such. Gaskell and Engels provide possible formulas for what marginalization looks like and, most important, for how England's sociocultural stratification works to subordinate and disempower its own domestic subjects. They also suggest that between the exploitation and dislocation of the laboring underclass lies absence and invisibility and that this framework is reinforced by the instrumentality of gender. Likewise, as postcolonial critic Trinh Minh-ha has observed, the very process of anthropological observation produces nothing of intrinsic value. Her critique of the ethnographic project as a marginalizing and silencing practice emphasizes its imperializing work. Under the scrutiny of the anthropologist, the colonizer surfaces as colonized and as nothing: "[C]olonizer and colonized have come to speak the same language. Don't complain of being alienated, for it is *we* who undergo the 'true,' quintessential alienation, we whose faith in our profession robs us of our *being* and reduces us into a *being nothing*" (Minh-ha 58).

Anthropology claims the authority not only of the observer-participant but also of the *subject* of the observation—not only the field of inquiry but its contents as well. Minh-ha states that anthropology bears "the will to annihilate the Other through a false incorporation" (66–67). In short, textualizing the lives and existence of

London's poor is not the same as incorporating them or as removing the barriers that marginalize them. Textualizing the nation's underclasses, strictly an ethnographic project, reveals a Victorian preoccupation with its own nationhood, its own fantasy of unity and solidarity and also the compulsion to amass knowledge concerning Others. Victorianist Patrick Brantlinger concurs: "[A]nthropological fieldwork is inevitably a form of spying . . . particularly so when . . . the information gathered is to be used for defending and enlarging the empire" (163). In the narratives I discuss the imposition of authority produces absence, invisibility, and appropriative intrusion that emerge between the idealization and exploitation of the poor and of women. However, these texts also serve to exhibit their subjects and perhaps to render them spectacles, insofar as they prepare them for middle-class consumption even as they aim toward a more inclusive interpretation.

In *The Condition of the Working Class in England,* Engels narrates a map of the city of Manchester that makes clear the positioning of working-class housing and territories, revealing the extent and ways in which the working classes were quite physically circumscribed to preempt their interference with the spaces occupied by the upper classes. The text and narration evidence the segregation of this population along class lines and the very physical, geographic establishment of the English domestic subnation. To the extent that Engels's map highlights the division of space and the cultural difference and segregation of the working classes from the middle classes, he effectively illustrates the status of working-class areas of Manchester as an unknown, an Elsewhere that is as invisible and hence as theorizable as "foreign" Others. To emphasize the material fragmentation of industrial urban centers, Engels provides a map that serves two purposes: First, it offers an outline of Manchester in its multilayered chaotic complexity; second, it marks the dividing line between the realms of existence of the two classes. Most important, the map locates in very concrete terms the gaps in space and experience between the polarized classes, much as the production of knowledge concerning foreign places served to distinguish the English from the non-English. Engels narrates his map but with difficulty: "Of the irregular cramming together of dwellings in ways which defy all rational plan, of the tangle in which they are crowded literally one upon the other, it is impossible to convey an idea. The confusion has only recently reached its height when every scrap of space left by the old way of building has been filled up and patched over until not a foot of land is left to be further occupied" (88).[9]

Engels's work (and other domestic ethnographies like it) suggests that the demarcation and marginalization of segments of the population begins "at home," as it were, and further proposes that such practices may even be endemic to the condition of England and the reaches of its capitalist enterprise. In an analogous gesture, following this hypothesis England may be seen to have "exported" a domestic practice, which is the culmination of both historical imperialism and typically Victorian processes of appropriation.[10] Of this dynamic, Mary Louise Pratt has observed: "[T]he textual apartheid that separates landscapes from people, accounts of inhabitants from accounts of their habitats, fulfills its logic The European improving eye produces subsistence habits as 'empty' landscapes, meaningful only in terms of a capitalist future and of their potential for producing a marketable surplus" (61). The bourgeois ideology that separates "spheres" not only along lines of gender and class membership does so through rigid material boundaries—walls and roads that would make it virtually impossible for the two classes to meet by chance. A venture into the slums would, therefore, of necessity be a foray, a deliberate and purposeful intrusion, and an excursion that is, for all practical purposes, a cross-cultural "travel." The aim of travel such as this would be, as was typically the case during the period, to amass and disseminate information. The preponderance and popularity of travel diaries, colonial journalism, and imperial administrative innovations during the period testifies to the desire for such knowledge of Others and Elsewhere.[11]

Engels uses the phrase "I have observed you" to qualify his knowledge of the English working classes and to further support the extent of his ability to comment on their condition (34). In the same stroke, he privileges his knowledge of Englishmen enough so as to be able to comment on their "true" identity and to align himself favorably with it. In order to establish such a connection, Engels relies on the transcultural currency of the gender hierarchy. Not only does he attempt to expose the exploits of the bourgeoisie and to substantiate the feelings of his working-class subjects, he also must, in the end, suggest that English working-class subjects have much in common with their fellow sufferers elsewhere. Engels's 1892 preface to the first English edition reflects on his earlier prediction concerning England's most assuredly becoming "the workshop of the world"

(40). As he puts it succinctly, "What is true of London, is true of Manchester, Birmingham, Leeds, is true of all great towns" (69). This prophecy serves further to legitimate his powers of observation and interpretive skills and also bolsters his position on the universality of working-class lives and conditions. The premise upon which *The Condition* is based is that the notion of national identity and "naturalness" of poverty are illusory. Engels's main argument, that the exploitation of the working classes in England is not an isolated incident but a constitutive part of a larger system of exploitation, challenges and extends the boundaries of social identity and universalizes the condition of those classes.

Engels and Gaskell qualify themselves as ethnographers often, possibly in preparation for the contentious depiction of England they will offer. Both subtly acknowledge that they themselves are unauthorized subjects, one as a foreigner and the other as a middle-class woman whose place in the domestic ideal is away from the scenes of impoverishment she describes. As a presumably objective (because removed) middle-class philanthropist whose main goal is to describe accurately so as to familiarize her readers with the realities of poor people's lives, Gaskell assumes the class privilege that this role proffers and also utilizes the distance from the working classes that would lend her task the authority of objectivity. In the role of the philanthropist, she intervenes in working-class lives without being subjected to them. She enjoys the privilege of relativist humanism since she can control her involvement with her subjects, always reserving the power to end that association at any time. Likewise, the financial help extended by philanthropists to the working classes is not really a material assistance but the *semblance* of it, since it is not intended to ameliorate their predicament in any permanent way. The figure of the philanthropist, a mainstay of Victorian culture, mediates many of the class and culture discordances characterizing the period and its literature. The intersubjective politics of philanthropy are such that there is no risk of the observer's becoming absorbed, subsumed, or overwhelmed by the subject; this positioning exhibits the same kind of ethnographic distance advocated by anthropologic practice in the early nineteenth century.

In these ways the philanthropic experience coincides with the anthropologic and ethnographic. Gaskell and the other recorders of sociocultural discord engage in a practice of observing and encoding that is appropriative in a very similar fashion. Their objectives in narrating working-class lives, their desire to represent and reproduce authentically their subjects for general consumption, and the final place of such narratives in the hegemony call to question their motives and their texts. It is Gaskell in the role of the philanthropist who makes every attempt to, but cannot, effectively extricate herself from the overwhelming degree of intrusion into the lives of the working classes: "*Whether the bitter complaints made by them,* of the neglect which they experienced from the prosperous—especially from the masters whose fortunes they had helped to build up—*were well-founded or no, it is not for me to judge.* It is enough to say, that this belief of the injustice and unkindness which they endure from their fellow creatures, taints what might be resignation to God's will, and turns it to revenge in too many of the poor uneducated factory-workers of Manchester" (*Mary Barton* 13). Presenting her work as devoid of bias or political assumptions, Gaskell ultimately must disavow any prior or "outsider" knowledge that might come to bear on her project, thus clearing her text of any ulterior motive. Gaskell claims, early in the novel, "*I know nothing of Political Economy, or the theories of trade. I have tried to write truthfully;* and if my accounts agree or clash with any system, the agreement or disagreement is unintentional" (38, emphasis added). This is clearly a false disclaimer, since the novel proceeds to analyze the identities and lives of the working-class poor in terms that are bourgeois political, Christian philanthropist in their ethics and presumptions, and ultimately nothing short of reactionary.

The ethnographic projects of Engels and Gaskell converge on the conclusions at which they arrive on the questions of morality and gender. Significant parallels emerge between the studies as they examine the geographic and material stratification of a city and its inhabitants. They characterize the poor as England's dispossessed, dislocated, *migrant* population. Their descriptions show the poor living in desolate and oppressive dwellings, overworked and underfed, at the mercy of the manufacturing class. In being disenfranchised the poor are exiles, much as middle-class unmarried women are social and cultural exiles. Like the subordinate spinster, the poor seem to have been integrally geographic, material exiles. The descriptions offered by Gaskell and Engels of the working classes, and the language in which they represent their subjects, suggest a correspondence between "redundant" and "excessive" women like those sent to the colonies and the working classes, both of whom occupy subordinate places in the cultural and social economy even as they are rendered invisible in radically different ways. For Engels, this feature of the working classes is best understood as a manifestation of the "attitude of the Bourgeoisie towards the Proletariat," and hence comes under the category of ideology; he considers its material manifestations in the workhouses: "To prevent the 'superfluous' from multiplying, and 'demoralized' parents from influencing their children, families are broken up . . ." (284). Engels highlights the dangers to morality posed by poverty and social disenfranchisement. In terms of gender, in particular, he points out that the natural order of things has been upturned since working-class women no longer know their domestic trade and no longer consider the home their sphere: "All the surplus which the acquisition of the necessities of life now yielded fell to the man; the woman shared in its enjoyment, but had no part in its ownership. . . . The domestic labor of the woman no longer counted beside the acquisition of the necessities of life by man; the latter was everything, the former an unimportant extra" (*Origins* 199). For Engels, then, the victimization of the working classes is manifested partly in the displacement of traditional gender roles. It is unsettling to the ethnographer of Manchester that "the wife supports the family, the husband sits at home, tends the children, sweeps the room and cooks" (167). He is as disturbed by this reversal of roles as Gaskell is unsettled by the heroine Mary Barton's challenges to gender prescriptions of woman's chastity and "superior" morality. For both authors, the problem is compounded by the inadequate socialization of women in the domestic arts; Engels presents the fact that unmarried women in particular are "wholly inexperienced and unfit as housekeepers" as one of the more dire "moral consequences of the employment of women in factories" (*Condition* 169). Ethnographies such as this also challenge the predominant, prevailing notions of "progress." The internal dynamics of class conflict and social inequities expose England, the nation, as divided and fragmented, so that it might be said to lack cohesiveness and coherence. Such a portrait of the empire is problematic, at the very least, as the quotation at the beginning of this chapter indicates, in that it subverts the imperial fantasy from *within,* from among the ranks of its own native subjects.[12]

In texts like *Mary Barton* the social map of England is expanded to reconcile a vision of "Other" lands as appendages to the nation. Foreign places, such as the colonies, are assimilated to produce a

vision of England as an economically and morally depleted place
within which individual agency and social change may no longer
prove possible. The incorporation of other spaces into the sociocultural map of England reconstitutes it as a nation, privileging a fantasy of economic self-sufficiency and cultural omnipotence over
both domestic and foreign Others. This imposition is particularly
the case with women, whose place in the cultural and national
economy is represented as problematic and most closely aligned
with the social-deficit cultural model. In the process of criticizing
the shortcomings of industrial "progress," some of the more important social novels of this period consistently make the point that
Victorian England is not where one would wish to be since it is
morally dangerous and that this nation cannot contain its subjects
successfully. Gaskell's novel argues this point as forcefully as does
Engels's nonfiction.[13]

In this novel, which arguably has a radicalizing mission, Gaskell
charts the terrain of the lives of working-class inhabitants of Manchester, following one family in particular. Gaskell's account concurs with that of Engels; the laboring classes' loss of the countryside
is compounded by the fact that this same land is now "occupied,"
colonized by the bourgeoisie. What used to be working-class terrain
is now the upper-classes' retreat from the industrial heart of Manchester, which, as Engels shows, the rich have abandoned. Much as
the colonies are the unseen, in Victorian literary culture the inner
city is both the source of the money and that which must not be
spoken of. Physical association with that rejected and abandoned
space takes on enormous symbolic and cultural significance, although its physical repulsiveness to those who are now done with
it cannot be underestimated.

TIME PASSAGES AND ESCAPISM

In charting the dynamic interplay among social classes, geographic
spaces, and the past and the present, Gaskell observes that countryside villages have now become places in which working-class people
no longer live. They are spaces that represent what used to be, as they
embody the consequences of the process of appropriation and the
damaging control by the emergent bourgeoisie of personal and public space: "Large houses are still occupied, while spinners' and

weavers' cottages stand empty, because the families that once occupied them are obliged to live in rooms or cellars" (*Mary Barton,* 59). The English countryside may be seen to represent an earlier phase of British capitalist imperialism, which concentrated for the most part on the exploitation of its own people. The country villages stand as colonial relics only in the fading memories of laboring-class city dwellers who live in basement rooms, virtually underground. In the present of *Mary Barton,* the 1840s, the symbolic and geographic positioning of the working classes has extensive implications for all subjects of the empire.

The internal, domestic migration of both the rich and the poor had by that time created a population of people for whom nation is a vague concept and who cannot easily be identified with it, despite the extensive efforts to coerce such an identification.[14] In contrast, the notion of "home" distinctly signifies the place that the urban working classes can no longer occupy, a place encompassed and subsumed by the nation. The notion of having been displaced and existing as a migrant, then, is not in any sense foreign, nor is the condition of living away from one's "home" and one's own "people." As historian Michael Hechter has argued quite persuasively, England's dominating imperial activities in faraway places such as India and Africa also are manifested closer to home, with its domination and appropriation of Scotland and Ireland: "Certain parallels may be drawn between the exploitation of the typical third world colony or neo-colony and that of Celtic periphery in the British Isles. Since the colony develops as an appendage to the metropolitan economy, and in this sense is used instrumentally by the metropolis, it most frequently serves as a source for primary or extractive products for metropolitan industrial manufacture and distribution or for food supply" (136). The patterns of the internal migration and the displacement working-class subjects share as their heritage have as their correlative the upward movement of the middle classes toward affluence. The latter appear detached from the implications of their own geographic mobility and pliancy, and exercise a peculiarly excessive degree of geographic agency. Gaskell observes, "At all times it is a bewildering thing to the poor weaver to see his employer removing from house to house, each one grander than the last, till he ends in building one more magnificent than all, or withdraws his money from the concern, or sells his mill to buy an estate in the country" (*Mary Barton* 59). Gaskell does not fail to note that the privilege of travel and movement from one carefully selected "place" to "another" belongs to the upper-class males, who clearly have a monopoly on mobility.[15] The upper classes' appropriation of the countryside leaves the English working class displaced and dispossessed of their "homes," much as the aboriginals of the colonies and dominions. When they are located after great effort (for, in the novel, one first becomes aware of where they are *not*), the poor in the cities live in abject conditions, in fact, places one would not want to "travel" to or visit, unless one had a specific purpose for doing so: "[Berry Street] was unpaved; and down the middle a gutter forced its way. . . . You went down one step even from the foul area into the cellar in which a family of human beings lived. It was very dark inside" (98).

There is also a geographic yet figurative Elsewhere that is to be found less materially within England itself. It is "not-Manchester." That is, Victorian culture as depicted in *Mary Barton* is forever defining itself in implicit contrast to an earlier time and perhaps quite a different place: Preindustrial or newly industrialized England. As Gaskell makes clear, the Elsewhere that many prefer to occupy is one of an England in the past. It exists only in a hallucination that produces a narrative of transcendence, a travel into a known place in one's memory. The countryside exists only in the mind of the elderly spinster, Alice, since it had been colonized by the affluent, and there was no going back:

> "Was it a pretty place?" Mary asks.
>
> "Pretty, lass! I never seed such a bonny bit anywhere. You see there are hills there as seem to go up into the skies, not near may be, but that makes them all the bonnier. I used to think they were the golden hills of heaven. . . ." (70)

In poetic language Alice remembers her childhood in the country in terms of the abundance of space and energy that are now rare in manufacturing towns like Manchester. It is a land that is now lost to the majority of British subjects and is recalled in narratives that are, however, inadequate travelogues. Like the cross-cultural travel narratives produced by the domestic ethnographers, they are recordings of places that are precious because they are lost. In this sense, the vast population of Victorian England, many of whom also sought a better future through emigration, are already dispossessed of their land

and their familiar, well-known places. Imaginative reconstruction and fantasies are their sole means of returning there. Much like the overseas emigrants, they are also guaranteed that they *cannot* go back; even if that idyllic Elsewhere still (if ever) existed, it would not be accessible to them. In practical terms, a return to a precolonized space is not possible for the British laboring class, since they also were transformed by the changing face of labor after 1815, when there was "an appalling amount of pauperism in many of the rural districts" (Hitchens xvi).

Gaskell's project in *Mary Barton* is to offer a map of Manchester quite similar to that drawn by Engels. Gaskell describes the trials, hardships, and the many virtues of John Barton, righteous factory worker. The pivotal crisis in the novel concern his daughter Mary, who is tempted to betray her class and to compromise her own virtue by submitting to the seductions of the morally degenerate and dishonorable Harry Carson, the factory owner's son. Mary's efforts at self-improvement through marriage are contrasted to her father's political activism; both fail to accomplish their goals, but Mary is represented as guilty whereas her father is clearly overpowered and defeated. Gender is persistently aligned with socioeconomic class, and Mary redeems herself and her class by marrying Jem, a virtuous working-class young man who truly loves her. The novel ends with the couple living in Canada. Both the mapping project and its implications are dismissed in favor of a figurative map that bears no concrete relation to England and makes no reference to the charted terrain of its slums. Gaskell's map points instead to spaces and places away from it. The map constructed in this narrative scrutinizes quite closely the details of working-class occupants' lives and circumstances, including their moral character as it relates to their material existences. Like that of Engels, this map includes the domain of the upper classes for the purpose of contextualizing the lower classes. Glimpses into the private lives of the manufacturing class serve to humanize them but also to widen the gulf between the two realities, so that there is no middle ground. The quirky worries of the affluent Carsons do not come across as pressing concerns and are inconsequential to everyone but themselves. However, unlike Engels's configuration, Gaskell's extension of the urban and social map continues until, by the end of the novel, we are not only outside Manchester but also out of England altogether. This manipulation of boundaries is a national practice, endorsing Engels's conclusion that

"what is true of Manchester is true of England" (*Condition* 69).These
working-class characters can find happiness only outside England,
since their morality and physical well-being are threatened by Victorian class stratification. Having barely survived numerous affronts to
their dignity, the characters are removed to the colony, where even
if their morality is challenged, we will not know of it or be troubled
by it; they will remain forever "rescued" from moral dangers just as
England will remain protected from their troubling existence, the
moral difficulties they present no longer accounted for within the
nation. Just as the poor have an Elsewhere in the past, they may now
also have one in the future.

In the context of 1840s Manchester, the past is a recurring fantasy also because the working classes are subsumed in the urban
structure that renders the middle class mobile and the laborers invisible. Thus, in harking back to the past by subjects who have cause
to dislike the present, specific remembrances function as self-willed
resurrections of a time and a place that was once and a condition
that is not possible any longer. Describing the working-class migration to the cities, Engels makes the same point as Gaskell: That the
internal demographics of England are changing, as is the very map
of the island. Both authors observe that to the extent that "the village grows into a small town, and the small town into a large
one . . . ," the village disappears altogether until it is no longer a
place of origin and so that, by extension, the internal migrants are
exiles (Engels, *Condition* 66). Consequently, the village and the countryside also become a kind of Elsewhere, a nonplace to which one
can retreat imaginatively to engage in fantasies of the past or of the
future. Caren Kaplan suggests that displacement may serve a central
cultural function: "When the past is displaced, often to another location, the modern subject must travel to it, as it were. History becomes something to be established and managed through tours,
exhibitions, and representational practices in cinema, literature, and
other forms of cultural production. Displacement, then, mediates the
paradoxical relationship between time and space in modernity" (35).
Such mystification explains the allure of the colonies as preindustrial
havens and also the growing appeal of the museum and the exhibition hall, in which the past is captured *as* an Elsewhere, that is, ar-
rested in the present moment.This symbolic exchange, by which one
can both possess the spoils of industrialization's excesses and be
spared its consequences, is abundantly evident in Victorian literature.

Gaskell's character Alice shows how the past becomes a site for escape, no longer incorporated in the material constitutionality of the nation, and is thus analogous to the colonies. Hence, despite the noted "peculiarly Victorian paranoia abound boundary order," England does not possess any solid geographic boundaries, nor can it claim *internal* consistency or immutability (McClintock 42).

In the context of high-industrial England, where active female sexuality was the preserve of working-class women, Mary Barton is asked to aspire to middle-class status by denouncing a legacy of licentiousness and unleashed passion. But Mary's great transgression is more encompassing than that: It lies in her desire for more than she is allocated by the capitalist bourgeois moral imagination. She seeks both romance and personal financial security; she wants both love and flirtation, as well as transcendence from her personal and social predicaments. The ghost of the "fallen" aunt, Esther, which appears throughout the novel to warn Mary against self-indulgence, serves to highlight the punishment and dire consequences for such self-interest. We learn that Esther became a prostitute as a result of having lived with a lover who would not marry her and having violated the imperative of marriage. Therefore, specifically as the penalty for sexual misbehavior, prostitution surfaces both as an option and as a threat. Here we are reminded of the prescription of self-sacrifice as the proof of feminine virtue and also of the censures against self-interest imposed on the laboring classes by bourgeois moralizing. Esther's ghost surfaces time and time again to remind Mary that women who openly claim their sexuality must be ostracized and that the penalties are severe for women who claim a sexuality outside the institution of marriage. The implication is that marriage sanctions female sexual activity and shields women from moral error and condemnation.[16] Mary Barton attempts to transcend her class through marriage but is punished with a figurative death. When she discovers that her father has killed her lover, she experiences a spiritual crisis that incapacitates her physically and mentally for many days. However, she is restored to life and to Gaskell's version of moral rectitude: She comes to love the working-class Jem unconditionally, is willing to sacrifice herself for her lover's sake, and is ashamed and repentant.

The one ingredient crucial to Mary Barton's happy ending is a specific combination of gender qualities that grant women moral responsibility for men, specifically, subservience to the middle-class moral imperatives of marriage and motherhood. The wife and

mother is the symbol of goodness and virtue and transmits hegemonic well-being. After all, it is following his wife's death that John
Barton falls both morally and politically. As we are told of Mary's
mother, "One of the good influences over John Barton's life departed that night" (58). In Victorian discourse the moral reform to
which Mary is subjected is often a prerequisite for a successful resolution to an impossibly difficult plot. However, that the reformed
Mary is rewarded with exile suggests an incompatibility between the
virtuous female and Manchester's poverty, much as emigrant middle-
class women were removed from England to preserve some of their
cultural and ideological value. Because this problem in conflicting
realities is irreconcilable by philanthropic, nondisruptive means, by
the very end of the novel the working-class heroes have been transplanted to Canada, where they are guaranteed a "happily ever after."
In an England that would threaten Mary Barton's purity by enticing
her to flirt with exploitative middle-class men as a means of survival,
the colonies and dominions are the antidote that puts her in her
proper place. Mary is happily married and a mother at the novel's
conclusion, in an old-fashioned happy ending that is not substanti-
ated by the world of the novel and is not guaranteed to any woman
in England. Echoing the emigration assisters' arguments that women
need a safer and more value-efficient place than England, Gaskell's
Canada is the contrast to what England has become and perhaps the
only space in which Mary may exist as a "normal," fully integrated,
and culturally acceptable woman. In the end, we see only a brief
glimpse of this new life, a short and frozen moment of being in
which happiness is a fantastic and clichéd image, delivered by an
ever-elusive narrator:

> I see a long low wooden house, with room enough, and to spare. the old
> primeval trees are felled and gone for many a mile around; one alone re-
> mains to overshadow the gable-end of the cottage. There is a garden
> around the dwelling, and far beyond that stretches an orchard. The glory of
> the Indian summer is over all, making the heart leap at the sight of its gor-
> geous beauty.
>
> At the door of the house, looking towards the town, stands Mary,
> watching for the return of her husband from his daily work; and while she
> watches, she listens, smiling;
>
>   "Clap hands, daddy comes,
>   With his pocket full of plums,
>   And a cake for Johnie." (*Mary Barton* 465)

The novel ends in a very different place from where it began. In the
early parts Gaskell maps out a configuration of subnation as encompassed by the nation in order to legitimate England's poor. As a representative of those who comprised the substandard population
within England, Gaskell's problematic woman is removed to a place
outside of England, the result of which is that the nation may no
longer be imagined to encompass an abandoned population.

The end of the novel offers very little description of the colony
as the heroine's new home, so that the Elsewhere is preserved as a
metaphor, the figure of a promise for a better future, the desire for
progress and its projected fulfillment. In the end, the nation is an excessively discordant and hence a dangerous place. Juxtaposed to the
complexity of Victorian working-class women's lives, the binary opposition established by Gaskell, pitting the whore against the virgin,
is exposed as the difficult and inappropriate bourgeois proposition
that it is. In her resolution to the conflict she describes, Gaskell ex-
patriates the virgin to a purer place and away from moral temptation, while the whore, Esther, is remanded to death. In thus salvaging
the heroes by removing them, and in depositing them into a *general
unknown,* the novel's conclusion also negates the narrator's frequent
reminder that we are to avoid "generalities" and to "let us now return to individuals" (223). In another sense, because she remains
problematic as a feminine figure, Mary Barton, virtuous although
tempted, in the end is much like her aunt Esther: "mysteriously absent" until "people [would grow] weary of wondering and [begin] to
forget" her also (64). The ending subverts earlier parts of the novel
where Gaskell insists on the materiality of this geographic and cultural ghetto, since clearly in the Elsewhere of the colonies all histories may be erased and all past actions revoked.

Between bourgeois idealizations and material exploitation, there
is the space of absence and invisibility. The process of deconstruct-
ing idealizations entails a confusing and chaotic encounter with the
details of exploitation as well as with the incompatibility between
the two. This paradox best summarizes the problem of the female
emigrant spinster, whose idealization as a woman is in perpetual
conflict with her economic destitution and societal neglect. For
spinsters in general, their place is no place, and their ideological import is in continuous strife with their material insignificance.
Gaskell's attempt to reproduce the very "soul" of the population she
studies has caused her to panic in her effort also to redeem, reclaim,

and resituate the working classes of the slums into the Victorian hegemony. Hence, she resorts to that conceptual and spatial depository for the limits of the Victorian imaginary, the colonies.

THE SPACES OF THE NOVEL AND THE NATIONAL GENDER ECONOMY

Class and gender exist within and beyond the parameters of the "literary," exhibiting textual tensions that call for narrative resolutions. Reading such social problems beyond the level of literary convention allows us to trace the social and symbolic "places" that the Victorian spinster may be said to occupy and to trace the ways in which "female space" is conceptualized in relation to "undesirable" women. The analysis that follows exposes some gaps in bourgeois patriarchal discourse, gaps that Homi Bhabha calls "slippages." These slippages comprise significant omissions in the plots examined here. One such instance of this concerns the impossibility of the fantasy of marital bliss and middle-class prosperity. Women's scholar Deirdre David has described them as comprising the "erasure of a narrative of corrupt exploitation of the native by a fable of uplifting salvation" and, I would add, of the subordinated English subject (46). Several texts serve to illustrate this discord well. Questions concerning the unmarried woman's cultural value are persistent motifs in the cultural and literary maps of England. The question of woman's fate is undertaken by George Eliot in *Mill On the Floss,* a novel that reflects much the same totality as *Mary Barton* and that locates resolutions to the problem of gender in a similar geographic and symbolic nonplace. In tracing the growth and social development of Maggie Tulliver, Eliot's novel poses the question of *where* an "undesirable" or excessively problematic woman might find her suitable place. It also examines the constitution of woman as undesirable not only in the usual moral-sexual sense that is fairly conventional for Victorian fiction (for it does do that, precisely) but also in terms of her economic predicament as predicated by her father's financial ruin. In this sense Maggie Tulliver's life parallels those of the unmarried middle-class emigrant women most closely. Unlike many such women who fell from economic grace, Maggie does not have far to fall since her litigious father has managed to lose most of their possessions by compulsively "going to law." However, Maggie's situation is emblematic since the middle class displays a relationship to social status that is neither economically nor socially stable, despite the many stolid conventions that worked to uphold it. Victorian social conventions were vulnerable to economic fluctuations, their ideological under-pinnings betrayed by an ambivalent and unstable materiality. Maggie's predicament most explicitly foregrounds the question of what to do with the unmarried and financially dependent woman— especially when she does not comply with the gender status quo and the domestic ideology that would have her marry *somehow*.

Questions of what to do with Maggie and whether there is a place for her are predicated on England's not being the place for her. After her perceived love affair with Stephen and her moral "fall," friends and relatives suggest to her that she might leave the country to start anew in a place where she will be anonymous. Maggie is en-couraged to emigrate as a way of disowning her past. However, the answer to the central dilemma is that the possibility of an Elsewhere is not really an option for her as she is determined to confront moral hypocrisy. Maggie refuses to leave and stays on in a community that has no place for her and does not know how to perceive her. As long as she remains unmarried, she is perceived as an anomaly and as a threat to moral propriety. She also refuses to marry, for personal rea-sons, although she knows that marriage would thrust her in a more acceptable light and redeem her socially. There is a suggestion in this plot that, in some instances, an Elsewhere is both essential to women's survival at the same time that it is not a possibility within the parameters of moral rectitude. Likewise, the genteel spinster stands opposed to class and gender stratification, since categorically, only working-class women were permitted not to marry while "genteel" women were not to be impoverished. Finally, Maggie's predicament also suggests that this question of woman's "place" transgresses the social, cultural, and class lines delineated by authors such as Engels and Gaskell. *Mill On the Floss* highlights the main cur-rents of the spinster's problematic relation to gender ideology and the institution of marriage, indicating that abstinence from marriage poses certain irreconcilable ideological and hegemonic problems.

Gender and "superfluous women" are dialectically linked to the colonial enterprise. The problem of gender subjectivity in relation to colonialism is illustrated from a very different angle by Charles Dickens's *Great Expectations*. Thus far it has not been acknowledged as bridging the symbolic gap between gender-based conflict and the

colonies.[17] A bildungsroman that spins a narrative of change and dis-
illusionment as does Eliot's novel, *Great Expectations* investigates the
role played by class in the realms of desire, fantasy, and possibility, and
in doing so addresses the prevalent intrusion of the colonies upon
the nation. The novel follows the life of young Pip, a poor child who
seeks financial and personal improvement in all the wrong places,
namely in Miss Havisham and her niece, Estella. In his growth
process, Pip comes to important awarenesses about society and class
but also about love and commitment. Both Estella and Pip are emblems of the fluidity of class and gender as categories of identity:
Estella as a woman-in-the-making and Pip as a bourgeois-male in-
progress. Each is much affected by Miss Havisham, who has adopted
Estella and oversees Pip's growth.

The plot accords primary agency to Magwitch, the ex-convict
who has prospered in Australia and who is the catalyst for the plot
development; in contrast, the bulk of the novel's thematic substance
lies in Miss Havisham. Magwitch is the source of new (colonial)
money, while Miss Havisham represents the old and unwanted: the
assignment of these two roles is telling in the ways it exposes colonialism's relation to gender within the dominant Victorian gender
prescriptions. Through Magwitch *Great Expectations* also facilitates
an examination of the ways foriegn lands and places are incorporated into domestic narratives, specifically those concerning class and
gender conflicts. More intstrumentally, the novel suggests some ways
in which those spaces are utilized in fiction. In this novel the Elsewhere proves essential in both ameliorating and exposing specific
disparities within the plot and within England. In this one product
of the Victorian imagination, the Elsewhere of the colonies figures
quite predominantly as an ingredient that impacts and shapes the
lives of British subjects and that is also denied. That the colonies' existence is represented as problematic to the Victorian domestic culture is interesting and suggests that "superfluous" women and
personal matters are dialectically linked to the imperial enterprise. In
this illustration of the interdependent and reciprocal antagonism between class and gender, the Elsewhere (in this case, Australia) represents a "relative value," the value of commodities that is based on the
by-products of problematic social relations as opposed to material
utility.[18] The colonies are important insofar as the empire profits
from their existence, even as their actual domestic influence is always
negated. In relation to the colonies, the "relative value" of Dickens's

character here reflects not need but preference; not material place but ideology.

The novel presents two women whose relationship to the institution of marriage is problematic, much as Pip's relationship to the middle class is furtive. But whereas his relationship to the rising middle class is to be seen as misguided by false knowledge and pretense, the women's relationship to marriage and romance is viewed as grotesque and anomalous, even in the eyes of Dickens (who arguably treats with suspicion and sharp criticism those institutions that maintain the hierarchy of social class and the requirements for its membership). In this gender-based conflict, Estella will never quite achieve the oppositional gender status to which she aspires; she is a woman who cannot actualize her goals and desires. In feminist theorist Monique Wittig's terms, Estella stands in opposition to the imperative that she must "correspond, feature by feature, with the *idea* of nature that has been established for [her]," that including motherhood and wifehood (9). And yet she cannot be satisfied without that identity. Estella and Pip are symbols of the fluidity of class and gender as interdependent categories of Victorian identity.

In terms of their place in the sexual economy, the difference between Miss Havisham and Estella is most obviously that the latter is still desirable and stands a chance at settling down in a conventional, middle-class married life. Miss Havisham confronts the blank stare of having no such "expectation" since she has surpassed the limits of desirability and is no longer valuable in the marriage market. This depletion of value renders Miss Havisham an "excessive" and "superfluous" woman. As the unequivocal unmarried woman of means, and thereby an anomaly, Miss Havisham also embodies subversive challenge to the domestic gender ideology. An antithesis to the domestic ideal, her house is dark and grim, her "marriage" a shrine to deceit and ruined dreams, In stark contest to the usual celebration of conjugal ease upheld by the ideology of domesticity, her situation suggests that the hope of marriage may, in fact, ravage women's lives. Pip observes: "I saw that everything within my view which ought to be white, had been white long ago, and had lost its lustre, and was faded and yellow. I saw that the bride within the bridal dress had withered like the dress, and like the flowers, and had no brightness left but the brightness of her sunken eyes. I saw that the dress had been put upon the rounded figure of a young woman, and that the figure upon which it now hung loose, had shrunk to skin and bone"

(87). Even though she herself represents the most troubling elements of unmarried women's subjectivity, Miss Havisham is nonetheless figurative "mother" to Estella, whom she makes every effort to educate in the arts of emotional unavailability and ruthlessness. This symbiotic relationship does not conform to the familiar dependent child and tyrannical parent scheme.[19] The desired end-product of that "mothering" process would be not only an unmarriageable young woman of means but also one who would deliberately subvert the domestic ideology by rejecting her expected compliance to it. Rather than be relegated to the role of the pitiful spinster, Miss Havisham poses a threat as one who is in a position to influence and is not herself subject to this normalizing institution. In being potentially redeemable for the institution of marriage, Estella defies easy categorization just as she is having difficulty defining herself, the central process in which she is engaged. In this respect she resembles the function of the Elsewhere in the novel, a place and a nonplace, a negative space that resists definition.

Estella stands somewhere between Miss Havisham's rebellion and every docile woman; she is neither good nor bad, but—like Pip—she is misinformed. Signifying the impossibility of sexual satisfaction in the absence of marriage (which is to assume its existence within marriage), Miss Havisham shatters the "myths" of domesticity and female virtue ideals.[20] However, her ridicule of marriage as an institution causes her also to forfeit desire and her own sensuality. The processes of loss and depletion ultimately yield the destruction of the prototypical old maid. With the loss of opportunities for happiness, Miss Havisham goes up in flames and is irrevocably consumed by her repressed passion and her hatred of the system that failed to protect her:

> I looked into the room where I had left her, and I saw her seated in the ragged chair upon the hearth close to the fire, with her back towards me. In the moment when I was withdrawing my head to go quietly away, I saw a great flaming light spring up. In the same moment, I saw her running at me, shrieking, with a whirl of fire blazing about her, and soaring at least as many feet above her head as she was high. . . .
>
> Though every vestige of her dress was burnt, as they told me, she still had something of her old ghastly bridal appearance; for, they had covered her to the throat with white cotton-wool, and as she lay with a white sheet loosely overlying that, the phantom air of something that had been and was changed, was still upon her. (414–15)

An indictment against formula of love and good patriarchal-capitalist fortune, Miss Havisham's identity is comprised of the shadow of what might have been, as is Estella's. Miss Havisham cannot be said to be more ghastly than the average spinster who carried her nonmarried status about with her in every situation and every social exchange. Her identity as unmarried woman follows her to the grave, even past the point of where she is burned beyond recognition.

It is interesting that Dickens should take such a position on gender when other representations of marriage in the novel are so astutely critical of how these matings occur and the artificial grounds on which they are based. Certainly it seem that, in Dickens, marriage is more than an ideal in which compatibility, compassion, and desire unite people. That he was not sure how to end the novel is also instructive, as is the fact that he concludes that Estella should be punished by the gender hierarchy. In the end, Estella has married a man for whom she does not care and who does not care for her, and she is defeated by the experience. Irony predominates here, specifically in the preponderance of conflicts in meaning and signification—she even has lost the bulk of her possessions. The promised rewards of marriage are not forthcoming for her, and the illusion of marriage as a solution has been shattered. Hence, even from within the institution of marriage, Estella signifies the impossibility of marital bliss. She proclaims, "The ground belongs to me. It is the only possession I have not relinquished. Everything else has gone from me, little by little, but I have kept this" (492). The possibility of the oppositional woman, who insists on participating in marriage as a socially transformative act and in maintaining her economic independence, is eliminated in this one stroke.

The strand of the plot that deals with marriage is intersected by another, not coincidentally one that pertains to an Elsewhere as the unarticulated portion of the formula for social training. This intersection also yields unauthorized English subjects. In all the instances where the Elsewhere is instrumental in shaping the ideological import of the novel, it serves its purpose in a negative manner: It subverts the plot expectation, it dupes the hero and/or heroine, and it upturns the logical course of events. In it "man" and "marriage" become foreign and inessential; in the context of the Victorian hegemony, they become the Other. The Elsewhere transforms the plot by introducing the unexpected and the unforeseen, the otherwise impossible, as is the case with Magwitch. This is most obviously apparent in Pip's coming into money and joining the middle class, which happens in a "magical" way that undermines the exclusivism of the middle class to which he aspires. Elsewhere's function in this novel, then, is ironic and subversive of the normative processes and the status quo, but it is also fantastic and extraordinary.

Elsewhere intercepts the rigid structure of Victorian class systems and gender prescriptions. Both Pip's and Miss Havisham's "expectations" are mediated by Magwitch, who is now, although returned to England, out of context. Magwitch serves as the indicator for how the intersections of class, gender, and the category of the nation are mediated by the agency of the trope of the Elsewhere. The Elsewhere has transformed him in ways that are crudely materialistic; it also serves as a point between his material affluence there and his continuing nonplace in England. Furthermore, it serves as the conduit between the failed establishments of class and gender boundaries in England (illustrated best in Miss Havisham, Estella, and Pip) and his status as a noncitizen, as cultural subject on the fringe. As an outsider in both the colonies and England, Magwitch mediates the predicaments which that same Elsewhere has created at home. According to the plot, Magwitch commits a grave error in crossing the ocean again in order to rectify the transgressions of the past, presently manifested at home although not in the "Elsewhere," Australia. His presence in England threatens to destabilize the elaborate illusion of economic progress, a fantasy that also is complicitous in establishing the pervasiveness of normative class and gender ideologies. Order is restored to the novel by way of the Elsewhere, as we see Pip leave to go "abroad" at the end. His perspective is so changed that he now proclaims, "I work pretty hard for a sufficient living, and therefore—Yes, I do well" (492). Patrick Brantlinger's observation that "the up-beat, pro-emigration propaganda of the many articles about Australia Dickens published in *Household Words* in the 1850s, obviously clash with the theme of the convict's return" (121) articulates the tensions between the real and the ideal. However, it is also consistent with the pro-emigration rhetoric that emigrants must not return, after all, and the horizon must be expanded outward in a linear progression, broadening the scope of the empire and the possibilities for poor Englishmen; the case seems to be that one must not revisit the dire conditions one has left behind.

The Elsewhere provides the means by which both class and gender prescriptions may be interrogated. Magwitch is linked to Miss

Havisham's societal ruin in becoming a rejected old maid, and also to Pip's moral temptation and near fall in attempting to embrace a class he does not understand and a woman who does not wish to be possessed. Jaggers's proviso—that we are to "take nothing on its looks; take everything on evidence. There is no better rule"— comments on the state of class and gender relations in the novel and problematizes assumptions concerning *anyone*'s cultural identity and social place (351). It serves to comment on the obvious givens of the plot but also appears as a refrain throughout: Miss Havisham is not who she seems, but neither are the other characters. More important, England and its culture are not as they represent themselves— nor is England's economy self-sufficient, its penal system just, or its women truly feminine. This discord is embodied in women who do not know their place, women for whom an appropriate ideological and cultural role had not yet been scripted.

One needs to question all appearances, and it is in this respect that class and gender surface as key indicators of the ambivalence underlying the facade of Victorian colonial discourse. As notable Victorian Alexander Begg was to point out in no uncertain terms, the bottom-line motivation of imperialism was monetary profit, and the relationship between empire and colonies was a dependent one:

> Our colonies are incomparably our best customers for our manufactures and while we are large purchasers in foreign marts for both food and raw material, we do not find there corresponding markets for our goods. . . . Nor must we forget that we are now fed from abroad. It is useless, nay foolish, to lament this fact. . . . Where should we be without our carrying trade, not merely for the import of our requirements and the export of our manufactures, but for that supply of the wants of other nations, which, by reason of our insular position, has fallen so largely to our share, and by means of which such large numbers of our people earn their living? (7, 10)

The problem that confronted England, of course, was the control of trade, or, as Begg put it, the fact that although England was involved in a one-way profiteering transaction, we may include emigrants among the transacted "goods" the other "raw" exports (10). Places that are not England, or that are recognized as not being England, both culturally and materially, figure in important ways in Dickens's *Great Expectations.*

There is no concrete evidence of the Elsewhere in this novel, just as there is no concrete description of it in *Mary Barton*. As I suggest in chapter 2, this ethereality works to maintain the very *general* usefulness of the Elsewhere when it may be construed in various and infinite ways as long as it remains an unknown. For the purposes of the literary and cultural productions discussed here, the Unknown is equivalent to the Elsewhere, and it is utilized as such.[21] The instrumental "Unknown" gleaned from these texts resembles very closely the unknown that is viewed as a challenge and a prompt for exploration and discovery by the colonies, by "uncivilized" lands in places that are not England. In the final analysis, perhaps the conceptual space of the Elsewhere remains vague and nondescript because it is so instrumental in the plot conflicts and their resolutions. There is considerable investment in maintaining to the colonies the level of commodification that emphasizes those of their qualities that are "imperceptible by the senses" (Marx 83). Employed in this way, the materiality of the colonies, and the nation's interest in it, are negated.[22] Elsewhere is both external to British domestic institutions and at the same time intrusive in its relation to them because it is so intrinsic to the empire's economic functions.

಄

What is the relationship of "superfluous" middle-class women to this literary, textually conjured Elsewhere? Given that the emigration of unmarried women was on the agendas of feminists, colonials, *and* the British domestic authorities, emigrant women are a significant factor in thinking about the kinds of values that were exported to the colonies, especially those that were in conflict with class and gender ideologies. The intersections among class, gender, and the Elsewhere in *Great Expectations* are remarkable and instructive insofar as the Elsewhere mediates and precipitates Miss Havisham's fall from grace as a new bride-to-be, just as it informs Estella's adulteration, her miseducation in matters of gender relations and social status. Perhaps most important, it is the Elsewhere that ironically informs and transforms Pip's own ideological education in matters of money and class loyalty. Tracing the practices and patterns attendant to female emigration reveals that in the Victorian hegemony, there was not a stark contrast between the constitution of home and Elsewhere, just as there was not in the minds of unmarried emigrant women, who by their very existence problematized such neat demarcations.

Based on such examples of the ways the Elsewhere mediates challenges to gender and class prescriptions in *Great Expectations,* it would seem that the ambivalent cultural value of emigrant women as exports to the colonies impacts on the domestic ideology of Victorian England not only as it was projected into the popular imagination, but also as it was transformed prior to its exportation and as it continued to mediate gender relations in England. It is precisely because the very issue of origins and cultural authenticity is put to question in this novel, and because the very origin of material wealth—regardless of social class—points to the colonies as it should, that this narrative speaks most forcefully on the extent to which England the nation "borrows" from the colonies for its continued "progress" and also its essential stratification. Likewise, it is because Victorian culture relies on an exchange in value between itself and its colonies, a relationship it denies, that Magwitch is as good as dead when he returns to England—not only because he was exiled but also because he embodies a truth about the source of money, wealth, and the speculating so common to the mid-Victorian period and at the same time so very objectionable. Finally, Magwitch's statement concerning his relationship to Pip serves as a metaphor for the colonies' relation to the nation: "I lived rough, that you should live smooth; I worked hard, that you should be above work . . ." (337). In another place, he says with characteristic bluntness: "If I aint a gentleman . . . I'm the owner of such" (339). Magwitch represents the possibility of an alternative mode of material and cultural production. He mainly represents the most unsettling proposition (and the concrete proof thereof) that the constitutive institutions of Victorian culture may, in fact, have as their main ingredient the symbolic gap and discursive absence maintained by the domestic uses to which the Elsewhere is put. This proposition is a difficult one to accept (and thus to incorporate into the cultural hegemony) because it suggests a reciprocity between England and the colonies disallowed by the imperial doctrine, and even a material subordination of the nation to the colonies' processes and internal modes of production.[23]

The conditions of the nation's relation to the colonies constitute a singularly controlled relationship and yield an ambivalent symbolic economy. *Great Expectations* suggests that the space between England and its colonies is very fruitful symbolic ground, for in that interval lie redefinitions of the value of gender roles and ideologies, and challenges to class boundaries. As such, it is in effect not only an undesirable intrusion on English domestic affairs but also—to borrow Bhabha's phrase—a "location of culture" that has unlimited potential to subvert and disturb the domestic institutions England sought to export as "pure" and unadulterated British raw material in exchange for colonial capital. The fantastic and illusory plots of this novel begin to unravel when the colonial intrudes on the domestic: Miss Havisham's present condition and pathos is to a large extent produced by the initial condition and proposition that a man may opt out of a marriage commitment by escaping into the Elsewhere, a place where the issue of accountability (the central theme of the novel) is moot. Likewise, her all-consuming passion would not have produced a socially displaced Estella, who claims at the end "I have relinquished all property," inheriting only the house, the symbolic site of Miss Havisham's and Pip's failed ambitions and hence the failure of "progress" (492). With his singular claim to a piece of Victorian culture, and as an ambivalent, unauthorized representative of the colonial context that maintains a degree of autonomy in relation to England, the exiled Magwitch manages to intervene and expose the transparency of the domestic ideology's fallacies.

The questions engaged in this chapter suggest that the notion of an Elsewhere is, in fact, intrinsic to the workings of the Here, so long as that Here also is seen to encompass what Disraeli called England's internal fragmentation, its "Two Nations." The problems that domestic ethnographers like Engels and Gaskell textualize in trying to map the underclasses of Manchester facilitate an invigorated appreciation of the specifics of domestic foreignness and hegemonic invisibility. As both *Mary Barton* and *Great Expectations* also suggest, when the problem of gender is added to this class-based fragmentation, the symbolic extension of the nation subsumes a promising Elsewhere. That emigrant women occupied a virtual nonplace within England contributes to an understanding of the conceptual and situational transition that was entailed in their leaving England to forge new possibilities abroad. In delineating the distinctions between England as "home" and the colonies and dominions as foreign places, we must conclude that in the domestic hegemony, there was not a stark contrast between them, nor was there such for unmarried emigrant women who, by their very presence, exposed the obfuscation of those boundaries.

Female emigration was neither culturally unique nor isolated. The systematic exportation of middle-class, "superfluous" women to the colonies followed the established patterns of general emigration but also the tradition of exiling problematic women. It had also long been enacted by the laboring classes within England. Although the emigration process managed artfully to renegotiate gender and class systems, female emigration did not in itself manifest any political innovation. Rather, the accommodation of unmarried women as a domestic problem prompted the extension and diversification of extant cultural practices. The condition of the lives of unmarried middle- and working-class women did not in itself prompt any cultural, political, or economic innovation. Rather, the accommodation of these unmarried women as a national problem prompted the extension and diversification of existing cultural and conceptual models. Given that unmarried women were "disposed of" in an already familiar and reliable manner (one that applied to the working classes traditionally), the only negotiation necessary must be directly and mainly relevant to the concerns surrounding gender. The significance of cultural exclusion and expulsion was already established, so that the main necessary hegemonic negotiation surrounding female emigration entailed the reframing of the category of gender. Such reframing poses the question of where the Victorian spinster's cultural value may lie. Furthermore, the invisibility of the Victorian laboring classes is analogous, in some interesting ways, to that of the "superfluous" woman. This chapter has worked to suggest that gender has its precise place among other domestic difficulties and that the colonial emigration of spinsters is analogous to the displacement and dispossession for the poor. The next chapter delves into the details of the personal and cultural displacement represented by the emigration of the unmarried woman.

Figure 4.1: Horrors of the Emigrant Ship, 1869. Courtesy of the Prints and Photographs Division, Library of Congress.

4

UNSAFE JOURNEYS

∂❧

Memory, Displacement, and Authority

GIRLS FOR AUSTRALIA—On an Emigrant Ship
A crowd had gathered on the wharf, and cheered as the great ship glided past
them. There was a waving of handkerchiefs, and cries of good-bye, but not one
of the girls cried in the conventional way. . . . The last you saw of the ship was
a row of excited faces in evident enjoyment at your ungainly leaps forward. One
would like to follow them to their new homes, and watch their lives take each
their own cause in the far-off country, where so many eyes are straining for the
arrival of such girls from the old country.

—J. W. Spender, *Westminster Gazette*, 1897

I n an article entitled "80 Stout and Healthy Looking Girls," historian Wesley Turner documents the scandal precipitated by the arrival of emigrant Irish workhouse women in Quebec in 1865. It appears that during the usual delays between their arrival and placement, the women occupied themselves with drinking and prostitution, and many failed to comply with prearranged placement plans, choosing instead to name their own destinations. The controversy surrounding these women's emigration and behavior reached England and was passionately taken up by many on both sides of the Atlantic. It is instructive of the main issues concerning the delicate relationship between the empire and its colonies and dominions. Critically foregrounding both the details and the implications of exporting women, the rhetoric surrounding this incident also defines the moral importance attached to female emigration. As Canadians objected to what they viewed as "'this wholesale exportation of vice from the workhouses to Canada,'" they also concluded that "'the morality of the country is as important as its money'" (Turner 42). They thus placed a trade value on morality and on the women who were supposed to be its vehicles of transport. What happens when these vehicles of cultural value are themselves compromised by the act of transport?

Of the many interesting features of the debate responding to the incident, two are most remarkable. First, the argument was made by the Limerick Poor Law emigration administrator that since, "'with the exception of the young women with illegitimate children, these females left Ireland with perfectly unblemished characters,'" perhaps the women experienced a moral fall because they became disoriented because they were accustomed to the structure and organization, the confines, of the workhouses (Turner 43). Stating that these same women had by and large been law abiding and had not caused any problems in their former domiciles, the only explanation remaining for their behavior was that they were out of their proper context, and that this had caused problems. Additionally, the women were "victimized by the temptations of the new world, that Canadian officials were to blame for not providing adequate supervision, and that the girls' true characters would in any case eventually resurface" (46). Beyond the boundaries of the institution of the workhouse, then, the women were easy prey in the presence of the immorality prevailing in the colonies. Clearly, they had undergone a transformation, but not one that rendered them completely altered.

A second point that surfaces in the emigration discourse, and that prompted a lengthy and involved investigation, concerned the morally corrupting influence on the culture of the emigrant ships.[1] The question was whether the moral fall of these women had not been precipitated by the seamen and the very space of the ship, and whether "the placing of so large a number of women on board a crowded ship where they are left to their own devices can only be productive of baneful results" (Turner 43). Although this disagreement was never settled to anyone's satisfaction, the point was made that "the women's demoralization clearly had begun during the sea voyage," despite assurances that "it had been an unusually rapid passage of a passenger ship," the *St. David,* and that the clientele and crew of this ship were of superior socioeconomic status, training, and reputation (43). The concern over morality lapses on board ship was a persistent one, however. The Victorian imperial administrator Sydney Herbert makes an impassioned argument in his 1851 essay for protecting emigrant women in transit, aboard emigrant ships that are clearly agents of corruption. He appeals to the public's concern for women's special vulnerability, citing "not less than eight cases . . . in which the single women have arrived [in the colonies] with characters notoriously tainted on the passage" (9). One new problem illustrated in the preceding example is that of the very process of travel for emigrant women, of their perceptions of their roles in the emigration effort, and of their agency, which may, at times, be in defiance of contractual agreements made on their behalf. The issues that surface are those that emerge consistently in regard to female emigration: The morality of the emigrant women, the colonies as receptacles of imperial "excess" and the complicity of the emigration assisters in compromising the colonies' preferences. As is suggested by the women at the center of the 1865 controversy in Canada, emigrant women exhibit a degree of agency and perhaps even rebellion, which rendered them problematic. They may ultimately even surface as resisting commodities.

The two figurative "travelers" examined here represent a problematic relation between physical space and social identity and suggest some of the more elusive subtleties of both the process and products of their commodification as unauthorized, unlegitimated cultural subjects. The Alices in Lewis Carroll's *Through the Looking Glass* and Elizabeth Gaskell's *Mary Barton,* very different characters in very different kinds of texts, figuratively exemplify the status of the female commodity in transit. Both texts scrutinize identities in flux and examine their relation to the difficulties of certain knowledge and recognizability in that context. They are instructive mainly in the ways they are valued as commodities in the context of Victorian culture, manifesting problematic relations to those contexts and to themselves as "transcendent" and yet complexly established cultural subjects. Current understandings of commodification as cultural practice also apply to the ways that the colonies are commodified until they attain a kind of "transcendence" and to the uses to which unmarried women are put in the imperial context. Both the colonies and the emigrant unmarried women are commodified to serve varying and conflicting purposes to the extent that use and meaning are in conflict. Carroll's Alice is well known as a child who persistently oversteps boundaries, the consequences of which actions make elaborate reference to the foundations of those boundaries. Alice's transgressions cause both the subject and her contexts to become refigured. Even as she looks forward to returning home, the "travels" and explorations of the young, rebellious Alice produce a vision of hegemonic alterity, a meaningfulness that easily can be seen to transform her point of origin, her familiar base of "home." In her status as commodity Alice highlights the ways subjects are conversely situated in regard to social relations in general. The two Alices also scrutinize the notion of difference embodied in the foreign "exotic," as attempts are made to appropriate and negate it. In this case difference is not negated successfully, since the young Alice does not achieve her goal of inserting herself into the unknown and adjusting it to her needs. She does not manage effectively to manipulate its meanings but remains a foreigner to it.

England's sending what it considered its "superfluous" women Elsewhere was mediated by the dialectic of emigration. As a result, the details of female transportation serve to comment on the Victorian hegemony and highlight the intersections of national and gender ideologies. The figurative journeys undertaken by the two Alices of this chapter traverse space that is ideological as well as geographic and material. This context facilitates a consideration of the issue of female agency. Chapter 3 worked to suggest that marginalized Victorian British subjects were in a state of perpetual flux and dislocation in their relation to the category of the nation, both ideologically and geographically. There is ample evidence, as with the political events to which *Mary Barton* makes reference, that working-class people regularly initiated acts of rebellion and insubordination. It is not likely that female emigrants were passive recipients of either legislation or social practice. The gender politics of cultural travel, which stands in contrast to the kinds of agency afforded Victorian females, support this possibility. Exploring the politics of displacement, this chapter investigates the possibilities of subversion as an ingredient in the emigration project. Subversion is variously associated with the Victorian female subject and subsumes her status as cultural commodity (which, as the emigration rhetoric suggests, was established fairly effectively by the 1880s). The questions that surface in this context concern the meanings attached to women's geographic mobility and the ways meaning is negotiated in specific rhetorical contexts. As noted in chapter 2, "superfluous" women were said by some to be most fit for emigration and colonial "duty" and were viewed as being potentially successful at enduring both transport and change. The literary, figurative journeys examined here offer an inroads to such questions and also suggest the limits of that potential.[2]

In the material and figurative "journeys" featured in Carroll and Gaskell, semiotics of travel are as culturally prominent as are its practical features. The perplexing ventures into the unknown of Carroll's Alice are attended by insurmountable and apparently arbitrary codifications of the traveling process, just as Gaskell's Alice, the perpetual imaginative traveler, confronts an idealized past that continues to be meaningful to her in her later years, if only as a Not-Here. The implications of both these kinds of travel for the emigrant women as commodities are significant insofar as imagining and/or remembering constitutes a symbolic space that bridges the Here with the possibility of an Elsewhere. Emigrant women had first to imagine themselves somewhere else, out of England, before they actually began to travel, much as the emigration assisters often were forced first to address the problem of Here—women's place in England—before they could make any compelling argument for placing women into foreign spaces. As some of the women were to exclaim in realistic assessments of their status in England: "I am exceedingly obliged to the Society for the privilege of coming to the Colony. I have been tolerably successful and hope to be able to return [to England] in a year or two. There are difficulties here as well as at home, but on the whole I think one's prospects are better here. . . ."[3] Even when they are forging into a frightening unknown, there is general recognition that the circumstances at home were ones the emigrant women chose to leave behind.

The details of this bridging process are illustrated in the example of these two characters, who come across as excessively limited in their self-conceptions and in their new and disorienting surroundings. This is easy to see in Carroll's heroine; Gaskell's spinster, Alice, is perpetually disoriented as she attempts to reconcile her present reality with what she had known "reality" and human existence to be in the distant past: the unspoiled countryside, familial intimacy, and the parent's relation to the child as protector. This second Alice suits the purpose of this study best, because she also embodies the woman who is sexually and socially dispossessed.

REMEMBERING: DISLOCATING IDENTITIES

Alice's adventures provide an allegory that articulates most explicitly the process of travel and transplantation as the fundamental experience of the emigrant. While *Alice in Wonderland* addresses some of these issues also, *Through the Looking Glass* deliberates the problems of constructed identity and dislocation much more explicitly, and does so in direct relation to the process of travel. Specifically, its emphasis on self-instigated travel puts Alice in a position similar to that of emigrant women, since she determines to breach the borders of the looking glass, decidedly a very different gesture from falling into travel. *Through the Looking Glass* is thus a more interesting text for the purposes of this discussion and is more immediately applicable to the dislocations that ensue in relation to the possibility of emigration. The parallels between the two sets of circumstances involving Alice and the emigrant women are extensive.

Literary critics and historians have observed that women traveled in the Victorian period as a means of getting away from male dominance as it habitually exerted itself in their daily lives. Critic Eva-Marie Kroller, in particular, states that many Victorian "women travelers went abroad precisely to escape the demands of their families in general, and their fathers, brothers, suitors, and husbands in particular" (91). She concludes, rightly, that to align these women with travel as a masculinist act of "penetration" is to ignore completely the position from which they traveled and their symbolic destinations. Whether it was "male dominance" as such that they sought to escape, it is clear that the imposition of the larger system of gender on the personal realm was oppressive to women and that they quite deliberately freed themselves from those pressures by travel. Furthermore, both curiosity—or the desire to know—and explorations through travel are emancipatory, empowering activities for those with freedom to move from place to place. Alice does not engage in those kinds of self-conscious motivations for engaging in exploration: Her travel experience is more intersubjective and immersing than emancipatory, although her curiosity alone would qualify as an emancipatory strategy. In this respect, Alice is reminiscent of the many Victorian "lady explorers" who looked outside their own culture in search of new spaces and new forms of knowledge. Some critics have seen this as a progressive movement. According to Margaret Strobel, "female travelers appeared to challenge Victorian gender norms and in many ways served as harbingers of New Women" (37).

In *Through the Looking Glass* Alice undergoes a number of unsettling experiences that put her in, and perpetuate, a state of disorientation and confusion. The experiences echo the intense uncertainty, anxiety, and confusion but also the wonderment emigrant women experienced in leaving England to chart out new futures for themselves in little-known places. While admittedly a silly tale about highly unlikely happenings, Carroll's story also works to represent and capitalize upon the very real fears of Victorian readers, themselves in a childlike state of awe and amazement before the specter of a globe stretching before them endlessly various and unimaginable notions of humanity and possibility in unimaginable modes of existence. Victorians' views of children and childhood suggest the imaginative economies upon which their visions of the colonies are based. Likewise, the connections between gender-based commodification in general and that of children are many, and the uses to which children and childhood are put are variously telling. As cultural critic Carol Mavor notes, Victorians "envisioned one's early years as a lost utopia" and hence as a constructed distant topos, an Elsewhere that came finally to be signified by the child and the condition of childhood. The fetishization of children and the colonies followed quite effortlessly, enforcing the possibility of the child as agent for the "lost utopia."[4] Mavor continues, "the material culture of Victorian childhood produced souvenirs of a time and place that never was—a true Neverland" (2). Both Alices are infantilized, just as the spinsters were infantilized, and just as the colonies are persistently represented as existing in the infantile phase of their cultural evolution. The symbolic significance of childhood and infantilization are instrumental governing notions in both Gaskell's spinster in *Mary Barton* and Carroll's precocious Alice as they confront their respective Elsewheres, a point to which I return later.

In Carroll's chapter entitled "Wool and Water," Alice's repartee with the figure of the Queen illustrates one specific feature of disorientation. To the Queen's statement, "One's memory works both ways," Alice is appalled and can respond only, "I'm sure *mine* only works one way . . . I can't remember things before they happen" (82). She thus exempts herself from whatever generalizations the Queen might make concerning everyone's memory but also distinguishes herself from both the Queen and others who are not like her. Similarly, she holds onto her sense of what is right and normal, even if it means opposing the formidable figure of the Queen. The final judgment stands, however, with the Queen's conclusion that "It's a poor sort of memory that only works backwards" (82). Exploration and discovery, the main subjects of Carroll's account of Alice's misadventures, are facilitated by the imaginary, by the ability to remember both backward and forward. Indeed, given the extensive displacement Alice experiences in her travels, remembering backward is a matter of survival, a necessity for remembering who she is and from where she comes so that she might return to that identity and place. It also guides her in her new environments by assuring her of her preestablished identity and "place" in relation to her new surroundings and by contrasting her place of origin to those she will occupy during her travels. Thanks to such differentiations, Alice therefore would be able to construct meaning of, and appreciate, the experience she is about to have as "travel," insofar as "travel" differs from the experience of staying put, of occupying a singular and fixed place, both physically and symbolically. In the context of the Victorian age, which prided itself on its mobility and transcendence, Alice's explorations are also "travels" in the sense of crossing the boundaries of space, knowledge, and culture and thus experiencing different ways of being.

Remembering in the conventional way, backward and into the past, will enable Alice to occupy the new places she visits as a "traveler"—an outsider looking in on a culture, place, and reality other than her own. Remembering backward will ensure Alice's return to her place of origin, either physically or ethereally through memory. Capable of such remembering, Alice can, in a sense, occupy both places at once. The paradox of remembering forward introduces itself to "Alice the Traveler" as a necessary ingredient to traveling "properly"—that is, in repeating an established dialectical relationship among knowing, traveling, and remembering. That is the message conveyed to her not by the place or people or recollections of what she has left behind but by the new creatures she encounters in the new land she explores. Suggesting that remembering forwards is another name for prejudice, the Queen says, for example: "The King's Messenger . . . is in prison now, being punished: and the trial doesn't even begin till next Wednesday: and of course the crime comes last of all" (82). In this context, remembering forward is like anticipating; it is a matter of imagining what is most likely to happen or what might happen, which minimizes the danger of acting inappropriately. The ability to predict is the power to foresee and thus to control a process in which meaning and experience are not consequential. Remembering forward also mediates the danger of miscalculating the likelihood of things, since consequences do not carry the weight they do in the order of things that constitutes a remembering informed by material experience. The elements of risk and chance that are part of travel are absent here otherwise. The Queen says that even if the Messenger is punished wrongly and unfairly, a little extra punishment is not a bad thing. This idea upsets Alice's linear thinking, which mandates that all actions have their predictable consequences and that evidence of proof always precedes judgment. Alice is disoriented by encounters that oppose her notions of causality, that is, the logical structure of sequences. More than anticipating, remembering forward is envisioning, imagining, and projecting. The power inherent in one's ability to influence outcomes is multifaceted, for remembering forward is meddling with (and potentially even changing) the future, since there is no concrete knowledge to support one's present actions but only possibility and fancy. Remembering of this sort is an imposition, an interference with the order of things that serves as a subtext in terms of Alice's acquired and established knowledge. Remembering forward is an appropriation, much as the empire's projections of an appropriated, commodified, and altered world was an assertion of its agency and fancy over that of specific others and over the multitude of transformations that would not have taken place if not for imperial interference.

This process of projection is epitomized in the established practices of Victorian anthropology and ethnography, the methods of which unfailingly situated the "here and now" in Victorian domestic culture as a materialization of "progress." According to this causality, objective reality becomes rationalized and appropriated as proof of the dominant hierarchy.[5] In the case of Alice's disorientation, the act of recognizing something as familiar pertains to knowing its essential features and functions in relation to oneself. The familiar and the known are also always knowable even as they change, as the "remembered" is as well. The activities of identifying and classifying beings, settings, and objects new to oneself is an act of appropriation insofar as they permit a linguistic and cognitive appropriation: "Guidebook descriptions of the geography and flora of a place are of course also an act of possession," says Kroller, especially since they render those same objects the "known" henceforth (94).[6] Definition entails appropriation and classification entails death, specifically because "naming, like a cast of the die, is just one step toward unnaming, is a tool to render visible what [has been] carefully kept invisible . . ." (Minh-ha 48). To the extent that classification fosters revision and ensues subsequent reappropriation and reconstitution, according to Minh-ha, it is diametrically opposed to the "heterogeneity of free play," an activity all too obviously lacking in, yet one that intrudes upon *Through the Looking-Glass* (49).

Practical, ever present, and in command of herself, Alice triumphs even in the predicament of her disorientation. She concludes very logically that "Of course the first thing to do was to make a grand survey of the country she was going to travel through. 'It's something very like learning geography' . . ." (45). And so geography or demography, naming the new places and things one encounters, becomes a central orienting task, or at least one that will counter any dangers of the absence of an identity one always has possessed and known. The new terrain and landscape become part of the body of knowledge possessed by the traveler, become incorporated into all the traveler already knows to be so. In light of this observation, the questions that surface—what does it mean to travel "right"? and what does it mean to not do it wrong?—suggest there is a kind of protocol one follows in traveling, a culturally circumscribed ritual; at least, that is what her fellow passengers tell her. "Don't make excuses," said the guard. Alice thought to herself: "Then there's no use in speaking" (47). In this context, speaking is equivalent to "making excuses" or to justifying one's place and reasserting one's authority.

The narrative language of travel experience situates the reader in the Here as opposed to the Elsewhere, to a more certain if contrived place. Prenarrating her experiences of travel and what Alice would say in retrospect makes implicit reference to her inherent ability to remember forward—that is, her ability to know that she may recollect, at will, the present moment in some future time and for a future audience, an imagined subject position that would render her more empowered over her surroundings. Travel narrating reveals a stark contrast between the Alice who offers her experiences to those who would seem to lack that experience, and the Alice who must understand for herself where she is and what her new status is to be. Significantly, the travel narrative differs from her ordinary speech and proposes the possibility of a voyeuristic narrator. Imagining herself as narrator and transposing herself from the present place and moment, Alice takes heart: "What fun it'll be when they ask me how I liked my walk. I shall say 'Oh, I like it well enough—' (here came the favourite little toss of the head), 'only it *was* so dusty and hot, and the elephants *did* tease so!'" (46). Such language, Mikhail Bakhtin notes, makes reference to the material by-products of social exchange, contrived and artificial things that pertain mainly to social exchange so that "each concrete utterance is a social act . . . a part of social reality . . . totally enmeshed in the communication event" (120). Hence the urgency in Alice's compulsion to project narrations of her experience.[7]

Alice's avowal to silence confirms the manifold dissociation she experiences of signs that do not signify in a recognizable way and that ultimately challenge the authority of her every perception. This phenomenon is succinctly applicable to the female emigrant, who in the process of inserting herself into an existing and established (although contested) cultural context does not possess the authority to manipulate contexts in order to authenticate or replicate her own reality. That emigrant women arrived in the colonies already "silent" is evidenced in numerous sources, both colonial and domestic.[8] It is not only in the foreign colonial context that the emigrant is "silenced," and not only in accord with her invisibility as a spinster in the domestic culture, but also in the course of the physical travel, during the course of transport. As historian Andrew Hassam infers from his study of travel diaries, unmarried women on board emigrant ships were censured and silenced to an unprecedented and shocking degree. What was contested was "their right to speak for themselves rather than to be spoken about, to have their voices heard" (71). Whether these women could or did in fact "speak" to the colonial condition or of their experience as "travelers" of sorts cannot be decided conclusively. What is more certain is that their speaking and naming do not constitute an appropriative act in an imperial sense, so that there is need to question their relation to such acts.

If we can view Alice as an unauthorized traveler because her status as a child and as a commodity allows for curiosity but not for categorical transgression, then we can see the many creatures she encounters as posing questions pertinent to the empire's presence abroad. The creatures Alice encounters are themselves inconstant in terms of power relations so that at times they speak as do the colonized. For them, "to speak is to exist absolutely for the other," for the colonizer, and quite typically, they fail to do so very effectively for her purposes (Fanon 18). In her efforts to assume a place of cultural importance, the emigrant spinster is analogous to the disoriented emigrant who has no tangible connection to "home" and no guarantee of a return to it. Alice occupies an inconclusive and indeterminate place in relation to the antagonism between colonizer and colonized. In "The Looking-Glass Insects" chapter, the tables are turned so that Alice, the spectator, becomes spectacle. The Guard, who clearly has considerable power over Alice's well-being, uses his own version of a much more intrusive looking glass to inspect Alice, the commodity-in-transit: "the Guard was looking at her, first through a telescope, then through a microscope, and then through an opera-glass. At last he said 'You're traveling the wrong way,' and shut up the window, and went away" (47). More important, Alice is scrutinized quite closely and then is criticized for doing wrongly what has nonetheless been her sole activity during this adventure: "'So young a child', said the gentleman sitting opposite to her . . . , 'ought to know which way she is going, even if she doesn't know her own name'" (47).

Encapsulated in Alice's predicament is the problem of concrete identity/established subjectivity as opposed to destination or "place." In this context, matters of etiquette are also matters of survival. To the question "What does traveling 'right' look like?" which confronts Alice, the answer that surfaces concerns the dissembling of the identity of the traveler *as* traveler. Once Alice's identity as traveler is undermined under the scrutiny of unknown codes, traveling translates into a fear of loss of her identity and her compulsion to name everything she encounters. She cries out in frustration, "well, at any rate it's a great comfort . . . after being so hot, to get into the—into the—into *what?* I mean to get under the—under the—under *this,* you know!" (56). In the process of attempting to name things, Alice is effectively commodifying the unknown things she encounters, much as ethnography claims the things it catalogues and much as commodification establishes or produces its own language.[9] Everything Alice thought she knew has been cast into doubt and indeterminacy, and she herself has ended up all "wrong." She is fearful of unnamed things, and this one fear differs from other irregularities

she has come across. Unnamed things are more threatening because
they are familiar and thus known to her but contextually unknow-
able. That is, they are not so in any communal or communicable
sense: They are unspeakable and hence undialogical. The process by
which disorientation and dislocation are effected, however, appears
to be mainly geographic, material. When she approaches the looking
glass and is able to look at both worlds, Alice stands on the periphery of the unknown but also of the known. In that moment, both are
only marginally *her* contexts, and neither one is that completely:
"what could be seen from the old room was quite common and un-
interesting, but . . . all the rest was as different as possible" (18). The
only practical use of a privileged perspective is the attainment of the
knowledge that one cannot know a place and a vantage point; to accomplish that familiarity, one must *be* there. Likewise, the consequences of an ordinary act in the course of ordinary events are
enormous. What could be observed from a safe distance, from within
the confines of "home," is knowable or made familiar by the act of
translation by the author of the travel narrative. On the other hand,
physical exposure is not mediated by the known to the same degree
and thus is essentially different.

The predicament confronted by Carroll's Alice is important to
my discussion of emigrant women's problematic positioning in the
Victorian imperial context. As a child Alice is precious and precocious, all that the woman could not be said to be, since she was excessive. Furthermore, imperial discourse does figure in this text, but
not as has been theorized thus far; the female's "place" in relation to
domestic and foreign spaces and the extent of her agency within
them do not yield her as imperialist. The objectification of the child
(and of childhood) produces a vision of the child as commodity in
the Victorian context, and it may be argued that Carroll participates
in and facilitates this. However, since Alice does not easily qualify as
colonizer, it would not suffice to class her, as does critic Daniel
Bivona, the "child-imperialist": "Like a good imperialist, . . . Alice assumes that because she comes to play a role in the 'creatures' drama
by virtue of her undismissable presence, she can thereby dominate it,
and successful domination must be the inevitable reward of comprehension" (158). Carroll's narrative does not suggest that Alice has
achieved any remarkable level of "comprehension." On the contrary,
her predicament lies in her inability to understand, which compromises her in her relation to the world and to others. Mavor observes

that "there is no way of demarcating [Alice's] innocence . . . from her guilt," despite the "period's obsessive devotion to the innocence of the young girl" (34). Alice's role is an ambiguous one. It is bound to remain so, both in relation to her own commodification and to her relation to the hierarchies of authority and legitimation as an observer and as spectacle, positions she occupies simultaneously.

Along these lines of rethinking the cultural status of women, historian Deborah Cherry's refiguring of the ambiguous placement of the female subject in relation to the dominant Victorian culture and to her status as both spectator and spectacle is quite useful. Her claim that the "domestic interior spaces of bourgeois Victorian women offered [them] a different order of visual gratification in which the gaze was 'that of equal or like'" urges a reconsideration of the subject positioning of these women (114). Given this proposition, it can no longer be taken for granted that middle-class Victorian women were perpetual passive recipients of the male gaze in the arena of commodity display, even within the domestic realm. Cherry adds that this kind of domestic feminine gaze "was not the 'mastering gaze' of the voyeur or *flaneur* but an exchange between women of reciprocal glances within spaces characterized by proximity" (114). If it was "enclosure" and containment that gave this "look" its "nonmastering" quality, women who are found outside the domestic realm may be conceived as possibly engaging in "mastering" practices. They also may be seen to have revised their general practice of "looking," insofar as their "proximity" and relation to one another as commodities goes. Cherry's thesis, then, allows for a rethinking of the female subject as exhibitionist and as voyeur, the prevalence of which in the Victorian imaginary is evidenced in Alice's transformations. In her rather indeterminate place in the Victorian hegemony, which mirrors that of the problematic middle-class single woman, Alice's subjectivity alters in accordance with her physical and geographic placement. Her essence and cultural value, in Carroll's account, is contextual. Hence Alice's predicament when she comes across the wood without a name:

> "This must be the wood," she said thoughtfully to herself, "where things have no names. I wonder what'll become of *my* name when I go in? I shouldn't like to lose it at all . . ."
>
> "Then it really *has* happened, after all! And now, who am I? I *will* remember if I can!" (56)

When the fawn says that it cannot remember its own name, the problem of identity and self-recognition shifts most clearly to reflect the importance of physical space and place. Remembering and knowing thus become localized and perhaps even geographic issues. This point is made most bluntly: "I can't remember *here*" (58). The suggestion is that when one "can't remember here," one may be able to remember "elsewhere," but one may *imagine*—if not remember—here. When forgetfulness befalls Alice and she loses her memory of objects she had been able to recognize and name in the past, the significance of place over an immutable and essential identity is emphasized incontrovertibly. Memory and comprehension return when Alice moves to a different spot in the wood. Like the emigrant to the colonies, for whom leaving England translated into a fairly irreversible dissociation from the known, and for whom a change of mind and hence return was not practically feasible, what Alice left behind is replaced by many unknowns, new places and experiences.

Even while invested with fantastic potential, the new places always pale in comparison, no matter how exciting they are. This issue of the limits of the imaginary and of memory also encompasses the pervasive hope among emigrant women that being in an entirely different and alien place would change everything: It would change both what they had always known to be true of their former life experiences and who they might become in their new contexts.[10] This experience is potentially liberating and highly creative, since it facilitates the creation of complex, often imaginative "provisional ways of being," modes of existence and thought that transcend and ameliorate the pervasiveness of prescriptive ideologies by virtue of existing outside them (Nixon 150).

REMEMBERING BACKWARD

I discussed Gaskell's *Mary Barton* in chapter 3 as well, in positing that the author's attempt to chart the existence of the lower classes is one domestic instance of the conceptual model for Elsewhere intercepted by gender politics. My discussion of *Mary Barton* here concentrates on the character of Alice, the spinster of the novel, and the sole character who circumvents subjective contradictions in her life by engaging in time travel. The past to which Alice travels represents a mode of existence that, as the novel evidences, is no longer possible and can be called forth only as an Elsewhere that holds a vague promise that cannot actually be achieved. The present moment, in contrast, is the most undesirable condition and place in which one can find oneself. Coming out of a period that marks poverty as a national condition, much as it was perceived to be by the emigration advocates and assisters, this novel offers an interesting instance of early Victorian social and literary commentary on travel. It addresses specifically the dilemma of limited mobility in Victorian England, mainly in movement from the countryside to the city and in imaginary travel through memory.

The Elsewhere of the past is nonetheless important in communicating to the new generations of laborers the existence of a different time and place that was once the province of the working classes. Alice's narrations of the past may serve as a sociopolitical caution against complacency and likewise as an alternative to the destitution represented by ruined women like Esther who have turned to prostitution. In that case, Alice's recollections mirror little Alice's process of transplantation and also become a projection of a more ideal state of existence, a kind of "remembering forward." More likely, however, recollecting an extinct place and time is a means of escape into a much less bereft, preindustrial English condition, a place in the past that can no longer be achieved. If that is the case, then the past to which Alice clings is somewhat like the colonies, in that it is "naive" and has not achieved progress, but unlike the colonies it cannot be redeemed. The world Alice left behind is a specific place in time and is now part of her consciousness, her memory. This alternative space is employed in complicating the limits of the Victorian imaginary. In her recollections Alice returns to a past time of lost innocence, her own childhood. In the present act of remembering, she regrets having been self-indulgent and disobedient, thus revising the memory she recalls so fondly. Implying that she would not have allowed herself childish behaviors now if she could revisit the past to change it, Alice transforms the past as she visits it. In the plot's present moment, Alice is a reformed child, an unnatural child, a childlike woman. She functions as the community's link to its collective past and as the embodiment of the community's now lost relationship to a nature that, once lost, becomes available again as a subject of scientific inquiry and study. As other characters confirm, it is an important feature of the laboring classes that they were not necessarily meant to dwell in slums, just as the grandfather inspects and analyzes

natural creatures, surprising the middle-class observer with his natural curiosity and the earnestness of his scientific pursuits. The
anomaly or exception, it follows, may begin to define the mass and
may even begin to resituate the marginalized from subjects to agents
of inquiry.

&a.

What significance is there in Alice's revisiting and, most important,
recalling the past? In the absence of self-determination and geographic mobility, one resorts to the mobility of the imagination and
undertakes a travel through time. Ideally, as experience the past
would serve to inspire and to inform, but it also may serve as a
model against which to scrutinize the present. For Alice, it is mainly
an escape from the ugly present; her translation of her personal
memories of the past may serve to highlight to her listeners that
something has been taken from them, that the present circumstances
must not be accepted or internalized complacently. In this way the
Elsewhere of the past serves as an "out" most literally in this novel,
just as the geographical Elsewhere comes into direct play in the plot
at the very end of the story. Escape into the past also represents a lost
innocence and purity, both of which are accessible now only
through the spinster as a woman material experience has not quite
spoiled. As the "anachronistic" creature she is, the spinster remains
untouched by life, unlike the other women in the novel whose preoccupations with pressing family needs and crises do not permit
time for remembering. Alice is the only living link to a past that is
imagined as being untainted by the present. Her peers, who shared
that past with her, are seen as too preoccupied by mundane matters
such as marriage, love, and politics. They are consumed by the urgency of their current predicament and are thus unable to fulfill her
role. Unlike Alice, they have no "out" to speak of, since their political and romantic plots fail. However, divested of any agenda or desire apart from returning to the past—which also negates the
present—and remanded to the cause of humanitarianism, Alice is
only marginally vital to her own community since she is at odds
with it in many ways: She is as inconsequential in history as she is in
social life.

Alice possesses a romantic and idealized relationship not only to
her past but also to her present. That is, her relations with others are

neither polarized nor conflicted—they are neither political nor otherwise strained since she serves the sole purpose of catering to, mothering, and subserving the world. Her significance is very contingent, then, and it may be viewed as a solely mediating, tangential one. Similarly, the past Alice describes exists only in her vivid narratives and recollections, and it is conjured up in the face of moments of utter defeat for the working classes. As an ironic ordering principle, Victorian class-based dispossession is unique in terms of gender and in relation to the institution of marriage. Alice serves as the embodiment of this dispossession and displacement, despite her unproblematic function in her present context; her attachment to the past constitutes her main distinguishing feature.

Alice wishes to return to the past, to a lost innocence that she can never recapture but that is nonetheless, despite its never having been such, persistently represented as an *actual* place in the past, and an ideal one at that. Simply in its contrast to the Here, which is overly difficult to understand and much too consequentially incriminating, the past, childhood, the countryside, all collude to form a far more desirable Elsewhere. However, if it is indeed the case that "it's a poor sort of memory that only works backwards," as Carroll's Queen ordains, then Gaskell's Alice is indeed a "poor" traveler. Lacking a vision into the future and absent any future prospects, her backward destination is Nowhere. Moreover, Alice's celibacy and martyrdom qualify her as the translator of the past and of history, just as they serve to infantilize her in the present moment. This Alice is also childlike, which in the worst of instances is equated to moronic. While she is available to all whom might need her, she is only marginally successful in ministering to the needs of others; Alice is said to be "too delicate-minded" to plan even the most simple visit, to manage even the most menial and trivial tasks that place her at a social center (65).[11] Anne McClintock's contention that "like colonial landscapes, the slums were figured as inhabiting an *anachronistic* space . . . a time beyond the recall of memory . . . [and having] little or no history" (121) applies well to Alice who, as a spinster, becomes the sole possessor of the memory that is missing in others and that is not manifested in the slums themselves, their physical surroundings, since they are also dispossessed. Likewise, Alice's memories are not intrinsically or essentially valuable because they are of little practical use to the urban underclass. Therefore, her symbolic usefulness and purpose, her serving to link the present problem to its origins, is at odds with both her own sense as truth-bearing being and the narrator's representation of her as virtuous in her altruism. Alice's main contribution to her community is a symbolic serving up of "the bread of her childhood," which ultimately does not suffice to remedy the evils that confront it (66). In her ineffectual role as potential nurturer and redeemer, Alice the spinster typifies the martyr, of whom Gaskell appears to approve especially and whom she exempts from the responsibilities and impossible constraints of both class and gender.

In every instance Gaskell juxtaposes the spinster to the self-interested working-class subject: John Barton's leftist politics cause him to become callous and insensitive to the needs of others; Mary Barton's desire to enter the ranks of the manufacturing class cause her to reject the virtuous man who loves her in favor of an illicit affair with the affluent Herbert Carson, the factory owner's son. The intersections of sex and class are clear not only in the central action of the plot, which calls for Mary's proper education in matters of love (which she must learn the hard way) but also in Alice's being a kind of vacuous "recorder" for this community and an agent through whom morality and innocence still may suggest their presence among the working classes. To be displaced and dispossessed, then, is not specific to the unmarried woman, but is a feature of the Victorian ethnography. Alice repeatedly recounts the process by which so many of Manchester's poor left their places of origin, the countryside, in pursuit of occupation in the repulsive yet invisible places of the city. Her recollections constitute a travel or ethnographic narrative that she shares with people who either have never been there, being second-generation urban laborers, or do not recall having been there. The most unsettling feature of her narrative is that it also serves to cast doubt on the present moment and reality and the very materiality of present circumstances and knowledge by recalling the most concrete feature of the past:

> Well, and near our cottage were rocks. *Eh, lasses! ye don't know what rocks are in Manchester!* Gray pieces o' stone as large as a house, all covered over wi' moss of different colours, some yellow, some brown; and the ground beneath them knee-deep in purple heather, smelling sae sweet and fragrant, and the low music of the humming-bee for ever sounding among it. Mother used to send Sally and me out to gather ling and heather for besoms, and it was such pleasant work! . . . It seems all like yesterday, and yet

it's a long time agone. . . . But I often wonder if the hawthorn is standing
yet, and if the lasses still go to gather heather, as we did many and many a
year past and gone. I sicken at heart to see the old spot once again. May be
next summer I may set off. . . . (70, emphasis added)

Members of the new urban laboring class have been "absorbed" by
the city's slums until they are intrinsic parts of it (much as the
colonies were said to "absorb" emigrant women) and until they are
as invisible as it (much as emigrant women were fantasized as being
"absorbed" by the colonies). If Alice's province was to reinsert these
dislocated subjects into the geography of England as nation, she
would be simple enough and quite productive. However, she articulates, imposes, and embodies a middle-class morality and approbation
toward the working classes that mainly translates into a paradox.
Alice is witness and living testimony to the laborers' displacement,
the process of their disinheritance and ghettoization. But she is also
the sole character who, as illogically as does the Queen in *Through
the Looking-Glass,* punishes them or accuses them without the benefit of her essential knowledge: Ultimately, their guilt lies in their
not being middle class. Utilized as an instrument of Gaskell's particular brand of middle-class morality, Alice repeatedly scolds and lec-
tures Mary Barton for entertaining notions of transcending her own
class, for not knowing her "place." As the narrative bears out, however, Mary's place is none—it is a nonplace. Insofar as she is an interesting cross between the working-class spinster and the author's
sentimental bourgeois projections (which are meant to humanize
her), Gaskell's Alice occupies a peculiar place between the other "superfluous" woman, the "genteel" emigrant, and her lower-class
counterpart. The example of Alice suggests a commonality between
the two classes of emigrant women, specifically one that is imposed
from above: The working-class unmarried female emigrant is as subject to the ironies of bourgeois commodification and moralization as
her "genteel" counterpart.

In Gaskell's formulation of the class struggle, Alice becomes an
emblem of the rift between body and soul among the lower classes
of Manchester, the violent extraction of a population from its preferred place and of their virtuous hearts and passions for justice
from the bodies and practical actions that defeat them. The only
living suggestion of the projected harmonious union of body and
soul is Alice, and hence she comes to signify all that is precious, too

valuable, and irretrievable. She comes to represent absence and contradiction. As a symbol of cultural and ideological disjunction, Alice is also an instance of the locus of values and ideals at odds with one another. Yet she is also a device used persistently to divert the conflict, and a fetish. In the context of the novel's conflicts, Alice is both central and inconsequential, both the self-sacrificing martyr and self-indulgent, both compulsively in service to others and incompetent. She is the quintessential gender anomaly, the excessive, superfluous spinster. Her life ends with a final travel, as she retreats both into the past and into the childhood she wants to reclaim: "[I]n this illness to the old, world-weary woman, God had sent her a veiled blessing: she was once more in the scenes of her childhood, unchanged and bright as in those long departed days; once more with the sister of her youth, the playmate of fifty years ago, who had for nearly as many years slept in a grassy grave in the little church-yard beyond Burton" (269). Recapturing the past is the principal escape from the present (her own death), but is also a journey back into childhood. Moreover, this escape does not constitute travel toward experience and change, but regression.

Gaskell's Alice is representative of proofs to the lie of woman's social utility as establishing the difference between her value and her "superfluity" and "excessiveness" or her redundancy—she subverts the bourgeois ideology and rhetoric that emigration automatically guarantees working-class women an unproblematic sexuality and gender identity because she is of the "servant" class. Rather, this example of Gaskell's attempt to confront the question of gender (and woman's cultural value) in relation to the subordinate classes exposes the inapplicability of the very solutions proposed by bourgeois gender ideology for its women and foregrounds the limits of its classist assumptions on gender's relation to class. Alice is important to our thinking about the cultural place and nonplace of single and emigrant women because she presents the wandering and displaced woman in ways that are significant beyond her class status and her shared experience with the laboring population of Manchester. She also illustrates the instrumentality of gender's relation to "place" and dispossession as they figured in the gender and class economies. The example of her life analogously features both the increasing diminishment of England as a naturally resourceful place and the increasing importance of venturing outside of it for value of various kinds. As the plots of this and many other Victorian novels bear out

(Gaskell's *Cranford,* Charlotte Bronte's *Vilette, Great Expectations,* and *Mill On the Floss* included), men are generally able to travel out of time and place, for short or longer periods of time and for various purposes.[12] For the most part, and apart from the overt efforts of assisted emigration, women had no such mobility.

DANGEROUS TRAVEL

Alice's preoccupations, adventures, and confusions call forth not so much the question of danger but the issue of single women's containment while in transit and their positioning in relation to destination, present location, and other passengers, and all of these in relation to their gender identities. The adventures serve as a point of departure for a cultural analysis, shedding some light on the viewer's participation in the construction of the Elsewhere and by extension on the traveler to that foreign place. The emblematic figure of the emigrant ship becomes a contested gendered space that sought to limit the visibility of unmarried emigrant Victorian women.

In addition to concerning itself with women's interiority, the rhetoric advocating women's emigration served further to privatize issues relevant to this phenomenon, highlighting "the advantage of private introductions to public advertisements" (Ross 315). As opposed to the expressed national mission of male emigration, which was easily construed and explained as serving a national function, the promotion of women's emigration was couched in personal and nonpolitical terms. It would seem that the emigration societies insisted on this privatization of the issue at the same time that they sought to control its representations and perception by the public. One 1894 newspaper headline that caused emigration organizers considerable embarrassment because it exposed to the public the women's "surplus" status read: "SINGLE WOMEN WANTED." Overexposure to public scrutiny had, in fact, been a concern for quite some time; an 1865 letter from South Africa proclaims the risks involved in publicity that mocked and commodified the emigration of women: "you cannot imagine the ridicule and disagreeable remarks that [one] advertisement caused," comments one correspondent (Monk 35). Publicity was a *general* strategy for colonial recruitment, many times promoted by agents who assisted for profit. Such motives were objectionable to all and were considered an obstacle to proper—that is, philanthropic—emigration efforts. The promotional efforts of shipping companies also posed problems to emigration philanthropists' efforts to guard the morality of emigrants, who made an "appeal . . . to the shipping companies to cease publishing flaring advertisements such as lured young men who came to South Africa" ("Immigration Question"). Furthermore, the voyage to the women's destinations also was viewed as dangerous. Monk describes in detail some of the hardships and dangers to which the women were exposed: "Crime and disorder on board were often among the hazards of mid-Victorian travel, particularly in the emigrant ships" (45). She cites the assisters' concern over these conditions as they applied to the women emigrants in particular: "In 1863 Miss Rye described as 'shocking and conducive to vice' the conditions at the dockyards where the emigrants had to wait until their ships were ready to sail" (54).

Popular accounts of the female emigration process are either sensational or sentimental in overinvesting the departure with emotional importance. Advertisements and newspaper accounts like the next one represent departure as a celebratory communal event, which is entirely positive because it bodes well for the emigrant women:

> . . . [H]ere on deck commotion still reigns supreme. A woman with a tearful, terrified face has come down to see her daughter off. . . . It cannot be said that arrangements are altogether luxurious, but the ship is one of the British India Company's, and is large and well-appointed. . . . Still it is emigrant life, and after all it is shipping away from our own shores materials of which, if all accounts may be relied upon, we are sadly in need. But they are free agents these domestic damsels—Few of us indeed are quite so free—free to go at any rate, but not for a time quite free to come back again. (*Evening News*)

Here, as in the passage with which the chapter opens, sentimentality is combined with excitement, anticipation, and even fear to produce a most sensational scenario, one sure to please the general readership. Sometimes, as in the "Girl Emigrants" passage cited next, reports diminish the emigrant's export value and desirability to her most crudely superficial, exterior characteristics:

> Girl Emigrants
> Though not required to be STRIKINGLY BEAUTIFUL, They must be above 4ft 8in, and in no way deformed or disfigured, even by a squirt.

They are not weighed for the voyage. . . . No matter what their age is, *the consent of parents must be obtained.* (*Daily News*)

Here the departure scene has a marketplace character to it. In yet other instances, as my earlier discussion of spectacle suggests, the awkwardness of overexposure and vulgar market practices was not limited to printed advertisements but to social activity as well. Accounts of the scenes surrounding the emigration of women make clear the impulse toward privatization of the entire process. An 1885 article from Australia reveals the spectacle of the emigrant single woman: "Whenever the announcement is made that an immigrant ship has arrived, and a number of the single women brought out in her are on hire as domestic servants at the Immigration Depot, a rush to the hiring-room is made, and for some hours there ensues a scene of jostling, pushing, struggling, & c, such as is not witnessed elsewhere except, perhaps, at a boat-race, and in some respects not even there" (Lockett 651). Public attention like this bore too close a resemblance to advertisements and caused much embarrassment among emigration assisters. Knowledge of these transgressions helps also to explain the assisters' efforts to keep the women out of the public eye. Such protective efforts were, however, antithetical to very process of appraisal and exportation (required for imperial marketing) to which emigrant women were subjected.

Unmarried women may be said to have existed outside of the recognized boundaries of domestic ideology and the sexual economy, just as they stand in problematic relation to these structures. In contrast, just as they were commodified for the purpose of colonial export at home, unmarried emigrant women appear within the context of the ship as spectacles insofar as they were isolated as problematic creatures onboard, whose visibility and public identity was contested not only on the ship (a place that becomes a microcosm for their status at home) but also as a distinct population within the cultural context of Victorian England and of England as locus of the empire. The following description of the emigration assisters' worries over female travel reveals the dynamic of the emigrant spinster's status as a commodity juxtaposed to other commodities and showcased for other passengers' consumption in public spaces. The next passage also highlights the author's views of the female emigrant's value as national and cultural commodity, specifically in relation to the dangers posed to the unmarried emigrant woman who is spectacularized and whose ambivalent status, her nonplace, becomes too obviously a threat:

> The difficulty of conveyance is not slight, though far from insurmountable. The cost of first-class accommodation is too great to be thought of, and in the crowded second cabin a delicately nurtured woman is liable to be injured in that which should be most scrupulously preserved—in her self-respect—the quality of all others most necessary to one who leaves friends, home, country, to make her way alone and unaided in a new world.
>
> . . . The strongest feelings of her nature may be suddenly called into play under the eyes of a hundred spectators. She may have to endure "the inexpressible torture of scrutiny without sympathy." The chief amusement of the inferior class of passengers is to observe one another. . . . A young girl in such society suddenly finds herself "the observed of all observers," and feels that her motives are being canvassed and possibly her actions misinterpreted. . . . The slightest false step exposes her to false imputations, and she falls in her own esteem by falling in the esteem of others. An unprincipled man has an immense advantage in her inability to escape from his observation; for he can see when to take the tide of feeling at the flood. (Rye, "Female Emigration Impartially Considered" 78–79)

The "danger" to which the emigration rhetoric makes constant reference lies in exposing the extent to which women are transacted; it lies in revelations of the secrets and "mysteries" of these women's valuations as commodities.[13] Suzann Buckley notes that "the passage-brokers, [who] receive[d] bonuses from the Canadian government . . . were more pecuniary than patriotic . . . [and] recruited indiscriminately," placing their numbers at 3,000 or so (29). False expectations also were created by this elaborate web of emigration profiteers, who commodified the experience more blatantly than anyone else. The danger of this spectacularization was thus not only metaphoric but also most material. Buckley explains: "White slavers, in the guise of benevolent ladies, practiced their wiles aboard ship, and at Canadian ports of debarkation. . . . The agents were guilty of other offenses besides lack of selectivity and protection. It was not uncommon for them to misrepresent conditions in Canada. . . . British female emigrants going to other areas in Canada ran similar risks" (31). Emigrant single women who survived such difficult journeys wrote home to warn others of the dangers and discomforts of the experience and to recommend, "in every question, as regards every Governess coming out here, . . . [that] they should come as

First class passengers" (Clarke 84). In the society of the spectacle, then, consciousness is transmuted to self-reflexivity and self-absorption on the part of commodities, a change not likely to have liberatory consequences.

Immorality concerns mainly refer to working-class women; the fear is that middle-class spinsters would lose caste or class integrity onboard ship.[14] The lower classes, whose relationship to commodification is not fetishistic, pose the threat of exposure, much as Magwitch poses the greatest threat to bourgeois imperial fantasies in *Great Expectations*. The *St. David* incident also makes abundantly clear the fears of assimilation and nondiscrimination posed by the intermingling of English subjects of different socioeconomic stations and accounts for the protective efforts made on behalf of single emigrant women by the emigration societies and others. The popular press paid much attention to the dangers of shipboard travel; discussions specifically emphasize the moral threats to unaccompanied women. One writer remarks on the reflection of this fact on the English character: "That any class—but more especially women—should ever need protection in British ships manned by British seamen, is a little humiliating; but so many instances of brutality and immorality have been proved, that the treatment of emigrants during their voyage is now occupying the serious attention of the Legislature" (Wills 228). The possibility of transformation and change of individual attributes believed to be intrinsic to those who fit neatly into a socioeconomic class (or who are firmly placed national subjects) then may be said to constitute the main threat of unclaimed spaces such as the ship and those only slightly more delineated spaces, the colonies.

To circumvent such dire consequences of the emigrant process, carefully controlled and charted points of relative safety were established for the space between the women's origins and destinations: "Reception Homes were an early essential in women's migration. An earlier emigration worker, the famous and remarkable Mrs. Caroline Chisholm, had founded one in Sydney in 1842, to shelter young women whom she found wandering the streets all night or sleeping rough in the shelter of rocks" (Monk 57). Emigrant women's very physical safety is a more comprehensive and recurring issue throughout the discourse on women's emigration, where the point is made repeatedly that women are as much in danger at home and during the voyage as they are abroad, if not

more. Education and domestication onboard ship were employed
to displace moral licentiousness and illicit social activity. Historian
Barbara Roberts confirms, "among the [emigration assisters'] concerns was the possibility that emigrant women would be on a four-
month trip with no matron, no surgeon and no supervision to keep
them apart from the crew. They would be dumped at Adelaide and
would surely become 'immoral'" (115).

Apart from its consistent gestures toward differentiating male
and female imperial roles, travel-narrative scholarship has a useful
purpose in helping to distinguish emigrant narratives from other
imperial rhetorical modes. The politics of travel as an act that is
identified with exploration, discovery, or amusement, is quite different from the process of travel as a means of relocating and thus
revising one's national identity in the act of making a new place
"home." Traveling for the purpose of emigration also necessitates
an equally elaborate process of definitively leaving one's original
"home" and country; this separation is permeated by the broader
implications of preparing for change and envisioning new places.
The politics of travel and observation apply to these two examples
insofar as they are mediated by the more pressing matter of having
to leave one's country and to make a very serious and drastic transition between acknowledging oneself as a British subject and becoming a British subject out of context. That women as travelers
are also voyeurs and, often, consumers of imperial exploits are important considerations that serve to problematize their accepted
roles in the gender economy, since in the Victorian hegemony
woman is consumer and object, but not voyeur.

The emigrant woman is both commodity and spectacle because,
by definition, she cannot be possessed, only traded. Her value lies
mainly in her relation to other commodities and to the processes of
commodification. This is so in terms of the prerogative assumed by
travelers but also in the dialectic of travel. English subjects could
conceive of the expanses beyond England's borders as within reach
and always in a subordinate relation to the nation and to themselves.
As destinations, the colonies and dominions approximate the closest
thing to perfection. The emigrant women in this study are similar to
women travelers in these respects. They differ mainly in their positioning not only in their relation to the colonies, which they hoped
to call "home," but also to the nation from which they emanated.
One of the key differences has to do with agency or, more precisely,

mobility, which emigrant women lack aboard ship as they do in the colonies. In this respect, they differ greatly from Victorian women travelers. One emigrant governess's letter reveals the stagnation that characterized her colonial life: "I have as yet seen nothing of Sydney, except to go to Church on Sundays. I am seldom outside the gate. I have been once into George Street in the two months I have been at Cook's River, so I cannot say a great deal about the Country or the City either."[15]

The events and narratives this study analyzes, then, are revealing both as travel writings and as something more than that. They are analyzed as documents that mark the transition between the ways in which the nation and its constituted Elsewheres are envisioned. (See also chapter 2). Transgressing the geographic boundaries of the nation is by far one of the main contrasts between travel and emigration, and a persistent concentration in this study. Self-evident as this distinction may seem, in travel one leaves with the promise of a return, whereas in emigration one leaves without that guarantee. This difference marks the experiential and symbolic significance of emigration, just as it lends distinct meaning to the imaginary space in between "home" and other places. This area is constituted by, and encompasses, the emigrant women's projections and desire for change but also the desire for what is left behind. In this respect, emigration and travel share the dynamic of leaving and arriving and also the sense of discovery insofar as it engages established knowledge. However, the contents of this imaginary and symbolic space are also distinctly different. Rob Nixon's definition of the "exile" as both debilitating and empowering in political terms serves to highlight the split subjectivity of the deconstituted national subject and also the potential for radicalness: "Th[e] creativity wrought from loss can be an asset" (150). Caren Kaplan's differentiations between exile and expatriation define more vividly the politics of the exile trope, specifically in exposing the interdependence of several social and political structures: "The Euro-American formation 'exile,' . . . marks a place of mediation in modernity where issues of political conflict, commerce, labor, nationalist realignments, imperialist expansion, structures of gender and sexuality, and many other issues become recoded" (28). Such new understandings of "exile" broaden the category so that it is equally appropriate and applicable to Victorian emigrant women.

To the extent that the emigrant experience is forced and the "home" changes in their absence, the place left behind is a sentimental place, static and intangible. In this sense, the "politics of memory" is equally applicable to both emigrants and exiles, although the finer intersubjective points remain decisively different (Nixon 151). Likewise, in *Sailing to Australia* Hassam notes the dynamic in emigrant travelers' relation to their destinations as opposed to their perceived origins and argues that both are subject to the traveler's imaginings. Onboard ship en route to the dominions, the emigrant is at once everywhere and nowhere, so that all places are "illusory": "The land of promise is always dreamlike because it is always a projection of the mind 'elsewhere,'" (187), he says, while "the promised land can never be reached; [it] was a place to which one looked forward, it was not a place at which one arrived" (188). Therefore, the emigrant's conception of the colonies (often misrepresented) is intricately meaningful in the sense that in part it represents her social desire, but it also calls for an examination of the colonial discourse that helped shape the vision of its fulfillment. The important focus for analyzing the emigration process, then, is not on destinations but on the symbolic preparations for transport.[16]

In their relation to the English nation and also to the British imperial mission, disenfranchised emigrant women occupy a place that is quite distinct. Emigrant middle-class spinsters (and spinsters within England) are a particular population that existed in a state of internal exile. They are culturally dissimilar not only in terms of their place in the Victorian imperial hegemony but also in their specific place in relation to the employment of gender ideologies and their social practices abroad. The difference between single and married women emigrating is emphasized by Hassam also, and it proves quite pivotal and symbolic in terms of the object that is in transit and the distinctly identified cultural values that are being transported and protected in the process: "In [certain] cases, women who had no voice in whether or not to emigrate might place more stress on the journey as part of a providential plan: to clergymen young single women were most likely to portray their journey in religious terms with themselves journeying towards a spiritual goal" (52). Domestic roles appear to have been imposed upon single women, according to Hassam, and greater restrictions were placed upon them than upon married women.[17] Unmarried emigrant women's activity onboard ship was curtailed to the extreme, especially by the matronly women who were their chaperones. Hassam notes that many of the shipboard diaries comment on the extent to which the very physical movements of these women were curtailed, and they were confined to their cabins. Even their language was censured. They were put under the guidance and control of married women, thus symbolically reproducing and establishing the very same hierarchy existing within England. As early as in 1841, an immigration official expressed concern over women he described as "unprotected and friendless females," unescorted and subject to danger (Roberts 121). Such concerns prevailed; among the solutions proposed by Caroline Chisholm was "to exclude single men from emigrant ships carrying single women, preferring a system of strict sexual segregation to the prevailing system of attaching single women to families on board ship" (Roberts 123). One argument for "protecting" emigrant single women spells out the presumption of danger quite explicitly. In this instance, the "heterogeneity" of its subjects threatens to render the ship an egalitarian society: "When we carefully consider the numbers and the condition of the passengers carried in such a ship, when we think of the conflicting interests, the mixture of sexes and ages, the different nations represented,—for Irish, German, and Welsh are constantly sailing together,—we naturally proceed to inquire what amount of discipline is exercised over so heterogeneous a conglomeration, and what care is taken that these masses do not morally fester and corrupt each others" (Rye, "Emigrant Ship Matrons" 27). This dissociation was as much a benefit and a loss to the spinster, who, as Cherry observes of female painters, enjoyed freedoms not granted to married women. However, the "independent life, living in rented accommodation and supporting themselves on earned income," did not become fully possible until the last two decades of the century (47). During the middle portion of the period, women's singlehood was considered "odd."

If women in general can be said to have been repressed and oppressed within the context of Victorian cultural economy, single women as sexual beings posed seemingly insurmountable contradictions in the cultural and gender economy. Their life aboard the emigrant ship can be viewed as a reified microcosm in terms of how they were carefully contained and subjugated. Insofar as their sexuality was contested, they were defined and treated as special-category subjects. Paradoxically, these women merited containment in the name of "protection" after their sexuality was rendered excessively problematic and hence undesirable, an unwanted component of their social and cultural identity. Whereas married female passengers were afforded various privileges and spaces, if not for the "chaperones" assigned to them, unmarried women fell in more with the "men and women who were strangers to each other [and who were] not infrequently berthed together in a space only a yard wide. There was no privacy" (Roberts 123). Hassam's observation that "the most severe incarceration . . . was reserved for the single women in steerage" (69) does not indicate a simple reproduction of the Victorian domestic power structures, does not reveal "an arrangement both physically and culturally [based on] an idealized image of the heterosexual family unit" (70). The spinster had no such place in the nuclear family but was positioned outside of it and was considered "excessive" in relation to it, just as she was clearly "excessively" problematic onboard ship.[18]

The emigrant ship is indeed a gendered space, but not in the way that Hassam suggests, since the incorporation of unmarried women in this divided space did not occur, as he implies, "naturally." Even so, very often the women initiated actions of rebellion and/or subversion of their enforced and exaggerated domestication. It is also significant that the *crisis* experienced by emigrants in transit had to do with the implementation of gender distinctions onboard ship more than with any intentional dislocation of their national identity. Hassam notes that "As British emigrants in British ships, the emigrants faced a challenge to their identities not so much from any breakdown from national identity but from a breakdown of gender roles" (149). That is to say, in the shared space of the ship, they had more difficulty in determining their relations toward one another than to the homeland they left behind and the one ahead. Following this idea to its logical conclusion, we have a better sense of the women's status in transit. Interestingly, this curtailment of activity is justified as much for their protection as for that of the other passengers; it is as if their very presence posed a danger to married women and all male emigrants. Part of what was being transported from England to Australia, in the cases Hassam documents, is the spinster's nonplace and nonauthority in relation to her married counterparts and also the threat she posed to the established hierarchy.

The forced domestication and even the segregation of single women onboard emigrant ships becomes a metaphor for the emigrant woman's identity as gender anomaly within the context of Victorian cultural hegemony. A consideration of the discourse relevant to the suitability of unmarried women for emigration reveals that, much like their cultural nonplace, their sexuality was problematic both at "home" and in their projected presence in the colonies and dominions. This tenuous sexual identity (both nonexistent and threatened) informs their cultural status as "excess" value in relation to the colonial project; it is also connected to the imperial accumulation of raw materials, markets, and the appropriation of culture, all of which constitute an "excess" of activity or agency. Attempts are made to deprive unmarried women of a sexual identity altogether, which presents a typically familiar contradiction: Much emphasis is placed on this negated sexuality, so that efforts to contradict its existence coexist with efforts to guard and protect it against possible exploitation of the "matrons" assigned to oversee the emigrant single woman during her journey, one eager emigration advocate writes that they "maintain discipline" and form "an essential part of [the] system" of female emigration (Rye, "Emigrant Ship Matrons" 27).

Unmarried women's negated sexuality thus becomes a metaphor for cultural value of a particular kind—that is, a contested cultural commodity. This indefinite status is epitomized in their public presence on board the emigrant ship. England exported the very same cultural commodities—women—that the gender and cultural ideology sought to insulate within the domestic realm. Such instances of negotiating and repositioning women within the national and cultural hegemony further support the view of the unmarried emigrant woman's assignment as a symptom of the cultural production of "surplus value." These problematics relate the concern with controlling single women's sexuality and the issue of women's sexuality as commodity. The single woman's domain is not "perversely private," then, as McClintock asserts, but is an elaborately *privatized* concern at the same time that the spinster is a public spectacle (6). It may be more useful, even, to think of the figure of the spinster as a public presence that is *perpetually* being privatized because she represents anomaly and contradiction in the domestic ideology that sought at once to contain her and to exempt her from that construction of collective identity. McClintock's observation that "domesticity denotes both a *space* (a geographic and architectural alignment) and a *social relation to power*" (34) affirms that the "value" with which women of the middle class were invested would undergo a translation as it was exported to the colonies since the purpose of "domesticity" as societal space *and* as a power relation shifted.[19]

ୟ

Little Alice's inability to travel both backward and forward testifies to the ridiculously difficult appearance taken on by the colonialist project in the eyes of English subjects, some tenets of which they espoused and others of which they could not in their own minds, lives, and constituted realities accommodate. It also mirrors the dual role required of English national subjects. A look at the past might facilitate a grander view of future possibilities, which may in turn define in more concrete detail the needs and desires of the English subjects in the present moment. This double or even triple projection is one that English subjects were required to adopt and undertake, however reluctantly; they were trained in the subject by example, through propaganda and rhetoric that exemplified the execution of this task. Questions of the process of imposition and visions of what ought to be, as of agency and oppression, are the necessary first step to showing how Victorian culture was changed by imperialism and by the exportation of its superfluous subjects. Such projection is also an act of incorporation and immersion of the observer-subject, especially in the context of Victorian culture, which precludes the possibility of objectivity and critical distance as activities distinct from spectatorship and commodification. This was the case with the ethnographers I discussed in chapter 3, but also with the anthropologists (as according to James Clifford) in their new appreciation of the ways in which all these categories are intrinsically segments of the "same" and known whole. It would not be suitable to view either the traveler or the observed foreign subject as constituting a segment of a linear and casual process of commodification, perusal, and spectacle. The reason such an attribution would not be prudent is that Victorian culture manifests a problematic relationship to materiality through its own obsessive materialism and the processes of commodification to which it gave rise to an unprecedented degree.

Recent feminist scholarship has argued, quite convincingly, that Victorian female-authored travel narratives are quite complex in several ways. Among these complexities, two are most relevant. First, women's travel narratives exhibit a liberated view of other peoples and cultures that seems to defy the oppositional and dominating view predominant in imperialist representations of foreign places, while they also embrace the imperialist initiative, which has been noted by Eva-Marie Kroller and Margaret Strobel. Second, travel narratives are often internally inconsistent; that is, many times they are self-contradictory in their descriptions and valuations of foreign cultures. As literary critic Sara Mills has noted, they alternate between description and prescription, and the narrators adopt various cultural and political posturings. This fact rightly suggests to Mills an ambiguity to Victorian women's relation to the empire and the colonization process. It would seem that in some respects, the female travel narrative, which often verges on the "ethnographic," is a permissive and comfortable medium for the child who wishes to appease her anxiety about being out of place. The process of toying with the idea of narrating her experience after the fact especially helps to remove her from her own immediate experience in a number of ways and also to allow her considerable control and influence over her contexts.

The process of dislocation that becomes clear in *Through the Looking Glass* involves a commodification that is multiple and complex. Alice's observations concerning her sense of identity and subjectivity are contextually defined, and her efforts to control or contrive that subjectivity point to the commodification of the traveler. Her attempts to "experience" these other places and her relation to them most self-consciously suggest that material experience and its cultural (symbolic or meaning-producing) interpretations can be construed as commodifying, even when the agent in this transaction is a commodity herself.

Invoking the notion of commodities as "social things" makes clear how Alice and the emigrant women were commodified for the purpose of export and yet exert authority. We may begin to appreciate the ways in which the commodified and circumscribed subject does, then, proceed to manipulate her relationship to other similarly commodified places and beings. We thus also are enabled to understand the role and position of the emigrant middle-class women, and to understand the intricacies of their commodification. Like the colonies, the female emigrant as displaced being is both object and subject, both material and immaterial. The degree of agency that may be ascribed to her is the locus of contest, as is her place in spaces both outside and within England. Given that "for the Victorians, the charm of buying childhood grew out of an active imagination that envisioned one's early years as a lost utopia," Alice herself can be said to represent a space/place in the imaginary that is significantly connected to the desire for another place for existence and an "out" the kind of which the colonies may arguably have represented (Mavor 2–3). Alice's venture through the looking glass proposes the matter of examining the roundabout ways in which the national subject and nationhood are constituted, since "In the dual relation of subject to subject or subject to object, the mirror is the symbol of an unaltered vision of things" (Minh-ha 22). Nationhood works to constitute the national subject by imposing upon that subject's margins of possibility. Likewise, projections toward emigrants' destinations constitute an escape from the present moment and present contexts. The promise of such escapes appears most vividly in an advertisement featuring the colonies as all that England is not, especially for emigrant women who seek to escape the confines of class:

> WHAT WOMEN MAY DO—The Colonial Lady-Help
>   The lady-help is only possible in well-established countries, where class distinctions are a reality, and not in the Colonies, where society is in a delightful state of topsey-turveydom, and a landed aristocracy unknown. But having been accepted as a factor in the labour world, she is becoming as popular as she is in England, and every year sees a larger number of refined, educated, independent women emigrating to the lands beyond the ocean . . . [where] women are scarce enough to be able to hold their ground against he demands of selfish employers, and to be in such request that labour values have not yet fallen a single point. (*WOMAN—For Women and Girls*)

In light of such fantasy production, traveling both forward and backward is not specific to nation-building but also is applicable to the everyday practical and ideological operations of the nation, its constant reiteration and perpetuation. At the very least, such a practice challenges imperialist, hierarchical notions of progress, especially in relation to questions relevant to identity and cultural subjectivities whose value is in flux. The next chapter explores the theoretical groundings and implications of the commodifying evaluations of the Victorian "superfluous" woman as domestic excess, both in sexual and in more broadly cultural terms.

5

QUESTIONS OF VALUE

ॐ

Female Identity as Excess

The family uses people, not for what they are, not for what they are intended to be, but for what it wants them for—for its own uses. It thinks of them not as what God has made them, but as the something which it has arranged that they shall be. If it wants some one to sit in the drawing room, that some one is to be supplied by the family, though that member may be destined for science, or for education, or for active superintendence by God, i.e., by the gifts within.

—Florence Nightingale, *Cassandra*

[S]o soon as it steps forth as a commodity, [a material form] is changed into something transcendent.
A commodity not only stands with its feet on the ground, but in relation to all other commodities, it stands on its head.

—Karl Marx, *Capital*

I n an argument for her own life and those of other unmarried middle-class women, Florence Nightingale notes the degree to which women's activity is curtailed. She cites incidents from her own life that have shown her that idleness in the lives of women serves a purpose and a function—the appearance of leisure and idleness that characterizes bourgeois lifestyles and class identity. The family, she contends, is one of the main institutions inhibiting women from overcoming their present limitations, and if women are to overcome, they must do so despite the dictates and norms of the family structure. The passage just quoted indicates, also, that as in the case of married middle-class women, the struggle for unmarried women lies in the enforced passivity that is imposed upon them. They must redefine their places in society first by challenging their roles within the family. Nightingale understood that, as a spinster, her value must not be defined along domestic parameters. She saw domesticity as an essential link in the patriarchal system of oppression permeated by self-interest and opportunism. It is due to this strife that the spinster's paradoxical relation to the institution of the family complicate her place in the dominant culture.

This study began by elucidating the concept of the Victorian "hegemony" as a way of locating emigrant spinsters in it. The chapters that followed outline the specifics of that problem in some detail and highlight the problems exposed by the discourse, the processes, and imaginings relevant to assisted female emigration. Questions have surfaced repeatedly, in these different contexts, regarding the unmarried Victorian woman's cultural place and hegemonic function. While I have attempted to address such specifics, several unanswered questions remain that lie at the very core of my analysis. Such questions pertain to the issues of female identity and cultural agency. They are best addressed in their historical and cultural specificity but also more broadly, conceptually and theoretically. This chapter attends to those lingering concerns and works to define, rather than resolve, the many cultural contradictions subsumed by the problem of the "genteel" female emigrant. It also explores some of the different possible understandings of the issues of gender identity, difference, and hegemonic function as they pertain to this problem. To present a distinct articulation of the ways questions of gender identity become employed in the emigration of spinsters, I turn to literary texts that provide symbolic instances of Victorian women's deviations from the bourgeois category of "woman." Such works address the question, how does the emigrant spinster qualify or fail to qualify as Victorian "woman"? That is, what is her relationship to that coalition of gender and other cultural domains that establishes the *legitimate* national subject, with distinct definitions and assigned functions within the Victorian hegemony? What is her relationship to commodity culture?

In his analysis of Victorian commodity culture, critic Thomas Richards comments that at the peak of culture's commercialization, "the body had become the prevailing icon of commodity culture, and there was no turning back" (205). In regard to the export of emigrant spinsters to the colonies, the processes of commodification of the body are engaged in a most interesting way. While these women's very corporeality was at issue insofar as they were seen to have no practical usefulness, their bodies also were persistently negated. Spinsters were seen as asexual because they were detached from the patriarchal processes that granted middle-class women some semblance of a sexual identity. They were not likely to reproduce outside of marriage, unlike working-class women who had little regard for bourgeois standards of propriety and hence were not as hampered by them. The genteel spinster's relationship to her own body and her sexuality is thus highly conflicted, contested as it is both from within herself and from without. A similar discordance is generally present in relation to Victorian female sexuality and sexual identity. The latter is not guaranteed, presumed, granted a priori but observed as present only when it is reiterated through social activity. Hence, what do we make of the fact that the performance of heterosexuality is absent on the part of the spinster, for all practical purposes? It does not follow that spinsters hence do not signify, sexually, for they continue to be valued based on that absence. Finally, there is this paradox: If female visibility is centered on the domestic sphere, is the emigrant spinster then invisible? Richards's interesting phrase to suggest the multiplicity of spectacle's functions, captures the emigrant spinster's various conflicting identities as commodity; he calls it a "semiotic medium" that pronounces, very boldly, a multitude of significations. The commodity, he says, is used "as semiotic medium . . . as spectacle" in the Victorian period following the Great Exhibition of 1851 (66). In the "semiotics of spectacle," commemoration takes the place of history, much as the unmarried middle-class woman is displaced by the woman who will benefit the colonies.[1] The spinster's function and purpose is no longer to survive and to live a meaningful life but to be of use.

Richards links the Victorian fetishizing fascination with commodities to simultaneous intimations of unavailability. He explains that "The Exhibition succeeded precisely because it elevated the commodity above the mundane act of exchange" (1990, 39). In these ways commodities are fetishized while their cultural value is controlled by a high degree of inaccessibility. Richards's scrutiny of the body as commodity affords possibilities for investigating the contradiction between the unmarried woman as commodity and also as "superfluous," redundant, undesirable excess. For Richards, figures of excess serve to mask and distort the processes and ends of commodity production. Likewise, insofar as emigrant women take on the role of "surplus value" for the purposes of trade, they expose the discrepancies in the causality professed by commodity-production rhetoric. His point, that "commodities [appear as] a means so powerful that they can realize themselves in the absence of any end," reveals the Victorian commodity as entirely self-absorbed and self-serving but also as having no practical use or purpose (126). In this intersection of Victorian fetishism and inaccessibility, commodities were spectacularized through the form of the Exhibit while their worth, appeal, and cultural value were controlled by a degree of frustration and discontent. Such formulations help us to understand the fact that the emigration societies attempted to market a commodity that did not exist in the conceptual framework of Victorian England—the morally virtuous working-class woman.

These questions of "excessiveness" are also apparent in the discourse surrounding women's assisted emigration, which makes clear the ambivalence toward women's emigration and also the tension in cultural imaginings of the colonies and of women. Looking at Victorian commodification practices enables us to examine the public phenomenon of female emigration, its seeking privacy and nonexposure, which stands in opposition to how things came to be valued during the period. It also allows us to consider the colonization of unmarried, problematic women in the midst of such definitions of rampant excess. In relation to these truths, the whole notion of "surplus" and "surplus value" become redefined. In this sense, and in reconceptualizing notions of value, it is most instructive that "the Great Exhibition created the sense of surplus that it is so often cited as evidence for," reminding us that materiality and ideology are inextricably bound in the "excesses" of Victorian England (Richards 28). How do these observations apply in terms of sexuality and sexual value, sexuality as socially consequential activity rather than as a condition of being? Specifically, how does this formula for determining value apply to the fact that sexual worth, the main category by which Victorian women are esteemed, is contested in the middle-class spinster?

The social and political significance of locating subjects and places as Elsewhere and as Other has been elaborated in different critical contexts. Like foreign places, national subjects always occupy distinct places within established parameters, whether national or hierarchically political, even when constituted as Other. Luce Irigaray notes that there is much about women's constructed identities that is evasive, that woman's social and cultural subjectivity succeeds in eluding the prescribed boundaries of definition and social function. But it is the very materiality of women's lives and places that is reiterated in social discourse, despite the abstractions to which women become subjected—abstractions that are likewise constitutive, in a reciprocal or independent fashion, of their material lives.[2] As Irigaray argues, what becomes most relevant in this context are the symbolic values attributed to gender systems and that such valuations serve to displace women, often rendering them invisible. Her formulations advocate a reconceptualization of cultural and semiotic systems as constituting an economy of indeterminacy and multiplicity. As has been illustrated thus far—in regard to the dangers of travel (chapter 4) and the "marketing" of emigrant spinsters (chapter 2)—the conspicuous visibility of emigrant women was deemed objectionable by the emigration assisters, especially when the emigrants were middle class. Whereas the emigrant spinster was most obviously out of context and a discordant image compared to the middle-class domesticity from which she was now alienated, attempts to shelter her from the public gaze sought to restore her connection to idealized femininity. Before the spinster was exchanged, some sort of value needed to be established for her, even if only a provisional one.

THE SURPLUS VALUE OF THE SPINSTER

Unmarried women keep surfacing as a problem in the Victorian cultural imagination. Often they are depicted as surplus, excessive commodities who confront difficulties in trying to make a place for themselves in society. They are alluded to surreptitiously as beings for whom England has no pressing practical use and no ideological or hegemonic "place." Representations of unmarried middle-class women confront the old adage that marriage is the proper resolution to any gender conflict. That particular portion of the Victorian domestic ideology is subverted by the infectious existence of the "spinster" and perhaps even the threat of joining the ranks of women who are un[re]productive and "superfluous" in the eyes of society. The terms "superfluous," "surplus," and "redundant" also constitute the middle-class spinster as problematic excess.[3] Seen as engaging in meaningless and unenduring occupations that merely consume time and energy, spinsters are potentially capable of depleting the Victorian hegemony and pose a threat to the projected cultural organicity of the nation. In being un[re]productive the spinster also stands as an accusation against other areas of British profligacy. As Catherine G. F. Gore, the author of "A Bewailment from Bath," put it in 1844, "Everybody knows that Great Britain is the fatherland of old maids," which highlights the fact that England is the only nation in the world that has failed to provide unmarried women with a suitable place in society (200).

If the middle-class Victorian woman's value was seen to lie in her perfect domestication, and if the unmarried working-class woman's value in her sexuality, then the middle-class emigrant spinster emerges as a hybrid. Where might *her* value reside? It does not, to be sure, lie in her social visibility, in her existence, or in her materiality and corporeality, and certainly not in her "spectacularity," since she was not sexual, not well off, and not a public figure. It is based instead in the "falsehood [that is] maintained by the organization of appearance" and in the negative relationship the commodity of the genteel emigrant spinster bears to her material place in society (Debord 153). The spinster's value also does not lie in feminine idleness, which differs from the standard valuation of middle-class women, whose idleness represents a positive and complementary excess of resources. Victorian women's activist Emily Davies's description of feminine idleness offers the starkest contrast to the spinster. The ideal middle-class woman, she writes, "feels no sort of impulse to take up any particular pursuit, or to follow out a course of study; and so long as she is quiet and amiable, and does not get out of health, nobody wants her to do anything . . ." (49). The middle-class wife is idle and superfluous, inessential, in a way that is quite distinct from that of the spinster, who clearly was compelled to take up some pursuit. The pressing problem posed by the spinster—what her society is to do about or for her—is precisely the problem that is evaded in the case of the married middle-class woman who had to fight for decades to problematize that idleness publicly.

In Victorian discourse the meaning and substance of the emigrant woman is inconsistent to the extreme not only in terms of how she was perceived and represented by her contemporaries but also in how she imagined and reimagined herself. Hence, personal testimonials do not provide adequate answers since self-conception and definition are only marginally indicative of the process by which women become reconstituted as cultural subjects. Furthermore, the fluctuations in emigrant spinsters' social and cultural significance often are dictated by sources other than the women themselves or even their immediate circumstances—that is, many times they originate quite entirely from without. Like Alice, Gaskell's spinster in *Mary Barton,* the spinster is imagined as establishing an important link between the here and now and a vaguely distant past. She even may be seen to embody a distinct anomaly in falling between class and gender categories. In sympathetic discourse, the spinster negates the loss of a past condition and place just as she encapsulates both the young virginal girl and the old maid. Persistent efforts to repackage spinsters sought to transform them into *national* commodities by convincing colonists that genteel spinsters could be of use to them. The emigrant woman embodies some of these contradictions in her *practical* value in the cultural economy, as compared to her professed importance to Victorian hegemony as an emblem of feminine virtue. As the Victorian Jessie Boucheret noted, the spinster's "departure would be an immense relief to the women remaining at home, but unfortunately, there is nowhere to send them, for nobody wants them either in the Old World or the New" (31). Outlining a formula by which women's value may be enhanced by their scarcity, Boucheret cites the problem concerning the cultural value of women—how very tenuous and uncertain it is. She proposes that the wrong class of men have been emigrating, thus positing that class is the source of the problem with "superfluous" women: "men who ought to emigrate very often prefer to remain in England" (35). In the process of exposing and examining the contradictions that render women excessive, Boucheret embarks on an analysis of the empire that situates the spinster in the context of much mismanagement, an inefficient economy and mode of operations. The insensible treatment of women with which she begins her essay ultimately locates the problem of the spinster's displacement in imperialism's paradoxes and leads to a critique of empire as the cause of her devaluation. Boucheret manages in this gesture to put the nation on display and to subject it to the scrutiny thus far reserved for the spinster: "What a strange spectacle does the great empire represent to the world! Savages doing Englishmen's work abroad; men doing women's work at home; and women starving, begging because they can get no honest employment" (41).

Even from within this profoundly racist framework, Boucheret makes an important observation about the extent to which the English economy and labor distribution have been diverted from domestic functions. In the context of the imperial muddle, the spinster is a pawn that has been displaced. But even in her nonplace of cultural and ideological uncertainty, the spinster as female emigrant is symbolically virulent. For her advocates and her critics the spinster represents both a lack and a conflict on a large scale: She has collapsed the intrinsic separation of the public and private spheres and serves as constant reminder, foreboding that "there is much moral wrong somewhere which requires to be remedied" (48). It is a strong comment on the spinster's identity that her advocates worked to define her in negative terms, since her identity was not to be found on a continuum with the established gender categories. In the essay "Old Maids" Victorian social commentator Charles Hamley illustrates the difficulty of constructing a definitive cultural identity and understanding of the spinster: "The spinster feels young among them who is separated from her former self by none . . . of the harsh breaks and dislocations which make people feel old. She carries her former self along with her, and can recall no point where the girl ended in the matron . . . something in her fate will express the fact that she has no master but her own will . . ." (100).

In considering the role of the unmarried woman in the context of Victorian culture, the paradox surfaces repeatedly that it may not prove possible adequately to simplify "superfluous" women, although efforts were made in that direction. They are ultimately not placed in some kind of restored and vital cultural economy, despite the fact that single women constitute a real population in themselves, give the prevalence of inescapable singlehood for women. In this context, spinsters implicitly challenge a number of social systems, including marriage. The traditional bourgeois plot resolution for women's limited lives, marriage, is negated by the impossibility of neat resolutions that the spinster represents. In fact, the unfeasibility of such a neat resolution constitutes a norm for a vast number of women during the period. It may be said to provide the necessary background to marriage, for the woman who is comfortably provided for repeatedly is the one who is married as well. The existence of the spinster is subsumed in the force of the normative ideologies that render marriage the only acceptable solution to the "woman question." It is worthwhile to consider the paradox of the predominant concern over unmarried women in relation to the ideology of domesticity and the extent to which the former mediated the latter.

Commodification implicates visibility, appearances, and finally spectacle but also the absence of the same; as a cultural problem, the emigrant spinster encompasses these dynamics, both prior to and during the process of emigration. Critic Guy Debord outlines the multivalent aspects of the spectacle, emphasizing what he calls "economy's domination of social life" and the spectacle's negative relationship to more basic economic functions and modes of production. Spectacle, according to Debord, is constituted by the convergence of desire and need with the negation of the forces in whose interests the spectacle functions:

> The present stage, in which social life is completely taken over by the accumulated products of the economy, entails a generalized shift from *having* to appearing: all effective "having" must now derive both its immediate prestige and its ultimate raison d'être from appearances. At the same time all individual reality, being directly dependent on social power and complexly shaped by that power, has assumed a social character. Indeed, it is only inasmuch as individual reality *is not* that it is allowed to *appear.* (16)

The spectacle of the emigrant spinster presents the obfuscation of the reality that the spinster is a subordinate class; the spectacle itself is meant to negate that reality. By the same token, in relation to Victorian spinsterhood, what is allowed to appear but does not exist is the image of the middle-class woman of means and dignity, whose place in society is always presumably assured. The poverty of Victorian spinsters is also their social marginalization, since bourgeois ideologies of femininity have material underpinnings and effectively perpetuate power hierarchies. In a sense, an ideology of femininity is being displaced by the spectacle of the Victorian unmarried emigrant woman, who is the terrible manifestation of a negation of life at a very rudimentary level. Hence, she qualifies as spectacle, insofar as the main ingredient of spectacle is negation. In Debord's terms, "the spectacle's essential character . . . [is] a visible negation of life— and . . . a negation of life that has *invented a visual form for itself*" (14). Desexualized in this manner, the spinster gains symbolic importance

in her relation to the nation. She posits the possibility of forgetfulness and of dislocation even as she embodies a violent clash between
her own past and her difficult present. The negation of her complexity and her predicament occurs at the moment when she is marketed as a colonial export, but also when she becomes the cultural
site of all that is frightful and undesirable in gender relations.

   In conceptualizing the emigrant female as an already-
commodified cultural subject, we are informed by Karl Marx's formulations concerning the constitution and positioning of
commodities in relation to other cultural and social "values." They
prove especially applicable to the status of the emigrant unmarried
woman as a paradoxical cultural subject, one who is at once precious
and superfluous. Marx problematizes and also renders more meaningful our understanding of how commodification works and how
its practices impact how commodities (in this case, women) are situated in relation to those systems that maintain and benefit from
their commodification. The quizzical statement, that occasionally the
commodity "stand[s] on its head," warns against construing commodification processes in linear terms. Rather, the commodity is
often a complex proposition that may, in fact, challenge the purposes
of its creation. This unpredictability is attributable in part to the
"mystical character" that commodities possess; this character "does
not . . . arise from [their] use value" (164), which accounts for why
"value . . . does not have its description branded on its forehead; it
rather transforms every product of labour into a social hieroglyphic"
(167). This distinction specifies that "every commodity is a symbol,
since, as a value, it is only the material shell of the human labour ex-
pended on it" (185), a relation that in turn points to the kinds of
labor invested in the production of the "superfluous" female emigrant.[4] Furthermore, the commodity may be viewed as an unstable
"symbol" since it is in a perpetual state of insubstantiation insofar as
its value is said (by definition) to lie both within and beyond itself.
This is the case with the emigrant female, who is at best a problematic commodity. Even when viewed in the bluntest terms, as export
to the colonies in the guise of national "good" or cultural product,
the female subject as commodity subverts and creates conflict in the
conditions of her commodification.

   If we accept that women are objects of patriarchal exchange, we
also accept that, categorically, women are commodities even prior to
the advanced commodity culture of the Victorian period. That is,

women are already "subjected" in a way that limits the extent of their potential values, movements, and identities, prior to any distinct act of commodification. The ideologies of domesticity and of femininity that prevail in Victorian culture are also the systematic means by which the main "value" standard of women is unrecognized and denied. Outside the institution of marriage, the exchange of sexuality and the very concrete bodies of women themselves are negated as determining their value so that when questions arise concerning the spinster's "use" value, this one key ingredient of the equation is not present. For instance, the vagueness that surrounds emigrant spinsters' nonplace is never connected to married women's legitimated "uses," their roles as mothers and reproducers of the race.[5] Therefore, the kind of worth that is attached to the spinster is not her actual potential value of reproduction but an artificial importance that is contrived and attached to her. In this respect, the spinster embodies the workings of "surplus value" which, as Marx puts it, "for the capitalist, has all the charms of something created out of nothing" (325). The peculiarities of this valorization highlight the extent to which "uselessness" is a characteristic the spinster and the bourgeois wife have in common in their relation to the dominant patriarchy: "By turning his money into commodities which serve as the building materials for a new product, and as factors in the labor process, by incorporating living labour into their lifeless objectivity, the capitalist simultaneously transforms value, i.e., past labour in its objectified and lifeless from, into capital, value which can perform its own valorization process, an animated monster which begins to "work," as if its body were by love possessed" (302). The valuation of commodities described here serves the interests of capital and can most aptly be described as "mystification." That is, the process of valuation of commodities entails the ingredients of insubstantiation and "valorization" as an exaggeration of actual material value. In Victorian discourse, the meanings of the unmarried woman are inconsistent to the extreme. In terms of the value attached to the emigrant spinster, she is either too precious or an enigma; what is not addressed in all instances of her exchange is her cultural situatedness, as that would contradict the valorization of ideologies of domesticity and femininity.[6] The very underpinnings of the middle-class wife's value (and the spinster "excessiveness") ultimately rest in the uses to which their bodies are or are not put for the purposes of patriarchal exchange, which is also what comes to be negated in the process of cultural translation.

The cultural construction of the spinster is a by-product of the events that rendered far too many women unmarriageable and the ideologies that colluded in determining the value of gender. Ultimately, as the early chapters also argue, the spinster problem is about more than the matter of women outnumbering men. In the context of the empire, British males achieve cultural status, money and power in the colonies; marriage is no longer lucrative for them, either socially or materially. Hence, at the peak of imperial activity, a more sanctimonious end, colonial expansion, has displaced the social institution of marriage. Consequently, the locus of masculinity's promulgation is not the domestic interior spaces but the infinitely promising Elsewhere. By extension, the ideological revision of domestic ideology accompanies revised imaginings of the category of the nation and its subjects. In the imperialist fervor, marriage and procreation are displaced as either vehicles or emblems of progress; they are replaced by a more global model of productivity. The prevalent worldview of Social Darwinism contributes to this shift by translating values not in terms of well-being but in terms of self-promotion and expansion, with an eye on the extension of those established systems to other places and seeking other contexts.[7] The late Victorian operative belief concerning social and national welfare appears to be that the individual bourgeois has outgrown his own physical boundaries. This observation also may be made of Victorian women as an inclusive class, since gender proscriptions were questioned by feminist writings and activism that explored alternative formulas for women's happiness.[8]

ACTING LIKE A WOMAN

Mid- and late Victorians retained Jane Austen's preoccupation with marriage and the desirability of thus being "placed" in the world of society and culture. However, they went even further than Austen in making the desirability of marriage a staple of art and literature and in problematizing it even more. The late Victorian perspective also differs since marriage becomes problematized by its many critics, among them feminists and other socially progressive types.[9] It would be difficult to point to a Victorian novel that does not scrutinize marriage as an extension of questioning social conventions and socioeconomic disparities. Indeed, many mainstream novels express an uneasy view toward marriage and its impact on women's lives. George Gissing's *The Odd Women* (1893) often is cited as the most explicit literary treatise on the problem of the Victorian spinster and on the question of women's socioeconomic dependency.[10] It offers a glimpse into the condition of the spinster, specifically as someone who has fallen from socioeconomic grace and is left destitute, alcoholic, desperate. Mirroring the typical scenario of Victorian spinsters' helplessness, the sisters depicted in the novel may have had some potential for self-sufficiency at one point in their lives but are now beyond the age when marriage might still be a viable possibility (the oldest being twenty-six) and can only vaguely fantasize of what they might do if they dared. The sisters' roles are fixed and often polarized; they are in a position just the opposite of agency.

Of the many Victorian novels that take issue with the unmarried woman, most important are those that comment explicitly on the issue as a social concern. The commodification and problematic status of the unmarried woman likewise are variously represented in the fiction of the age. Fiction that gained popularity in the later decades of the nineteenth century facilitated the public visibility of the spinster and guaranteed her exposure as a domestic social problem. That is, fiction makes public pronouncements concerning unmarried women as it addresses an inclusive general public—both the bourgeois class to which the genteel spinster belonged at one time and the one she may now be forced to join, the working classes. It is not surprising, perhaps, that popular literature is the most incisive of all since it removes spinsters and their problems from the insularity of bourgeois refinements and privacies, appealing as it does to a diversity of readers. When sensational and popular novels take on the problem of the spinster, the issue ceases to remain the preserve of the upper classes and instead is exposed to a broader and more diverse scrutiny. Examining the narrative strategies employed in such novels helps us to arrive at a more specific understanding of societal perceptions of the spinster and the problems she poses. One may even read such novels much like the nonfiction discussed in chapters 1 and 2—as historical and cultural documentation of a particular kind and as pertinent narratives of the cultural status of the "genteel" unmarried woman.

One novel in particular unequivocally engages these same issues of women who must exist outside the institution of marriage and thus on the fringes of proper, respectable, and exclusive society.

Wilkie Collins's *No Name* offers a disapproving analysis of marriage and bourgeois morality and also of the middle-class readership it exposes as hypocritical. The explicit ways it does so qualified it for harsh criticism when it first appeared in serial form in 1862. While George Gissing seeks to promote sympathy toward the ostracized spinster, Collins provokes righteous anger against the social injustices perpetrated against women. Critic Mark Ford rightly notes in his introduction to the novel that *No Name*'s "ambivalence over [moral absolutes] proved especially controversial," even when compared to the harsh treatment generally given most sensational novels.[11] *No Name* treats frankly those institutions the Victorians saw as sacred as it calls into question the foundations of their morality. In this respect Collins has surpassed even the transgressions of Charlotte Brontë and George Eliot in his celebration of the rebellious unmarried woman.[12] The novel follows the lives of two sisters who are suddenly left alone without provision; they are proclaimed "Nobody's Children" (109) when, following the death of their parents, it is discovered that they were born out of wedlock. The two sisters take very different approaches to their predicament: Norah, the older sister, opts for the expected option for survival and becomes a governess, while Magdalen seeks to avenge herself and her sister and to reclaim their inheritance. Together, the two sisters' stories delineate the predicament of the spinster and also underscore the prohibitions that obstruct the possibilities of women's happiness and self-actualization. The heroine, Magdalen, is the profligate daughter who defies convention and mocks tradition and "place" by attempting to assume for herself a number of identities. Fascinating in the way that she presumes to perform a number of roles and initiates acts of mimicry, Magdalen transgresses all boundaries of acceptability and normalcy in the context of Victorian morality, sexual conduct, and gender roles. She is the rebellious woman triumphant.

These particulars of the novel coincide with other, realistic depictions of Victorian spinsters' lives. The two sisters are first encountered in the throes of the narrative that explains the cause of their predicament: Their father dies unexpectedly, having failed to educate his daughters in the practical matters of making a living and supporting themselves. Reflecting bourgeois practice, Mr. Andrew Vanstone, as "the master of the house" (4), lovingly humored his daughters yet also shielded them from life's worries, preparing them only for a life of dependency. Collins criticizes such social complacency harshly and castigates the domestic ideal for failing women; he suggests that women need protection not so much from the harshness of the "real world" they often are contrasted to as from the goodwill of patriarchs and the protective ideologies of gender. The novel also supports the historical fact that in the context of Victorian economic superfluity and rampant production of excess, within the family there was also the incapacity to provide financially for any woman other than one's most pressing responsibility. In light of this, the proposition of "dependency" becomes dangerous for women and is an ever-present irony noted by a great many Victorian women, among them Florence Nightingale and the women's rights advocate Frances Power Cobbe.

The case of emigrant spinsters makes clear the cruel paradox that patriarchy promotes a dependency for women that it cannot support. Hence, Magdalen is horrified when she discovers that she and her sister are "left dependent"—in this particular setting, dependency is a stark term when it is not accompanied by even marginal remuneration or protection. Rather, it is a technical, legal term meaning destitution, pronounced upon them by their family lawyer, following their parents' deaths and their subsequent disinheritance (105). It becomes abundantly clear through the course of the novel that dependency is not a good proposition for women, although men would insist on it as a necessary ingredient of feminine moral virtue. The novel argues most powerfully that women do, in fact, need to be prepared for every contingency and that there is no stability or security within the domestic realm—that, contrary to sentimental fantasies predominant in Victorian culture, the home is not sanctified. Left with nothing in the world, not even their proper names, Magdalen and Norah must make do somehow. The question posed by their dilemma is: What is a woman to do when she finds herself on her own, in the midst of an opportunistic society that has expectations of women but absolves itself of any responsibility to them? Left without money and failed by the men who should protect her, Magdalen's very character is challenged so that the change in her circumstances becomes a fundamental change in her identity.[13] Away from her familiar surroundings and family, she takes on an exotic and mysterious appearance, suggesting that her identity thus far has been shaped by her social and class status. Now that she has lost both class and money, she is merely an outcast who is vulnerable to every influence: "There she stood, in her long black cloak and gown, the last dim light of evening falling tenderly on her pale resolute young face. There she stood—not three months since the spoilt darling of her parents; the priceless treasure of the household, never left unprotected, never trusted alone—there she stood in the lovely dawn of her womanhood, a castaway in a strange city wrecked on the world!" (155). The predicament detailed in *No Name* and the fate to which the heroines are subjected are emblematic of the fate of many spinsters who had to provide for themselves in a society that denies women's self-sufficiency and does not permit female independence. When Magdalen rebels against poverty and obscurity and rejects the passive renunciation that is expected of her—in short, when she definitively renounces dependency and becomes an active agent on her own behalf—she encounters many difficulties. Her radicalness lies in her refusal meekly to accept her fate and her fall from social grace, and also in her attempts to subvert the very customs that oppress her. She attempts to use marriage toward her own ends. She actively courts and marries her cousin, the introverted and pathetic Noel Vanstone, who is now in possession of the fortune that was once hers.

Pretense and transgressing one's proscribed social roles is not permitted for "dependent" women, however, and Magdalen's every effort at independence is foiled. In one of the most powerful instances of "mimicry" in the novel, Magdalen co-opts the rituals of romance and courtship, employing them for the purpose of regaining her wealth In making a mockery of Noel's egotistical (but quite conventional) claims of love, Magdalen also mocks romance as an appendage to domestic ideology. According to the dictates of ideal femininity and the standard romance plot, Magdalen would have played a subordinate role in a drama of love initiated by Noel. In contrast, although she is repulsed by him, Magdalen uses her beauty—her very desirability—to seduce him into restoring her estate to her and her sister. That she should use marriage to serve her own self-interest makes Magdalen a most objectionable unmarried woman. In seeking to marry for money, she makes visible the hidden motivation in the institution of marriage: the perpetuation of existing hierarchies. As if understanding this precept rather too well, Magdalen suits herself and attempts to play the institution against itself to recover her lost fortune.

Like Gissing's "odd woman" Monica Madden, Magdalen Vanstone discovers that marriage is a difficult proposition, even when used as a ploy to manipulate the law for her own purposes. Thinking that they could use conventional rules and traditions to their advantage defeats both Magdalen and Monica. They also find, through their respective marriages, that marriage does not suffice to relieve women from many of life's predicaments. In accordance with the domestic ideal, marriage also must conform to the dictates of romance and preservation of the social strata; it may not be entered into deliberately as a means of survival. Collins's meaning here is that this is, in fact, how marriage traditionally has functioned; but it is taboo for single women of no means to appropriate this system for their own use. The alternative to such tactics toward self-determination is the spinster's acceptance of her lot, when her only acceptable means of living is a demotion to a lower class and her removal from bourgeois society. This, of course, is no alternative at all. In the end, both sisters are married off quite happily, and the many problems they encounter and expose remain forever unresolved. Ultimately, Magdalen fails to attain an existence apart from the institutions that failed her in the first place.

No Name proposes that the problem confronted by Magdalen is not only a matter of misguided loss of values on the part of their cousin and his father. Rather, the conditional protectiveness of the ideology of domesticity is exposed as dubious. Chivalry, in this novel's illustrations, is all too obviously a myth it behooves Victorian women not to accept. Through the examples of Noel Vanstone and his father we see that men not only fail to fulfill their assigned roles as protectors of women, they are also ruthlessly self-interested. The ideology of domesticity also works against the unmarried woman in other ways. Prepared for nothing but marriage, spinsters are indeed poorly qualified for the independent existence their new status requires. One of the key problems illustrated here is precisely that moral rectitude often substitutes for socioeconomic status and that, in the absence of recognizable forms of class differentiation, it can serve to establish some socially desirable distinctions. Moral rectitude, in other words, can stand in for—or is exchangeable for—economic privilege. In the case of spinsters of reduced means, this substitution is expected. According to that standard, as a rebellious woman, Magdalen has forfeited any and all status and has no place in proper society. This example also suggests that the societal sanction against women who do not conform to a single circumscribed role is expulsion.

In the context of such overwhelming restrictions, how might the abject exert cultural influence and/or act against authorized institutions?[14] Part of the answer rests in the plot development, according to which such transgressions result Magdalen's being disinherited in yet another way. She is totally removed from the society that disowned her until, in the end, she becomes invisible. She can no longer have any contact with her sister, the virtuous Norah, who passively accepts her victimization. She also must have no contact with the governess, Miss Garth. Both "proper" women are in turn forbidden to acknowledge Magdalen publicly at the risk of losing what little social status they have. The women's efforts to maintain contact with one another despite social prohibitions becomes a significant portion of the plot, as is their individual acknowledgment of social mandates. These and other instances in the novel closely reflect the kind of internal, domestic exile incurred by genteel spinsters. The punishment of exclusion is a retaliation for Magdalen's having illicitly donned the identities of a good, marriageable woman and a good spinster-governess. As she herself remarks to her agent, her becoming an actress is more unforgivable than leaving her family and wandering the streets alone: "Captain Wragge, when you first met me on the Walls of York, I had not gone too far to go back. I have gone too far now" (192).[15]

Magdalen's influence as a wayward woman would seem to be quite powerful, if even the slightest association between her and Norah or Miss Garth can cause their societal ruin. The power of the spinster may not be in helping herself, then, but in influencing the lives of others. As Miss Garth explains in a letter to Magdalen, Norah's employers hired her on the "positive condition that . . . she should never permit you to visit her at their house—or to meet her and walk out with her when she was in attendance on the children" (254). As a former "dependent" governess herself, Miss Garth concludes her directive to Magdalen by diagnosing the problem confronting single women who choose a path other than that of the subservient and humble governess: "Your way of life, however pure—and I will do you the justice to believe it pure—is a suspicious way of life to all respectable people. I have lived long enough in this world to know, that the Sense of Propriety, in nine English-women out of ten, makes no allowances and feels no pity" (254). In no uncertain terms, societal opinion does not care about the details or truths of one's circumstances; it mercilessly delivers pat indictments that the individual is powerless to contest. Like mimicry, assuming different identities in this novel "radically revalues the normative knowledges of the priority of race, writing, history," so that to repeat the activity that is more or less an imposition exposes it as such and subverts its very premises (Bhabha, *Location of Culture* 91). Its systems and premises are exposed as contrived and fragile. The mimic and mimicry serve to alter the very functions and processes they mime mainly in that what is being reflected and performed in the "mimic" are portions of the authentic (that is, the imperialist). That authenticity is comprised mainly of the ambivalence and the insecurity of the "authentic" subject. "Mimicry" enhances our understanding of the spinster who, even as a distressed gentlewoman, retained her previous class identity. She continues to act from that place even as she was no longer of that class, financially and socially. Even in her status as poor and socially disenfranchised woman, the spinster is nonetheless seen as someone who is not intrusive and for whom the domestic sphere is the proper one, although it must undergo some revision in order to accommodate her.

Bhabha and Irigaray recognize in mimicry an element of rebellion and subversion since the performativity of mimicry is also the locus within which it deconstructs its subject. For Bhabha, mimicry consists of the comparisons between the native and the imperialist, a comparison that is initiated by the imperialist. This comparison generally serves to distinguish "them" from "us" but also allows for partial identification between Others and imperialists. Bhabha notes this relation as also marking the close connection between mimicry and mockery. In the colonial context the "mimic man" or subject "is the effect of a flawed colonial mimesis, in which to be Anglicized is *emphatically* not to be English" (*Location,* 87). The end of cultural production, in this process, is difference that is not entirely foreign. Bhabha assigns the possibility of subversive agency to the native behind the mask but also to the mask. Similarly, what is being reflected in the spinster and in the governess is a version of the Victorian hegemony, an understanding of its workings, always implying that it operates on exclusion and reprobation for deviation of any kind. Yet it is precisely the space of experimentation and performance that is opened to the spinster as social outcast, and this becomes a very meaningful and fruitful space.

Magdalen's intense bond with her sister illustrates the extent to which her identity is conflicted. Separated from Norah by their social constitution as binary opposites, Magdalen defiantly appears at Norah's workplace. She gazes at her sister from a distance, from beyond yards and roads and walls, and sees her carry out the duties of a governess. Although Magdalen violates social mandates when she visits her sister, this transgression reflects positively on her because she does so due to "the higher and purer longing to see her sister's face again, though she dare not discover herself and speak" (*No Name,* 220). Magdalen is compelled to approach her sister, whom she loves greatly, without revealing her presence. She appears as a ghost and disappears again without being seen and without having disturbed propriety or her sister's prospects. While Norah has done as she was expected in becoming a governess, she is not depicted as having made the right choice. When Magdalen looks at her from distance, she seems pitiful in her new role: weak, unhappy, and made painfully aware of her excessive status in the household of her employers. On the contrary, the visit is also important in moral terms, since Magdalen's very proximity to her more virtuous and suffering sister highlights to her the degree to which she has strayed from standards of acceptability:

> She made a wide circuit on the grass, so as to turn gradually and meet her sister, without exciting suspicion that the meeting was contrived. Her heart beat fast; a burning heat glowed in her as she thought of her false hair, her false colour, her false dress, and saw the dear familiar face coming nearer and nearer. They passed each other close. Norah's dark gentle eyes looked up, with a deeper light in them, with a sadder beauty, than of old—rested all unconscious of the truth on her sister's face—and looked away from it again, as from the face of a stranger. That glance of an instant struck Magdalen to the heart. She stood rooted to the ground, after Norah has passed by. A horror of the vile disguise that concealed her; a yearning to burst its trammels and hide her shameful painted face on Norah's bosom, took possession of her, body and soul. She turned and looked back. (221)

This scene reveals that while she must assume social invisibility, Magdalen also enjoys a distinct autonomy as pariah and errant woman. Her power to observe the relatively immobile Norah, whose every action and word is closely monitored by her employers, manifests itself in her very physical movements as she witnesses the governess caring for her charges and enduring harsh treatment. Magdalen's relationship to her sister is such that the two women combined may constitute one whole. They are contraries, each representing a prevalent facet of Victorian womanhood at opposite ends of the limits of femininity. Through the relationship of the two sisters and the righteousness of Magdalen's rebellion, the novel negotiates these two polarized femininities and deliberates the question of Magdalen's moral guilt or innocence.

The spinster also is represented as an empowered figure in the characterization of Miss Garth. When Miss Garth explains that society will ruthlessly punish Norah and herself for Magdalen's transgressions, she functions as patriarchy's agent. She is society's instrument, reinforcing and sustaining its power to dictate the lives of single women and to curtail their options. The spinster (Miss Garth) is a beloved surrogate mother and teacher in life's ways to the two sisters, but she is a great deal more. She is the site of hidden resources, a matriarch and a masterful negotiator between several different and often disparate "places" in culture. Financially, Miss Garth is able to take care of Magdalen and Norah better than their own mother had been able to do, since she has been setting aside some of her earnings over the years and has sole ownership of her own money. In this particular plot, the governess is the mediator between Norah's poverty and her new professionalism, and she is also the link between the law and lawyers and the two sisters' interests. She is an essential link between all the important facets of the story, its characters, and the institutions that govern them.

Magdalen appears to have learned from the industriousness of Miss Garth but also has deduced that ideally one would use the authority granted governesses for emancipatory purposes. Therefore, she dons the older woman's garb when she visits Noel Vanstone to demand restitution of her and her sister's inheritance. In that guise, Magdalen delivers the accurate indictment of selfishness and greed against Vanstone. Her exclusion from even the world of respectable servitude is the paramount penalty for having committed the crime of severe social and gender transgressions and for assuming identities other than the marginal one assigned to her. Likewise, this expulsion emphasizes the vulnerability of the governess, whose only marketable feature and characteristic is her moral standing. A great portion of Magdalen's "dangerousness" lies in her having known other roles, other possibilities, and from having manipulated these roles and characteristics, thus exposing their very tenuousness and artificiality. However, each time Magdalen assumes a different identity, whether as an actress or as a disguise, in effect she also becomes invisible. This is a common occurrence in Victorian fiction, which does not often succeed in representing female rebellion and subversion.

Several Victorian novels feature women for whom the domestic bliss promised by convention and bourgeois mythology was not an option. These women are remanded to remote corners of society and respectability. Spinsters often are seen lurking in the shadows of the stage occupied by women who are either married or sure to be so before long. Their lot in life is difficult and they themselves are invisible either because they are disqualified from mixing in the company of women whose status is secure or because they are allowed a singular function—that of the governess. And yet, as *No Name* also suggests, the governess exhibits different kinds of agency, some of them oppositional, even from her marginalized place. This is most vividly the case with Charlotte Brontë's famous spinster heroines, specifically Lucy Snow in *Vilette* (1853), which charts one woman's journey toward fulfillment.[16] Charlotte Brontë's works make clear that the figure of the governess is important, especially when she is viewed as a more acceptable translation of the spinster. She represents the proximity of economic hardship to middle-class pretensions. In emphasizing this contradiction, she is an anomaly and a paradox but also, conceivably, a threat. As critic Mary Poovey observes, the governess presents many problems to the Victorian hegemony, both as a *working* middle-class woman and an unmarried one:

> If even middle-class women could and did work outside the home, then women might not be naturally dependent or destined (or content) to be mothers; if they did not always marry, then marriage might not be the only unit of social organization (155).
>
> The governess is [important] because of the proximity she bears to two of the most important Victorian representations of women: the figure who epitomized the domestic ideal, and the figure who threatened to destroy it. . . . [T]he very figure who theoretically should have defended the naturalness of separate spheres threatened to collapse the difference between them. (127)

The figure of the governess is thus a choice location for the tensions between gender and class identities as encountered in the "distressed" middle-class spinster.

There is much that is daring about *Vilette,* insofar as it undertakes to represent the spinster's powerful sensuality and passion. It is perhaps because of this passion that Lucy is seen most often alone and isolated, her passion a well-kept secret. She visits the garden after dark so that she might be alone with her thoughts, overwhelmed by emotions for which she can find no outlet. It is abundantly clear that in the context of spinsterhood, Lucy's feelings are a major liability; she is encumbered by them since her situation precludes the appropriate forms of their expression. As a governess, Lucy's identity is rigidly circumscribed since she is expected to consist of no more than her professional duties. She is expected to be simple and predictable, at once transparent and unseen. Lucy recognizes that the expectation is that, as a spinster, she will be a "mere looker-on at life" and not an actor in it (131). The expectation also is that she will be silent and unobtrusive, "thinking . . . [her] own thoughts, living [her] own life in [her] still shadow world" (109). As little more than an appendage, the spinster has no legitimate place of her own, standing as she does independent of legitimating accompaniments. Also, high premium is placed on her serving others while sacrificing her own desires and wishes. In her role as teacher, as in any of the other roles allowed her, any activity that surpasses the expected range of behaviors would be objectionable. It is no surprise, then, that Lucy roams about at night and appears quite literally as a ghost. She carves out a dark corner for herself, even in the midst of a ball, "withdrawing to a quiet nook, whence unobserved [she] could observe—the ball, its splendors, and its pleasures passed before [her] as a spectacle" (131).

Lucy's new situation abroad, however difficult, is nonetheless an improvement over those available to her in England, where she was companion to an elderly woman until she died. She recognizes that as a teacher she has more privileges than she could have hoped for since, as she acknowledges, "my qualifications were not convertible, not adaptable" (280). With Madame Beck, her new employer, Lucy is simply a teacher and has the most important things of all—her freedom and time to herself: "I was not *her* companion, nor her children's governess; she left me free: she tied me to nothing—not to herself—not even to her interests" (280). Madame Beck grants Lucy this freedom as if it were a precious gift; the moment of its endowment is repeated and rendered in Lucy's mind in the original French, granting it a most important, binding authenticity: *"c'est ce que je ferai"* (280). Lucy is also happy to be able to escape the restrictive confines of her professional roles by disappearing into nonsocial spaces, places from which people are remarkably absent and in which she is no longer spectacle. She is capable of escaping her confinement, which in this case is not only the school where she teaches but also limiting social interaction with other people:

> At first I lacked courage to venture very far from the Rue Fossette, but by degrees I sought the city gates, and passed them, and then went wandering away far along *Chaussees,* through fields, beyond cemeteries, Catholic and Protestant, beyond farmsteads, to lanes and little woods and I know not where. *A goad thrust me on, a fever forbade me to rest; a want of companionship maintained in my soul the cravings of a most deadly famine.* I often walked all day, through the burning noon and the arid afternoon, and the dusk evening, and came back with moonrise. (147, emphasis added)

Lucy's freedom is the freedom to roam, to enjoy the luxury of solitude, to move beyond the confines of work. She uses this freedom to the fullest so that her walks become acts of symbolic importance. They enact her transgression of gender and other social boundaries. Escaping the city limits, she walks through places not known to her and in which she is herself unknown. In this way she exercises control over her very identity and the possibilities of her very agency. She also rejects the realm of the known that is oppressive to her (namely, her awareness of the limits imposed by her circumstances) for the mysterious and the unknown that hold the promise of infinite possibilities.[17] In her mind, the England she has left behind becomes a fond memory and increasingly a malleable space she can reimagine in idealizing terms. Thus, Lucy's independence may be produced by the very structures that confined her.

These ways of understanding agency and performativity help us to see that it would have to surface (as it does in the guise of acting) in narratives that question identity and subversion in relation to gender prescriptions. *Vilette* includes an acting scene as well as several moments of ecstatic, passionate moments of semiconsciousness when Lucy crosses one threshold to embrace another in terms of her sexuality and her wants and desires. When she is coerced into participating in a play, Lucy discovers that though she would not have opted to take on such a challenge, she is well suited to role-acting: "Cold, reluctant, apprehensive, I had accepted a part to please another: ere long, warming, becoming interested, taking courage, I acted to please myself" (131). Pursuing this exercise of taking on identities and deploying multiplicity, Lucy is free to pursue her many possibilities. As she observes, courage and rebellion may come from being a shadow, discrete, an unknown, as long as she can still observe from the shadows: "I felt . . . an inward courage, warm and resistant. In this matter I was not disposed to gratify Dr. John: not at all. With a now welcome force, I realized his entire misapprehension of my character and nature. He wanted always to give me a role not mine. Nature and I opposed him. He did not at all guess what I felt: he did not read my eyes, or face, or gestures; thought, I doubt not, all spoke" (298). Lucy (and the narrative text of her life but also of the novel) embraces a number of possibilities at once, at the same time that she is limited and circumscribed from every direction, socially and ide-ologically. She is able to transcend those limitations by the novel's end, to step outside of them and to become critical spectator to the rituals of heterosexual practices in the garden; she is not only voyeur empowered to observe, she is also participant. In the end, Lucy Snow has both marriage and property, and the freedom from societal con-ventions that accompanies marriage, since her husband conveniently dies at sea shortly after their marriage, leaving her a house and a school of her own. While she regrets that she has lost the man she loves, Lucy is now safely established in a school of her own and has realized every Victorian middle-class spinster's goal of self-sufficiency and independence. She is now "spared the pain of being a burden to anybody" (268), and she is transformed into the ideal-ized, virtuous, and independent woman she has wanted to be: "to work for herself, that she might burden neither kith nor kin" (268). Thus Brontë delivers the antidote to the predicament of the spinster.

GENDER AND AGENCY

Irigaray's work accounts for gender in the process of commodifica-tion and exchange, taking into consideration the material conditions of women's subjectivity. She addresses the possibility of agency for the commodified emigrant woman, who may be seen easily as inan-imate in the great scheme of interactions between men in power among themselves and between empire and colonies:

> In our social order, women are "products" used and exchanged by men. Their status is that of merchandise, "commodities." How can such ob-jects of use and transaction claim the right to speak and to participate

in exchange in general? Commodities, as we all know, do not take themselves to market on their own; . . . So women have to remain an "infrastructure" unrecognized as such by our society and our culture. The use, consumption, and circulation of their sexualized bodies underwrite the organization and the reproduction of the social order, in which they have never taken part as "subjects." (84)

Looking back to the mention of Gayle Rubin's very useful work on the marketing of women in the introduction of this study, we encounter again the concept of woman as Victorian commodity that is exchanged among men and whose value is perpetually in flux. On the basis of her gender status, the unmarried middle-class woman who finds herself financially dependent must discover different ways of asserting a cultural importance. The problem that remains is that concerning their agency: how might they be said to exert any agency at all, from such a subordinate place? While it is important to acknowledge that unmarried women were commodified, this commodification does not preclude their own agency in the imperial context. Their one consistent quality was that they remained materially, physically inaccessible to the bulk of spectators. Hence, excess or "surplus" as a condition was valued at the same time that the nation argued the case of its own efficient productivity. As with the example of the Great Exhibition, both the high premium placed on maximized productivity and the sense of affluence and overabundance that it claimed as a benefit were dialectically negated as a concern in the Victorian hegemony. The "surplus" or excess of products or goods had to be desirable, if inaccessible. The notion of "surplus" and "superfluity," as applied to unmarried middle-class women, then, serves as the locus of these contradictions.

For the analysis of gender politics that Irigaray offers, "mimicry" holds a different kind of importance. Mimicry, for Irigaray, answers the question of woman's subservience to the patriarchal status quo and also her immobility and silence. Her concept of mimicry is used to address the question, "[H]ow . . . are women, that 'reality' that is somewhat resistant to discourse, to be defined?" (85) and also: What is the process by which women might become "speaking subjects"? (88). Finally, Irigaray asks, "[H]ow . . . can any articulation of sexual difference be possible," given the symbolic order's rejection of women? (110). However, women are not completely absorbed in the act of mimicry. As Irigaray notes, "the mimetic role itself is complex,

for it presupposes that one can lend oneself to everything if not to
everyone. That one can *copy* anything at all, anyone at all, can receive
all impressions, *without appropriating them to oneself,* and *without adding
any*" (151). The point is that mimicry also impacts on identity and
that through it one potentially becomes further enmeshed in those
practices that serve to subjugate one's agency in the first place. In
this analysis female agency is employed through mimicry since there
is no possibility of a woman performing any role (particularly empowering ones) without also adopting the means of that power by
way of the behavior itself, which is a recognizable and hence symbolic aspect of that power. For women, mimesis is about exposing
exploitation and marginalization. Irigaray elaborates:

> To play with mimesis is thus, for a woman, to try to recover the place of
> her exploitation by discourse, without allowing herself to be simply re-
> duced to it. It means to resubmit herself—inasmuch as she is on the side
> of the "perceptible," of "matter"—to "ideas"; in particular, to ideas about
> herself, that are elaborated in/by a masculine logic, but so as to make "vis-
> ible," by an effect of playful repetition, what was supposed to remain in-
> visible: The cover-up of a possible operation of the feminine in language.
> It also means "to unveil" the fact that if women are such good mimics, it
> is because they are not simply resorbed in this function. *They also remain
> elsewhere.* . . . (76)

The female mimic opens herself up to the ideologies that rule her
life. It makes the most sense to consider the spinster using an amalgamation of these two concepts, so that the category of gender is accounted for and can be incorporated into the equation of power and
into the politics of subject positions, mimicry, and performance. Irigaray makes clear the distinct differences proposed by gender in female subjects' mimicry. The genteel spinster, we have seen, does not
qualify for any easily recognized social category. As a hybrid caught
in the ideological rifts between woman's materiality and her ideological place, the emigrant spinster problematizes gender's conventions. And yet, as the novels here suggest, at all times she may pass
herself off as her counterpart. The spinster possesses the inherent
ability to mimic proper womanhood, and this is one of her powers:
She can implement exchanges in gender and class identities to serve
her own interests.[18]

Accounting for the specifics of women's constructed subjectivities in the production of cultural meaning and value entails much

dissonance and incongruity. Only then can we begin to locate the spinster's social indeterminacy without disallowing the significance of physical places and material transplantation. The concept of "mimicry," as articulated by Homi Bhabha and Irigaray, makes it possible to locate the Victorian spinster in the context of the period and the culture. Insofar as it feigns accurate representation but is clearly and overtly imitative, mimicry interrogates authenticity, evoking distinctions in power and legitimacy, between privileged and subordinate subjects. If we grant that acculturation is a possibility within England as without it (which, as argued earlier, may be quite appropriate), the ways in which one becomes "acculturated" and to what extent may be analogous to similar imperializing impositions on non-English subjects. The identification between empire and its undesirable subjects is always only "partial," as Bhabha terms it, and—given that she is between classes and exists in the structural rifts of the hegemonic strata—the membership of the spinster to any social and economic class can be only "partial" (*Location of Culture* 87). What is re-established through "mimicry" is a statement of the proximity between us and them, a semblance of being human, whole, civilized, and significant, on the part of the natives. In a similar gesture, the middle-class spinster is disowned by her culture and yet is still bound to it, in terms of her virtue and in her relation to certain features of culture, such as morality. Domesticity surfaces as the most equivocal area, the place that best illustrates the concept of mimicry. The domestic space is the one spinsters are expected to occupy, but not really. The figure of the governess, the middle-class woman who is no longer technically a member of that class, is "like" the other women of her class, enough so as to qualify to acculturate their children; they share some of the same cultural features but not others, namely their relation to domesticity. As Emily Davies noted in 1866, "men have no monopoly of working, nor women of weeping. The sort of distinction it is attempted to establish . . . is for the most part artificial, plausible in appearance, but breaking down under the test of experience." The spinster exposes the "theory" of absolute and untroubled difference (and gender division), as Davies contends would need to happen "in practice" (14). It is precisely this artificiality that was exported to the colonies alongside the spinsters, who bore it for their nation.

Leaving England and remembering England are tropes that reveal much about the colonization and emigration processes, as they do about the popular imagination. England is both a place and a condition, both an experience and a confusion, for Lucy Snow and Magdalen Vanstone. However, the most dynamic aspect of the emigration process is the projection forward into the colonies and the remembering "backward" into what has been left behind. What is reconstructed in the act of remembering is not the precise place that the emigrant once occupied but the imaginary spaces she wished she had, those very spaces and relations that had been forbidden to her. In leaving England, she can claim those spaces and relations as her own plus forge some new ones. A material and geographic boundary is asked to serve an ideological and political function as women's advocates send their heroines to the unknown and the endless possibilities offered by the cities in an effort to achieve a similar end: They attempt to provide a different contexts for women, whose circumstances and positions proved far too limiting and victimizing. In the process, the nucleus of the family, of the cultural community, and of the nation as institutions are problematized. Franz Fanon's point, that "there are close connections between the structure of the family and the structure of the nation," applies very well to the case of unmarried emigrant women (141). Insofar as "the family is the miniature of the nation," while "the family represents in effect a certain fashion in which the world presents itself to a child" (141–42), imperial expansion has its cultural analogue in the changing significance of the family—indeed, in the transformation of the domestic sphere. Patriarchal power operates within the family much as England functioned relationally to the world. Nationhood and the "nation" serve as an alternative and less restrictive signifying model for those among the English who sought to effect some kind of change in their own lives but also in the meaningfulness or ideological import of those lives.

A type of substitution is taking place with the emigrant spinster whose distressing circumstances are projected into an unrealizable fantasy of dignity in the colonies. The substitution is both within the spectacle itself and within the offering, the gesture. On both counts, the colonies and the women, material compensation is supplanted by moral and cultural compensation, much as aesthetics overtook material need, as Thomas Richards argues (*Commodity Culture of Victorian England*, 61). If it were not for the fact that much of the commodity's value serves a symbolic function alone—that is, remains totally inaccessible to most spectators at the exhibit—at this cultural moment "surplus" might be said to be a positive value. It was, in any case, a positive product of the commodity obsession evidenced by showcases such as the Great Exhibition. Richards notes, "more than anything else, the Exhibition projected an image of surplus" and "actually helped to create the sense of surplus that it is so often cited as evidence for" (28–29).[19] That substitution parallels the one that took place within and around the spectacle of the Great Exhibition, through which the mother nation, owner of all spectacles and all values, made apparent to the world and to the colonies its material and cultural superiority.

And yet the overriding concern cannot be dignified privacy but successful exportation, that is, bringing spinsters out into the world. The spinster remains culturally valuable only insofar as her colonial valuation and the imperial exchange transaction succeeds. By its very definition, the centrality of the commodity calls attention to itself and to its material foundations, at the same time that it must work overtime to oversignify in other contextual ways as well. However, the features of the commodity's production and constitution must not suggest a solely symbolic agency. Guy Debord has observed that "each commodity . . . unconsciously actualizes something of a higher order than itself: the commodity's becoming worldly coincides with the world's being transformed into commodities," culminating in the "complete colonization of social life" (43). This colonization, Debord emphasizes, is epitomized in the spectacle (29). Emigrant spinsters could be invested with cultural value only insofar as their exchange could be assured. That part of the equation, of course, had been in development for centuries in England. However, the commodification of the "markets" or the colonies as plausible and receptive destinations for unwanted women had yet to be established.

Material truths become social myths in the impasse between excessive symbolic value and material *lack*, the signifying remnants of ideological prescriptions. Spinster novels generally concentrate on marriage or its failure as a feature of the past that is always pressing on the present moment. Unmarried women look into the past at a moment of chance or missed opportunity that has rendered them "spinsters" the rest of their lives. Like Gaskell's *Cranford* (1853), the meaning of spinsters' lives, the fluctuation in their cultural value, is to be found not in the conditions of their present lives but in the past. At the same time, spinsters are depicted as totally unprepared for their changed circumstances from relative independence and comfort to complete dependency. More than being not an asset to their societies, they are also a liability because they have not made an easy transition into the present moment. Such "anachronisms" combine with the specter of lost status and lost security to suggest that the past moment in which the novel is set continues to impinge on the present and that it may not serve to change the present.[20] Given the complex relationship I have suggested between a problematic domestic subject and the rhetoric of imperialism, it would not be feasible to establish a linear model of causality and progression in examining the role of emigrant women in the imperial project or concerning the individual's relation to the empire. But the relationship one holds to empire and to one's own nationalism is not simple or predictable. Furthermore, as the cases of Carroll and Gaskell suggest in chapter 4, literary texts do not immediately and directly evidence the ways cultural contradiction permeates discourse. This complexity is compounded by the open-endedness and variability of notions of the nation and national subjectivity and also by the complex relationship between the nation and the national subject.[21]

The spinsters one encounters in novels and in Victorian nonfiction also present a number of possibilities for understanding how gender functions in constituting social and cultural subjects. The figure of the spinster is persistently one that is promising, rebellious, and progressive; at other times, the spinster is the epitome of reactionary politics. In the literature, as in the social history, working to resolve the problem of the spinster's nonplace means working to demystify it, and also to examine the power dynamics of that nonplace which is also an extremely problematic place. What at first seems a contradiction—viewing a nonplace as the locus of conflict—is simply a negated realm that may be relegated to the domain of ideology. The spinster's cultural and ideological "nonplace," then, is an instrumental space in the sense that she exists somewhere in between morally upright and fallen women, the authorized national subjects and the immigrant and the foreign native, as she exists both in the literature and culture as well as always beyond, beyond its purview.

Given emigrant women's complex and dynamic cultural identity, and given the demonstrated shifts and contradictions in the constitution of their identities, but especially given their intricately unique relation to the imperialist project and to the cohesiveness of notions of nationhood, we can begin to see them finally not only as cultural commodity in transit but also as a cultural and national conduit of sorts. Their very agency becomes an important but secondary feature of their persistent identification as somewhere in between Here and There, Us and Them, assimilated versus foreign, male and female, Same and Other. This is an impossible yet interesting position in which to find oneself.

NOTES

1. Small portions of this introduction, specifically those dealing with the "post-colonial" problem and definitions of "hegemony," appeared in an earlier form as the introduction to the collection *Imperial Objects: Victorian Women's Emigration and the Unauthorized Imperial Experience.*

2. The work of Martha Vicinus has persistently problematized the status of the unmarried woman in the context of Victorian culture in general. Her *Independent Women: Work and Community for Single Women, 1850–1920* focuses on exploring the tension between the domestic front and woman's function within it.

   Some other relevant sources on the subject are: Laura Brodie, "Society and the Superfluous Female: Jane Austen's Treatment of Widowhood," 697–718; Joy Parr, "The Skilled Emigrant and Her Kin: Gender, Culture, and Labour Recruitment"; Laura Doan, ed., *Old Maids to Radical Spinsters: Unmarried Women in the Twentieth Century Novel.* See also Joan Perkin's chapter, "Making Their Own Way: The Lives of Unmarried Middle-Class Women" in *Victorian Women* and Sheila Jeffries, *The Spinster and Her Enemies: Feminism and Sexuality, 1880–1930.*

   In *Uneven Developments: The Ideological Work of Gender in Mid-Victorian England*, Mary Poovey notes the repressiveness of middle-class gentility, specifically within the context of marriage. See her chapter on Caroline Norton and the Matrimonial Causes Act, "Covered But Not Bound."

3. See also Anne McClintock and Rob Nixon, "No Names Apart: The Separation of Word and History in Derrida's '*Le Dernier Mot du Racisme.*'"

4. I use the term "Elsewhere" throughout this study, realizing that it is invested with much diverse meaning. My uses of it are deliberately multivalent. The conception of the Elsewhere that I use throughout is a composite that includes the unknown and the foreign (such as colonial cultures), the already appropriated features of imperialized spaces, and also that which must always be exoticized at the same time that it is eliminated or subjugated. The Elsewhere is not England and is not the colonies either. It is, rather, a complex space between those entities and is employed for imperial uses in many of the contexts I discuss throughout this study.

My understanding of this concept encapsulates the contradictions of imperialism. It is closely aligned with Edward Said's notion of "structured irony" that permeates British articulations concerning colonized places. In the terms that Said studies, such places are seen to exist beyond the influence of the empire, while on the other hand they are always approximated to it: "On the one hand, there was a collection of people living in the present; on the other hand, these people—as the subject of study—became 'the Egyptians,' 'the Muslims,' or 'the Orientals.' Only the scholar could see, and manipulate, the discrepancy between the two levels" (*Orientalism* 234). The obfuscation is as elaborate and deliberate as its clarification is elusive and specialized.

5. Such histories have been written by Dee Birkett, Charlotte Macdonald, Patricia Clarke, Una Monk, and James Hammerton, all of whose work I make use of throughout my study.

6. See Patrick Brantlinger, *Rule of Darkness,* especially his chapter on Thackaray, whose views on imperialism appear to change from one novel to another. The instability of views on imperialism is also explored in the essay by Aijaz Ahmad, "Postcolonialism: What's in a Name?"

7. It will become apparent, in the discussions of commodification and cultural value that follow, that my reading of Marx on these subjects is sometimes standard and sometimes not. For example, I take the liberty of extending the significance and meaning of "surplus value" (as have other scholars of the Victorian period) to emphasize its excesses. In analyses of Victorian commodity culture, "surplus value" is no longer a positive value but a site of appropriation, irony, and contradiction.

8. There is a general consensus among historians that the 1880s constitute a turning point in British economic progress and a turn to a more service-industry oriented domestic economy. On this specific point concerning the peak numbers of emigrants, see C. E. Carrington's study on the 1920s, *The British Overseas: Exploits of a Nation of Shopkeepers,* and James Hammerton's study, *Emigrant Gentlewomen: Genteel Poverty and Female Emigration, 1830–1914,* for figures on the 1880s.

CHAPTER 1

1. As I suggest later, the specific numbers for female emigrants vary in different accounts. I offer this figure as an average of sorts, based on all the studies I have consulted, including Hammerton, Macdonald, and others.

2. Maria Rye, "Emigrant Ship Matrons" 25. This is an excellent source for the available statistics on female emigration; tables and charts offer details on numbers of passengers and their ages and marital status, among other factors.

3. Jean Jacques Van-Helten and Keith Williams, "'The Crying Need of South Africa': The Emigration of Single British Women to the Transvaal,

1901–1910." This article is quite useful although it covers a somewhat later period, because it highlights the interplay between gender and race ideologies as they pertained to emigration rhetoric.

4. Women's Branch of the Oversea Department, "The Opportunities Offered to Women," *Britain's Call from Overseas: The Need and Scope for British Women in the Dominions and Colonies,* 2. Henceforth, cited as *BCFO.*

5. The degree to which Victorian England may be said to have "traded" its citizens for different, more desirable ones is also suggested by the existence and activities of the following organizations: The Jewish Board of Guardians, founded in 1905, assisted the emigration of 3,091 individuals; The Jews' Emigration Society assisted over 11,000 to emigrate; The Jewish Emigrants' Information Board, which assisted potential emigrants by providing essential information. The whole notion of emigration, then, takes on a much more sinister flavor in the context of visible signs that it was motivated by class, gender, and race/ethnicity exclusionism (Ibid., 97).

6. Monk's description of emigration's difficulties continues with "Except in South Africa, the recruitment of governesses was a piece of work which virtually ended in the eighteen eighties," while general emigration numbers continued to rise (43).

7. See Barbara Roberts, "Daughters of the Empire and Mothers of the Race." The history of Victorian feminist activism for female employment suggests that efforts to bring about women's financial autonomy were indeed a priority and were carried out in conjunction with efforts for all other political reforms. Among the societies formed to address the problem was Jessie Boucheret's "Employment Society." Clearly, these organized efforts to employ women were politicized as segments of the feminist project, unlike the emigration efforts, which were pointedly not feminist-political in their rhetoric and affiliations. For a more elaborate discussion of Victorian feminism and the female employment agenda, see Philippa Levine, *Victorian Feminism 1850–1900,* specifically chapter 4, "Employment and the Professions: Middle-Class Women and Work."

8. In 1886, the FMCES was absorbed into the Colonial Emigration Society and thus was fully associated with apolitical philanthropy and further removed from feminist actions toward employment reforms (Hammerton, *Emigrant Gentlewomen* 142). However, the association between feminism reform and philanthropy remains problematic in the Victorian context, and these two social arenas often overlap. For a most illuminating discussion of this problem, see Barbara N. Rammsack, "Cultural Missionaries, Material Imperialists, Feminist Allies: British Women Activists in India, 1865–1945."

Sidney Herbert's appeal on behalf of the emigration assisters in *First Report of the Committee of the Fund for Promoting Female Emigration* highlights the distinctions often made between political radicals such as feminists and the more altruistic philanthropists.

9. Sidney Herbert, M. P. *First Report of the Committee of the Fund for Promoting Female Emigration,* note 40. See also, Thornton Leigh Hunt, *Canada and South Australia.*

10. Quoted in Hammerton, *Emigrant Gentlewomen,* 125. The source of this information is the *Report for the National Association for the Promotion of Social Science* 1862 (808–9).

11. In *The Governesses: Letters from the Colonies, 1862–1882,* Patricia Clarke adds:

> In all, 302 women were sponsored by the FMCES, including those women sent out in 1861 and the early part of 1862. . . . To the end of 1872, 158 emigrants were assisted by the Society. Of these, 87 went to Australia, 33 to New Zealand, 20 to South Africa, 9 to Canada, 8 to the United States, and 1 to India. For the years 1880 to 1885, 86 were assisted, 42 to Australia, 15 to New Zealand, 12 to South Africa, 14 to Canada, 2 to the United States and 1 to Russia. (19)

12. These "Rules" were listed in all FMCES pamphlets, 1880–82.

13. See chapter 5 for a more elaborate discussion of the Victorian unmarried woman's cultural value and the ways in which she may or may not qualify as "woman."

14. This much is suggested by all the existing studies, as well as the available documentation of the FMCES at the Fawcett Library. For additional information on the sources available at the Fawcett Library, see Paula Hamilton and Janice Gothard, "'The Other Half': Sources on British Female Emigration at the Fawcett Library, With Special Reference to Australia."

15. That Maria Rye used emigrant letters in her possession to combat criticism and accusations of her emigration work is a thoroughly and repeatedly documented phenomenon. This was, in fact, an established strategy for her, as for discussions concerning colonial emigration in general. Among others, John M. Robson has noted that letters and first-person accounts of colonial life proliferated during the period and were printed in popular venues. See his *Marriage or Celibacy?: The Daily Telegraph on a Victorian Dilemma* (194–95).

16. Cited in Samuel Sidney, *Female Emigration: As It Is, As It May Be,* 3.

17. Also telling is a letter to Mrs. Joyce, Secretary, from Madeline Goutley, "Lady Superintendent": "I keep boxes full of letters I receive from the girls you send out so that any time you wished to know about anyone I shall be pleased to tell you all I know. There are comparatively few who do not write." July 4, 1899. Fawcett Library. South Africa Committee.

18. Letter from Miss G. Diffield, published in November 11, 1893. An informative collection of letters published in *Gentlewoman* and other newspapers and journals, is collected in the Fawcett Library, *Scrapbooks.*

19. Eric Hobsbawm's discussion of the shifts in Victorian economy and employment in *The Age of Empire: 1875–1914* is most instructive; he notes that there was a new and marked emphasis on service professions following 1880. His-

torians generally note an economic and labor shift in the Victorian period after 1880.

In *Emigrant Gentlewomen,* Hammerton correlates to these changes a shift in emigration patterns, when he observes that "After 1880 the numbers alone are for the first time, large enough to confirm the readiness of genteel women without prospects to risk the hazards and uncertainties of emigration" (178).

20. In *England in the Nineteenth Century: 1815–1914,* David Thompson notes that "By 1870 British capitalists had sunk some £700,000,000 abroad, whereas in 1850 the total had been only some £200,000,000" (164). In the most concrete terms, then, the investment in the future wealth of England was located outside of England itself, specifically during the later decades, and the nation's hopes and dreams may be seen to have lain there as well.

21. In *Britannia's Daughters: Women of the British Empire,* Joanna Trollope concurs with the general characteristics of the memsahib as "idle, frivolous, and luxury loving" but proceeds to make apologies for them: "but that was in large measure India's fault rather than their own" (125). Blaming the colony is a standard response among imperialists.

CHAPTER 2

1. *To Intending Emigrants.* Leaflet advertisement distributed by the Australian government's emigration agency in London.

2. "The Colonial and Indian Exhibition," *Westminster Review* (1886): 51.

3. Pamphlet. Women's Branch of the Oversea Department, "Britain's Call from Overseas" (1897): 2.

4. Along these lines, see the article "Prosperity and Industrial Emigration from Britain During the Early 1850s" by William E. Van Vugt, which analyzes the emigration patterns to the United States among laborers. Van Vugt marks the correspondences between the national economy, the types of workers emigrating, and their destinations.

5. Thompson's account, *England in the Nineteenth Century,* suggests that the queen deliberately used the colonies as political tools and as a means to control her public image (171). See also Adrienne Auslander Munich's *Victoria's Secrets* on the same subject.

6. W. W. Carrothers offers this statistical explanation of "excess" that is representative of Victorian analyses of the problem and that reveals an agist bias; in other instances the problem is viewed as being compounded by the character of the colonies themselves:

[B]etween the ages of 15 and 45 there are just 700,000 excess females. . . . The ideal age for women to migrate would be between 20 and 30. Beyond that age the possibility of natural and pleasant assimilation overseas diminishes. Another difficulty presents itself in the Dominions themselves. The major part of the male surplus is situated in the outlying rural districts. That women can find a life of real enjoyment in these districts is true. But the conditions call for exceptional qualities of both mind and body. (275)

In her own study, *Rights of Passage,* Helen R. Woolcock also notes the pre-occupation with emigrant women's ages and describes how emigration policies were devised to address this issue:

Regulations attached to the application forms clearly stated the eligibility criteria: age limits were forty years for men and thirty-five for married women, couples could not be separated or leave behind children under eighteen years, no widows or widowers with young children would be accepted, the men had to agree to work for wages. Only single women aged between eighteen and thirty-five years, of "exceptional character," sound in body and mind with written evidence that they had been "in service" need apply: those with illegitimate children were definitely not eligible. (36–37)

See also Carrington's *British Overseas,* which gives a full and detailed account of life in the colonies as well as each colony's imperial history. Carrington's accounts are rendered more interesting by the fact that he writes from an imperial perspective. He also offers a series of maps that dramatically illustrate imperial expansion.

7. Many letters in Clarke, *The Governesses,* support this claim. See also chapter 1.
8. It is widely known that the elimination of natives took many forms in the course of imperial expansion; among them, disease and violence. Lemon and Pollock note that "In Tasmania the aboriginal population was exterminated and in Victoria nearly disappeared" (90).
9. Very briefly, here is some essential information on the colonies that were most popular as emigrants' destinations (after the United States, not a colony). This information is listed in John Hale, *Settlers: Being Extracts from the Journals and Letters of Early Colonists in Canada, Australia, South Africa and New Zealand.*

Australia was described as "an emergency solution to a problem in social sanitation" (114). Convicts were first sent in 1787, plus freepersons and their families. There was rapid growth after the discovery of gold in Victoria, 1851. Aboriginals were hunted (114).

New Zealand was considered an instance of "reluctant imperialism" because of persistent resistance from the Maoris, which peaked in intensity in the 1840s (304). Annexed by Cook in 1769, a constitution was set up in 1852 to make New Zealand self-governing.

South Africa was valued mainly as port of call. From the 1870s onward, "Cape Town came to deserve its description as the gilded hostelry on the road to India" (205). Holland ceded it to England in 1814; assisted emigration was adopted to avoid territorial loss to the Kaffirs. English became the official language in 1825, and colonial status was granted in 1843.

10. Paton, ed., 94. According to Paton, "since 1885 no emigrants have been introduced into [South Australia] at the public expense" (16); it is noted that "good servants are rare [in New Zealand] since so many of the young women prefer the more independent life of the shop or factory" (31).

11. See Terri Lovell's discussion of the relationships among gender, ideology, and material circumstances in *Consuming Fiction*, 96.

12. Feminists who were very active at the time were involved in a number of related causes, among them women's employment, revising the matrimonial, divorce and property laws, and also increasing political representation for women. See Levine, *Victorian Feminism*, and Barbara Caine, *Victorian Feminists*.

13. Loeb, Miller, and Richards have opened much-needed new possibilities for thinking about the excessive materialism and commodity-obsessiveness of the Victorian period, and they have initiated a necessary series of analyses of Victorian material culture. See Lori Anne Loeb, *Consuming Angels: Advertising and Victorian Women;* Andrew Miller, *Novels Behind Glass: Commodity Culture and Victorian Narrative;* Thomas Richards, *The Commodity Culture of Victorian England: Advertising and Spectacle, 1851–1914;* and Thomas Richards, *The Imperial Archive: Knowledge and the Fantasy of Empire*.

14. However, insofar as a "productive ambivalence" is the object of imperial discourse, and insofar as "the stereotype is an ambivalent mode of knowledge and power," the analogy is only partially congruent, and is deliberately ambiguous (*Location*, 67, 66).

15. Letter from northwest Canada, 1893, quoted in Monk, *New Horizons*, 114.

16. *Evening Telegraph* June 23, 1894.

17. In *Britannia's Daughters* Trollope comments, "It must have been a relief, after the unrelenting social codes of England, not only to be able to pick and choose, but also to feel oneself in a position of equality and sometimes even of superiority" (66).

South African wages were lower and positions less desirable, but at least there were openings there for governesses long after they ceased to be desirable in other colonies:

South Africa might have paid as handsomely as other colonies but the demand for governesses endured there far longer than elsewhere, well into the 1880s and 1890s. At first in Australia and new Zealand, some sixty frantic ladies might beseech each new arrival from England to teach her children, but demand waned after 1860, partly as economic depressions hit the colonies and partly as governesses left their families and set up schools, creating securer employment for themselves but fewer jobs for their fellows. (70)

18. Characterization by Mrs. Ellis in *Daughters of England*, quoted in Catherine Hall, *White, Male and Middle-Class: Explorations in Feminism and History*, 87.

19. As Bhabha puts it, "if the ambivalent figure of the nation is a problem of its transitional history, its conceptual indeterminacy, its wavering between vocabularies, then what effect does this have on narratives and discourses that signify a sense of 'nationness'?" (*Nation and Narration*, 2).

CHAPTER 3

1. The authority with which emigrant letters were invested as truth-revealing observation accounts works to support my contention that observation is an imperial activity. See chapter 1 for a list of emigration apologists.

2. See also Peter Keating, ed., *Into Unknown England, 1866–1913: Selections from the Social Explorers*, which includes domestic ethnographies of England's slums by lesser-known authors. Most offer physical geographic descriptions as well as moralistic commentary.

3. However, as I have elaborated, the category of women is not subsumed by the category of the poor because radically different concerns exist in the two populations and also because class identity and membership are not contingent on monetary assets or prospects alone.

4. Of course, James Clifford (*The Predicament of Culture*) is not alone in finding cultural and geographic boundaries meaningfully interconnected. Clifford Geertz (*The Interpretation of Cultures. Selected Essays*) remains very useful for this kind of transcultural analysis.

5. Insofar as "ethnography is, from beginning to end, enmeshed in writing" and that "the writing includes, minimally, a translation of experience into textual form," these domestic sociography texts illustrate the project of the domestic ethnographer and situate the middle-class reader as voyeur of the same (Clifford, *Predicament of Culture*, 25). Such textual and social projects initiated the typically Victorian documented preoccupation with subjects whom the English middle classes did not know and with whom they were not immediately familiar.

6. See the two important studies of cultural stratification in Victorian culture and beyond: Andreas Huyssen, *After the Great Divide: Modernism, Mass Culture, Postmodernism;* and Bram Dijkstra, *Idols of Perversity: Fantasies of Feminine Evil in Fin-de-Siecle Culture.* Both studies situate gender and women in popular culture and illustrate the correspondences between women and the masses.

7. Clifford's points concerning Bakhtinian polyphonic texts are most interesting in how this concept applies to the project of ethnography and textual production: "A 'language' is the interplay and struggle of regional dialects, professional jargons, generic commonplaces, the speech of different age groups, individuals, and so forth" (*Predicament of Culture*, 46). The kind of language and multiplicity of meaning that are so apparent in Victorian women's travel narratives is especially apparent in Dickens's novels; especially where Dickens re-

creates local dialect and Cockney speech, which is very often, a single novel can be seen to encompass a number of languages and several cultural perspectives or vantage points at once. The novel as a form also may be viewed as encompassing diverse subjectivities and to speak for them, although that authority is not already granted but assumed and earned by the author.

See also Marjorie Stone, "Bakhtinian Polyphony in *Mary Barton:* Class, Gender, and the Textual Voice." This discussion of shifting narrative voices is a more sympathetic reading of Elizabeth Gaskell's interventions.

8. See chapter 1 for a more elaborate illustration of this distinction.

9. Friedreich Engels reiterates, "To confirm my statement I have drawn here a small section of the plan of Manchester" in *The Condition of the Working Class in England,* 88.

On this same issue, see Adan Ferrin Weber's *The Growth of Cities in the Nineteenth Century: A Study in Statistics.* This is a thorough and extensive study, considering not only population figures but internal migration and other such changes as well. The author's perceptions of declining numbers are as revealing as the statistics themselves, suggesting to us how such information may have been perceived in the nineteenth century.

10. Homi K. Bhabha notes in *The Location of Culture* that the operative dynamic principle here is knowledge-based appropriation: "cultural difference is the process of the enunciation of culture as 'knowledgeable,' authoritative, adequate to the construction of systems of cultural identification" (34).

11. One bizarre account of this compulsion for amassing colonial knowledge occurs in Francis Gatton's 1900 essay, "Identification Offices in India and Egypt," which proposes the employment of bureaucratic tools for identifying native peoples. While Gatton admits that he has not actually visited India, he makes impassioned arguments for the need of acquiring as much certain information as possible:

> If a map of the world were tinted with gradations of colour to show the percentage of false testimony in courts of law, whether in different nations or communities, England would be tinted rather lightly and both Bengal and Egypt very darkly. So, whether it be from the impossibility of identifying the mass of natives by their signatures, or from the difficulty of distinguishing them by name, or from their roving habits, or from the extraordinary prevalence of personation and false testimony among them, the need for identification office has been strongly felt in both India and Egypt. (119)

In this case, what is sought by bureaucratic (scientific) means is a way to document natives' moral licentiousness, which is presumed a priori. These texts are typical of nineteenth-century anthropologic accounts that predate anthropology as an established discipline. The anthropologist's involvement in the subject matter is minimal but extended further and further as the field grew and methodology and theory developed. As the field of inquiry and observation broadens, so does the observer's authority over his/her subjects. There are, of course, countless examples of this dynamic.

See also C. A. Bayly, "Knowing the Country: Empire and Information in India." This important essay takes into account not only formal and institutional methods of information-gathering but also networks of informants, spies, and so on. Bayly makes a compelling argument for the relationship between accumulation of knowledge and England's political hold on India.

12. Anne McClintock notes in *Imperial Leather: Race, Gender and Sexuality in the Colonial Contest* that the correspondences between domestic and imperial ethnography, specifically in relation to explorations of England's slums. She observes that, "drawing on the imperial progress narrative and the figure of the journey into the interior," these kinds of narratives employ "the language of empire and degeneration" (120).

13. There are many other novels that depict England as an undesirable space for virtuous beings, male and female. The long tradition of social-protest novels offers countless examples of the ongoing critique of English domestic conditions.

14. Many historians have argued that the working classes were urged to identify with imperialist interests. See especially John M. Mackenzie, *Propaganda and Empire: The Manipulation of British Popular Opinion, 1880–1960.* See also, C. A. Bayly, *Imperial Meridian: The British Empire and the World, 1780–1838.* Another excellent source on imperializing strategies abroad and their domestic representations is A. P. Thornton's *Doctrines of Imperialism.*

15. This is also the case in *Mill On the Floss;* Stephen is free to "travel" after the scandal with Maggie breaks out, while Maggie's only options are to hide away and/or disappear. She decides to stay, to her detriment.

16. However, marriage is not meant to do this much. In the novel, Mrs. Carson used to be a factory girl but is now well-to-do with a big house and husband and children, but she must deny her past in order to exist as a middle-class woman. If what Mary wants is to join the ranks of those few who have transcended class boundaries through marriage, she also must disown her past.

17. In his introduction to the novel, Angus Calder offers what amounts to the standard interpretation of *Great Expectations:* "*Great Expectations* has two major messages. One is, that in a class society there is justice for the rich, but none for the poor; so that in the absolute sense (the Christian sense, he would have said), there is no "justice" at all. The other is that class divisions sustained by wealth destroy the bonds of fellowship which should exist between man and man, and can condition even a morally sensitive person such as Pip to act badly" (24). This reading of the novel's tensions is typical in rendering Victorian culture (and its texts) quite insular, without the fissures created by the colonial presence.

18. See Marx on commodity production in *Capital,* vol. 1, and my discussion of the same in chapter 2.

19. Monika Rydygier Smith, "The W/Hole Remains: Consumerist Politics in *Bleak House, Great Expectations,* and *Our Mutual Friend.*"

   Smith comments astutely that "the Victorian order is, in fact, a violent order—that violence is a structural, not merely an individual, problem," and that this is what is depicted in the many relationships in *Great Expectations* (5). However, her point that "in relation to Estella, Miss Havisham replicates the pressures and coercions ingrained in the power structures of Victorian society" (13) and that "the particular vulnerability of children is conveyed in the many images of violent ingestion" is problematic (11). In "Daughters of Empire and Mothers of the Race," Roberts sees the novel as depicting the dysfunctions of the family structure in a critical light. In the case of Estella and Miss Havisham, then, Estella is the child and Miss Havisham the abusive parent; this interpretation seems to overlook the possibility of women's relation to other women as mentors and the possibility of alternative family structures and dynamics, and rather accords too much primacy to the patriarchal family model.

20. See Evelyn M. Romig, "Twisted Tale, Silent Teller: Miss Havisham in *Great Expectations.*"

   I disagree with Romig's view of Miss Havisham as "mythmaker." Romig comments: "Fairy tales, of course, are related to myth, and mythmaking is the activity of Miss Havisham . . . she sees herself in terms of sacrifice, an object to replace the decayed wedding cake on the bridal table and to be eternally consumed by death as she has feasted on sorrow and revenge" (21). However, it seems to me that it would be just as easy to see Miss Havisham as narrativizing her life experience and preserving, in however satirical a manner, the details of her victimization so that she may make sense of her life. Miss Havisham is macabre, but perhaps not unreasonably so, given the loss of her many "expectations" as a moneyed young woman.

21. Yet, this is not an Unknown in a negative or frightening sense, an unknown that other texts tend to treat as the feared, to be approached with some trepidation.

22. Nonetheless, this "insubstantiation" is paralleled by self-absorbed efforts to document, survey, and make knowable the colonies' very physical features, thus appropriating their perceptible features.

23. The Elsewhere is functional only insofar as it is contrived as Other, as different from ourselves, but it also must be, as Bhabha's definition of "mimicry" emphasizes, *of* us: Like the colonized, this instrumental Elsewhere must be different from, and yet the same as, the Here—"almost the same, *but not quite*" (*Location of Culture* 86).

CHAPTER 4

1. Una Monk cites several emigrant letters that comment on shipboard conditions, as does Patricia Clarke. One such letter from a young governess who

sailed to Australia in 1862 says: "The Saloon passengers objected to the 2nd Class on the Poop (rather unusual exclusiveness, I believe), consequently a large number of free emigrants and passengers were huddled together in a dense mob on the decks and the noise, filth, drunkenness and swearing were altogether frightful . . . Providence was very gracious to us or with such a reckless drunken mob we should never have reached our destined port safely" (Monk, *New Horizons* 45). Some women seem to have had a better time of shipboard travel, but the stories are generally quite horrifying.

2. N. N. Feltes, in *Modes of Production of Victorian Novels,* and Andrew Miller in *Novels Behind Glass,* discuss the artificial divisions often drawn between literature and a presumably distinct category of "culture."

3. Miss M. A. Knightley arrived in Melbourne March 9, 1865, and got a position as a teacher in a government school. Quoted in Clarke, *The Governesses,* 7.

4. See also Linda M. Shires, "Fantasy, Nonsense, Parody, and the Status of the Real."

5. On this extreme and illogical rationalization, Van Helten and Williams observe:

> Within the framework of evolutionary theory there was an implicit research program, consisting of ordering ethnographic data in the probable sequence of cultural development. The conclusion of this process—contemporary Victorian culture—as known and the beginning could be surmised. What remained was to collect data on primitive contemporary and prehistoric cultures, develop ethnographic descriptions that described the cultural attributes of as many cultural systems or stages as possible, and order them according to their relative occurrence on the developmental ladder. (31)

6. Eva-Marie Kroller reviews some of the scholarship on this subject and renders an interpretation of women's travel narratives that emphasizes their ambiguous ideological positioning, both in terms of women's relation to British imperialism and their relation to the foreign cultures they observed.

7. The lesson that Alice gleans from this experience is that concerning the sociality and materiality of linguistic signification as outlined by Mikhail Bakhtin in *The Formal Method in Literary Scholarship: A Critical Introduction to Sociological Poetics:* "The connection between meaning and sign . . . in the word taken concretely and independently of the concrete utterance . . . is completely random and only of technical significance. Here the word is simply a conventional sign. There is a gap between the individuality of the word and its meaning, a gap which can only be overcome by a mechanistic linkage, by association" (120). Similarly, Gaskell's Alice escapes her present loneliness and poverty by narrating her childhood and the increasingly elusive collective past of the urbanized working classes.

8. It can be argued that the figure of the governess and of the "odd woman" in many Victorian novels is also a portrait of the silenced unmarried woman.

Chapter 3 analyzed these kinds of texts, but the category is not limited to novels and texts that deal with these subjects explicitly.

9. Commodification is transformed into language, but commodification also *creates* a language of its own, according to Guy Debord in *Society of the Spectacle* and Franz Fanon in *Black Skin, White Masks.* See also my discussion in the introduction.

10. Patricia Clarke, in *The Governesses,* notes that there were "problems stemming from the emigrants' expectations" of the colonies, which were too high (76).

11. Interestingly, in this respect Alice resembles very closely the spinsters in Gaskell's *Cranford,* who are of an entirely different class. This and other such discursive correspondences suggest—once again—that unmarried women's social and cultural "usefulness" is questionable, regardless of their class affiliation.

12. Will's indenture with the merchant marine in *Mary Barton* affects both his cultural and monetary value. He becomes a source of much-needed money but also triumphs as hero and literal character witness in the novel's most critical moment.

13. See also Basil Greenhill and Ann Giffard, *Travelling by Sea in the Nineteenth Century.* This study shows that conditions on emigrant ships contrasted sharply for travelers of different classes, so that ships were strictly segregated according to class.

    In *Society of the Spectacle,* Debord makes clear the distinctions between commodity and spectacle when he says that in the spectacle "the commodity contemplates itself in a world of its own making"; he posits this understanding as the antithesis of the "consciousness of desire and the desire for consciousness," which he sees as constituting struggles toward equality and liberation (34). Deborah Cherry also suggests this in her "Differencing the Gaze" chapter in *Painting Women: Victorian Women Artists,* as does Andrew Miller in *The Imperial Archive: Knowledge and the Fantasy of Empire.*

14. See the fascinating new study by Joy Damousi, which pays a great deal of attention to the moral concerns attending women's emigration and women's presence in the colonies: *Depraved and Disorderly: Female Convicts, Sexuality and Gender in Colonial Australia.*

    Other excellent sources on this topic are: Margaret Tennant, "Maternity and Morality: Homes for Single Mothers 1890–1930" and Raymond Evans, "Soiled Doves: Prostitution and Society in Colonial Queensland—An Overview."

15. Quoted in Clarke, *The Governesses,* 96. Letter by Mary Bayly, governess to Australia, March 22, 1867.

16. Deirdre David also takes up this kind of analysis in her *Rule Britannia: Women, Empire, and Victorian Writing,* when she extends her argument to point to certain lines of Tennyson's poetry as "domesticat[ing] empire, mak[ing] it an extension of British loyalty to the Queen, in the image of 'boundless homes' spreading throughout Britain's 'broadening' territories, *the emphasis on a rounded unity* intensified by the strong assonance" (171, emphasis added).

17. In regard to gender roles, Andrew Hassam's analysis in *Sailing to Australia: Shipboard Diaries by Nineteenth-Century British Emigrants* has some blind spots. He discounts information that suggests the emigrant ship was a gendered place and specifically suggestions that the division of space was not so neatly or effectively instituted: "The cabin is made 'home' by its occupants adopting roles appropriate to the Victorian home, the woman adopting the dominant role of the housekeeper, the male accepting the superficially subservient role of handyman. In these ways, the spaces of the ship are being invested with identifiable cultural meanings and the 'snug' cabin marks out the culturally designated space of 'home'" (63). The version of "home" described here is rather sentimental in that it assumes it to be a comfortable middle-class dwelling and to a degree reinstates bourgeois ideals.

18. Based on Hassam's account, if women sought to domesticate their new temporary "homes" on board ship, unmarried women were both coerced and forced to domesticate their own as well. They had no help with their domestic duties on board, and additional duties were invented to keep them occupied and out of trouble.

A plea for qualified matrons to oversee working-class females invokes the ideal female emigrant:

> The number of single women in government ships varies from fifty to three hundred. An efficient matron is expected to attend to their personal habits, *to live with them,* . . . to find them suitable employment, in cleaning, washing, needlework, etc., as well as to give them religious instruction, and to teach them reading and writing; in short, to see that the time on board ship is spent in training them for domestic service in the colony, and in inducing such habits as will make them useful members of society, instead of their being, as is too often the case, ignorant of household duties and disinclined for labor, when they soon lose their character and become a burden to the colony. (Rye, "Emigrant Ship Matrons" 29)

19. The applicability of these formulations is further elaborated in light of Marx's intricate definition of the commodity, specifically as it relates to the reflectivity of the constitution of commodities in context: "What chiefly distinguishes a commodity from its owner," we must remember, is "that it looks upon every other commodity as but the form of appearance of its own value" (*Capital,* vol. 1, 97). Hence, the single emigrant woman reflects rather than establishes or even substantially embodies her own value. The antithesis of this proposition is that the owner is the commodity's single source of value definition.

CHAPTER 5

1. In Anne McClintock's analysis in *Imperial Leather*, "the social semiotics of visibility" (98) is a way of understanding the different ways power is exchanged

and claimed in social gestures and activities that highlight the prominence and importance of one group over another.

2. As Judith Butler suggests in *Bodies that Matter: On the Discursive Limits of Sex,* in order to address this type of power relationship adequately, we may need to reconstruct our very basic working definition of materiality: "What I would propose in place of these conceptions of construction [as power that acts] is a return to the notion of matter, not as site or surface, but as a *process of materialization that stabilizes over time to produce the effect of boundary, fixity, and surface we call matter*" (9). Butler adds that "construction is neither a subject nor its act, but a process of reiteration by which both 'subjects' and 'acts' come to appear at all. There is no power that acts, but only a reiterated acting that is power in its persistence and instability" (Ibid., 9).

3. These terms were used fairly widely to describe spinsters during the Victorian period, as I elaborated in chapter 1.

4. One obvious point concerning commodities always must be kept to the forefront of their analyses: "it is plain that commodities cannot go to the market and make exchanges of their own account," as Marx has argued (*Capital,* vol. 1, 96), because the value of commodities is determined from without, and hence contexts and the specificity of historical moments is paramount. The concept of fetishism articulates most fully the discordant rift between value and nonvalue invested in emigrant women. Fetish is also the imposition and projection of value where, in fact, there is only the absence of desirability and exchange value. Sexual purity, in short, is the basis of cultural marketability for the emigrant women in question.

5. Of course, motherhood is valorized in Victorian culture, as I elaborated in chapters 1 and 2, but even there in the most ethereal, aestheticized terms. See Anna Davin, "Imperialism and Motherhood," which outlines the heightened valorization of motherhood in the service of empire.

6. Marx's explanation of the process of "valorization" emphasizes the production of "excess" value: "If we compare the process of creating value with the process of valorization, we see that the latter is nothing but the continuation of the former beyond a definite point. If the process is not carried beyond the point where the value paid by the capitalist for the labour-power is replaced by an exact equivalent, it is simply a process of creating value; but if it is continued beyond that point, it becomes a process of valorization" (Ibid., 302). The "valorization" of marriage is also the mystification of marriage. Marx's conception of this dynamic suits the Victorian spinster's valuation as excess very well.

7. Social Darwinism is a common precept in the second half of the Victorian period. While quite complex as a dogma, it mainly aligns itself with the concept of "survival for the fittest," which it applies to social problems, naturalizing poverty, suffering, and inequity on the basis of merit.

8. In *White, Male and Middle-Class: Explorations in Feminism and History,* Catherine Hall has observed that "Schoolmistress, lady companion, governess, wife,

independent lady living in genteel penury, these were familiar routes for a middle-class woman in this period. . . . It is these changes which provide the context for the feminist demand in the 1880's for more training and employment for women" (175).

9. Feminists, of course, put their best energies into combating the abuses of marriage and fighting for women's protection from legal and personal losses. See two good studies on Victorian feminism, one comprehensive, the other more selective: Levine, *Victorian Feminism;* Caine, *Victorian Feminists.*

10. Some such readings are: Rita S. Kranidis, *Subversive Discourse: The Cultural Production of Late-Victorian Feminist Novels;* Martha Vicinus, *A Widening Sphere;* and Elaine Showalter, *A Literature of Their Own.*

11. See, for instance, the article cited by Ford, Margaret Oliphant's unsigned review for *Blackwood's Magazine* (1863). The most controversial aspects of the novel concern Collins's praise of the illicit relationship between Magdalen's parents and especially his justification of the heroine's illegitimacy.

12. In Eliot, I am thinking specifically of Maggie Tulliver in *Mill On the Floss.* In Charlotte Brontë, Lucy Snow in *Vilette,* which I discuss below.

13. See the article "'Neither Pairs Nor Odd': Female Community in late Nineteenth-Century London," by Deborah Epstein Nord for an interesting discussion of Victorian women's relationship to the city and specifically how it may have proven liberating for unmarried Victorian women. There are, in fact, many suggestions that the city is a "topos" of a distinct kind for women who were dislocated within Victorian society.

14. McClintock uses the terms "abjection" and "abject" in *Imperial Leather* to describe the condition and process via which the dominant culture disowns its subjects. This term is most applicable to the status of the emigrant spinster.

15. Also of special relevance is Bhabha's assertion in *Location of Culture* that "in order to be effective, mimicry must continually produce its slippage, its excess, its difference" (86). That is, mimicry is both the production of verisimilitude and of difference but is also the site of reproduction of a kind of relativism that nonetheless insists on defining and controlling cultural value at the site of that "slippage." Therefore, the social identity of the spinster always will be comprised of what she is not (an acceptable model of the middle-class female) as well as who she has been (a marriageable woman of the middle class). Finally, she might be said to mimic her former self as she mimics her present, ambivalent status in society. This concept brings us to Bhabha's other main claim, that which emphasizes the potential for subversion on the part of the mimic: "The ambivalence of mimicry—almost but not quite—suggests that the fetishized colonial culture is potentially and strategically an insurgent counter-appeal. . . . Under cover of camouflage, mimicry, like the fetish, is a part-object that radically revalues the normative knowledges of the priority of race, writing, and history. For *the fetish mimes the forms of authority at the point at which it deauthorizes them*" (91, emphasis added).

16. It is significant, I think, that Brontë wrote as a spinster, as one who perceived and spoke from within the cultural and personal spaces she describes.

17. Julia Kristeva would say, in fact, that Lucy is embracing the semiotic and through her wanderings away from the familiar and the known experiences *jouissance* (*Desire in Language: A Semiotic Approach to Literature and Art*). My meaning and use of the concepts of the symbolic and system of signs and signification is more in line with its sociological use by Barthes in *Mythologies* and (as illustrated here) by Richards, *Commodity Culture of Victorian England,* and by other scholars of material culture.

18. One indication of this is that when we see her in the colonies, the emigrant spinster is proud and demanding. See Charlotte Macdonald, *A Woman of Good Character: Single Women as Immigrant Settlers in Nineteenth-Century New Zealand;* Patricia Clarke, *The Governesses,* and earlier references for descriptions of emigrant spinsters abroad.

19. Most important among Richards's observations is the implicit suggestion that while surplus commodities were being contained, categorized, and specified, they also "appeared to be expanding profligately in every direction possible," thus defying the very process and ends of the Exhibition (*Commodity Culture of Victorian England* 27).

20. As I discuss in chapter 4, the concept of "anachronisms" as being out of step with "progress" is instrumental in the constitution of the emigrant and domestic spinsters.

21. In a similar way, remembering (and, I would add, traveling) "forward and backward" establishes a multilayered correspondence between England and the colonies.

WORKS CITED

Ahmad, Aijaz. "Postcolonialism: What's in a Name?" In E. Ann Kaplan, Roman De La Campa, and Michael Sprinker, eds., *Late Imperial Culture*. New York: Verso, 1995.

Althusser, Louis. *Lenin and Philosophy and Other Essays*. New York: Monthly Review Press, 1971.

"Answers," *The Queen*. September 8, 1894. Fawcett Library, *Scrapbooks* 1BWE 3/1.

Auerbach, Nina. *Communities of Women: An Idea in Fiction*. Cambridge, Mass: Harvard University Press, 1978.

Baines, Dudley. *Emigration from Europe, 1815–1930*. London: Macmillan Publishers, 1991.

Bakhtin, Mikhail. *The Formal Method in Literary Scholarship: A Critical Introduction to Sociological Poetics*. Cambridge, Mass: Harvard University Press, 1985.

Barr, Pat. *The Memsahib: The Women of British India*. London: Secker and Warburg, 1976.

Barthes, Roland. *Mythologies*. New York: Farrar, Straus & Giroux, 1972.

Bayly, C. A. "Knowing the Country: Empire and Information in India," *Modern Asian Studies* 27:1 (1993): 3–43.

———. *Imperial Meridian: The British Empire and the World, 1780–1830*. London: Longman Group Ltd., 1989.

Begg, Alexander. *Emigration: A Paper Read at a Conference, Indian and Colonial Exhibition, London, July 23, 1886*. London: H. Blalock, 1900.

Bhabha, Homi K. *The Location of Culture*. New York: Routledge, 1994.

———, ed. *Nation and Narration*. New York: Routledge, 1990.

Birkett, Dee. *Spinsters Abroad: Victorian Lady Explorers*. London: Basil Blackwell, 1989.

Bivona, Daniel. "Alice the Child-Imperialist and the Games of Wonderland," *Nineteenth Century Literature* 41 (September 1986): 143–171.

Booth, Charles. *Labour and Life of the People in London. The Charles Booth Collection, 1885–1905*. Brighton: Harvester Press, 1988. Originally published 1889.

Boucheret, Jessie. "How to Provide for Superfluous Women." *Woman's Work and Woman's Culture*. London: Macmillan, 1869.

Brantlinger, Patrick. *Rule of Darkness*. Ithaca, N.Y.: Cornell University Press, 1988.

Brodie, Laura. "Society and the Superfluous Female: Jane Austen's Treatment of Widowhood." *Studies in English Literature*. 34:4 (1994): 697–718.

Brontë, Charlotte. *Vilette*. New York: Signet, Penguin Group, 1987. Originally published 1853.

Buckley, Suzann. "British Female Emigration and Imperial Development: Experiments in Canada, 1885–1931." *Hecate*. 3:21 (July 1977): 26–40.

Butler, Josephine. "The Education and Employment of Women." URL http://www.indiana.edu~letrs/vwwp>

Butler, Judith. *Bodies that Matter: On the Discursive Limits of Sex.* New York: Routledge, 1993.

Buzzard, James. "Victorian Women and the Implications of Empire." [Review essay.] *Victorian Studies.* 36:4 (Summer 1993): 443–453.

Caine, Barbara. *Victorian Feminists.* Oxford: Oxford University Press, 1993.

Calder, Angus. "Introduction." *Great Expectations.* New York: Penguin Books, 1985.

Carrington, C. E. *The British Overseas: Exploits of a Nation of Shopkeepers.* Cambridge: Cambridge University Press, 1950.

Carroll, Lewis. *Through the Looking Glass.* Boston: International Pocket Library, 1956. Originally published 1871.

Carrothers, W. W. *Emigration From the British Isles.* London: Cass, 1929.

Chapman, J. "Emigration." *The Westminster Review.* 102:40 (1874): 25–38.

Chaudhuri, Nupur, and Margaret Strobel. *Western Women and Imperialism: Complicity and Resistance.* Bloomington: Indiana University Press, 1992.

Cherry, Deborah. *Painting Women: Victorian Women Artists.* New York: Routledge, 1993.

Cixous, Helene, and Catherine Clement. *The Newly Born Woman.* Trans. Betsy Wing. Minneapolis: University of Minnesota Press, 1987.

Clarke, Patricia. *The Governesses: Letters from the Colonies, 1862–1882.* London: Hutchison, 1985.

Clifford, James. *The Predicament of Culture.* Cambridge, Mass: Harvard University Press, 1988.

Collins, Wilkie. *No Name.* New York: Penguin Books, 1994. Originally published 1865.

Colls, Robert, and Philip Dodd, eds. *Englishness: Politics and Culture, 1880–1920.* London: Croom Helm, 1986.

Constantine, Stephen, ed. *Emigrants and Empire: British Settlement in the Dominions Between the Wars.* Manchester: Manchester University Press, 1990.

Craig, Isa. "Emigration as a Preventive Agency." *The English Woman's Journal.* 2:11 (January 1, 1859): 289–297.

———. "Emigrant Ship Matrons." *The English Woman's Journal.* 5 (1860): 24–36.

———. "On Assisted Emigration." *The English Woman's Journal.* 5 (1860): 235–240.

Damousi, Joy. *Depraved and Disorderly: Female Convicts, Sexuality and Gender in Colonial Australia.* Cambridge: Cambridge University Press, 1997.

David, Deirdre. *Rule Britannia: Women, Empire, and Victorian Writing.* Ithaca, N.Y.: Cornell University Press, 1995.

Davies, Emily. *The Higher Education of Women.* London: The Hambledon Press, 1988. Originally published 1866.

Davin, Anna. "Imperialism and Motherhood." *History Workshop Journal.* 5 (1978): 9–65.

Debord, Guy. *The Society of the Spectacle.* New York: Zone Books, 1995.

Dickens, Charles. *Great Expectations.* New York: Penguin Books, 1985. Originally published 1861.

Dijkstra, Bram. *Idols of Perversity: Fantasies of Feminine Evil in Fin-de-Siecle Culture.* New York: Oxford University Press, 1986.

Doan, Laura, ed. *Old Maids to Radical Spinsters: Unmarried Women in the Twentieth Century Novel.* Urbana: University of Illinois Press, 1990.

Donaldson, Laura. *Decolonizing Feminisms: Race, Gender, and Empire-Building.* London: Routledge, 1993.

Eliot, George. *Mill On the Floss.* New York: Penguin Books, 1985. Originally published 1860.

Engels, Friedreich. *The Condition of the Working Class in England.* New York: Penguin Books, 1987. Originally published 1845.

————. *Origins of the Family, Private Property, and the State.* New York: Penguin Books, 1985. Originally published 1884.

Errikson, Charlotte. *Leaving England: Essays on British Emigration in the Nineteenth Century.* Ithaca, N.Y.: Cornell University Press, 1994.

Evans, Raymond. "Soiled Doves: Prostitution and Society in Colonial Queensland— An Overview." *Hecate.* 1:2 (1975): 6–24.

Fanon, Franz. *Black Skins, White Masks.* New York: Grove Press, 1982.

Feltes, N. N. *Modes of Production of Victorian Novels.* Chicago: University of Chicago Press, 1986.

"Female Emigration." *Evening Telegraph.* June 23, 1894. Fawcett Library. *Scrapbooks.* 1BWE 3/1–3, Box 22.

Ford, Mark. "Introduction." *No Name.* New York: Penguin Books, 1994.

Frost, Lucy. *No Place for a Nervous Lady: Voices from the Australian Bush.* Sidney: McPhee Gribble Publishers, 1989.

Gaskell, Elizabeth. *Cranford.* New York: Oxford University Press, 1972. Originally published 1853.

————. *Mary Barton.* New York: Penguin Books, 1970. Originally published 1848.

Gatton, Francis. "Identification Offices in India and Egypt." *The Nineteenth Century.* 48:3685 (1900): 118–126.

Geertz, Clifford. *The Interpretation of Cultures. Selected Essays.* New York: Harcourt Brace, 1973.

Gissing, George. *The Odd Women.* New York: Penguin Books, 1983. Originally published 1893.

Gore, Catherine G. F. "Bewailment from Bath; Or, Poor Old Maids." *Blackwood's Edinburgh Review.* 55 (February 1844): 199–201.

Greenhill, Basil, and Ann Giffard. *Travelling by Sea in the Nineteenth Century.* London: Adam and Charles Black, 1972.

Greg, W. R. "Emigration or Manufactures." *Westminster Review.* 40 (August 1843): 101–122.

————. "Why Are Women Redundant?" *The National Review.* 28 (April 1862): 434–460.

Grey, Mrs. William. "Old Maids, A Lecture." London: William Ridgeway, 1875.

Hale, John. *Settlers: Being Extracts from the Journals and Letters of Early Colonists in Canada, Australia, South Africa and New Zealand.* London: Faber and Faber, 1950.

Hall, Catherine. "Rethinking Imperial Histories: The Reform Act of 1867." *New Left Review.* 208 (1994): 3–28.

———. *White, Male and Middle-Class: Explorations in Feminism and History.* New York: Routledge, 1992.

Hamilton, Paula, and Janice Gothard. "'The Other Half': Sources on British Female Emigration at the Fawcett Library, With Special Reference to Australia." *Women's Studies International Forum.* 10:3 (1987): 305–309.

Hamley, Charles. "Old Maids." *Blackwood's.* (July 1872): 94–108.

Hammerton, A. James. *Emigrant Gentlewomen: Genteel Poverty and Female Emigration, 1830–1914.* London: Croom Helm, 1979.

Hassam, Andrew. *Sailing to Australia: Shipboard Diaries by Nineteenth-Century British Emigrants.* Manchester: Manchester University Press, 1994.

Hatton, Noel. "The Future of Single Women." *The Westminster Review.* 121 (January 1884): 151–162.

Hechter, Michael. *Internal Colonialism: The Celtic Fringe in British National Development, 1536–1966.* Berkeley: University of California Press, 1975.

Herbert, Sidney, M. P. "First Report of the Committee of the Fund for Promoting Female Emigration." London: Her Majesty's Stationer's Office, 1851.

Hickok, Kathleen. "The Spinster in Victoria's England: Changing Attitudes in Popular Poetry by Women." *Journal of Popular Culture.* 15:3 (Winter 1981): 119–131.

Hinde, Andrew P. R. "The Marriage Market in the Nineteenth Century English Countryside." *The Journal of European Economic History.* 18 (Fall 1989): 383–392.

Hitchins, Fred H. *The Colonial Land and Emigration Commission, 1840–78.* Philadelphia: University of Pennsylvania Press, 1931.

Hobsbawm, Eric. *The Age of Empire: 1875–1914.* New York: Pantheon Books, 1987.

———. *Industry and Empire: From 1750 to the Present Day.* New York: Penguin, 1968.

Hunt, Thornton Leigh. *Canada and South Australia: Disposal of Waste Lands and Emigration.* London: A. Cole and Company, 1839.

Huyssen, Andreas. *After the Great Divide: Modernism, Mass Culture, Postmodernism.* Indianapolis: Indiana University Press, 1986.

"Immigration Question: Meeting in Capetown," 1894. Newspaper Clipping. Fawcett Library *Scrapbooks* 1/BWE (3/1–3) Box 22.

Irigaray, Luce. *This Sex Which Is Not One.* Ithaca, N.Y.: Cornell University Press, 1985.

Jeffries, Sheila. *The Spinster and Her Enemies: Feminism and Sexuality, 1880–1930.* London: Pandora Press, 1985.

Kaplan, Caren. *Questions of Travel: Postmodern Discourses of Displacement.* Durham, N.C.: Duke University Press, 1996.

Keating, Peter, ed. *Into Unknown England, 1866–1913: Selections from the Social Explorers.* Manchester: Manchester University Press, 1976.

Kranidis, Rita S. *Subversive Discourse: The Cultural Production of Late-Victorian Feminist Novels.* New York: St. Martin's Press, 1995.

————, ed. *Imperial Objects: Victorian Women's Emigration and the Unauthorized Imperial Experience.* New York: Twayne Macmillan, 1998.

Kristeva, Julia. *Desire in Language: A Semiotic Approach to Literature and Art.* New York: Columbia University Press, 1980.

Kroller, Eva-Marie. "First Impressions: Rhetorical Strategies in Travel Writing by Victorian Women." *Ariel.* 21:4 (1990): 87–99.

Lemon, Anthony, and Norman Pollock. *Studies in Overseas Settlement and Populations.* London: Longman, 1980.

"Letter to Emigrants." 6/23/1888. Fawcett Library. *Scrapbooks.* 1/ BWE/ 3/2, BWEA Scrapbook 2.

Levine, Philippa. *Victorian Feminism, 1850–1900.* London: Hutchinson, 1987.

Lockett, Jeannie. "Female Labour in Australia: An Appeal for Help," *The Nineteenth Century.* 18 (October 1885): 651–656.

Loeb, Lori Anne. *Consuming Angels: Advertising and Victorian Women.* Oxford: Oxford University Press, 1994.

Lovell, Terri. *Consuming Fiction.* London: Verso, 1987.

Macdonald, Charlotte. *A Woman of Good Character: Single Women as Immigrant Settlers in Nineteenth-Century New Zealand.* Wellington: Bridget Williams Books, 1990.

Mackenzie, John M. *Propaganda and Empire: The Manipulation of British Popular Opinion, 1880–1960.* Manchester: Manchester University Press, 1984.

Mangan, J. A. *Making Imperial Mentalities: Socialization and British Imperialism.* New York: Manchester University Press/St. Martin's Press, 1990.

Manochie, Captain. *Emigration: Advice to Emigrants Especially Those With Small Capital.* London: Olivier, 1848.

Marx, Karl. *Capital: A Critique of Political Economy.* Vol. 1. New York: Penguin, 1990.

Mavor, Carol. *Pleasures Taken: Performances of Sexuality and Loss in Victorian Photographs.* Durham, N.C.: Duke University Press, 1995.

Mayhew, Henry. *London Labour and the London Poor: Cyclopedia of the condition and earnings of those that will work, those that cannot work, and those that will not work.* London: Griffin, Bohn & Co., 1862.

McClintock, Anne. *Imperial Leather: Race, Gender and Sexuality in the Colonial Contest.* New York: Routledge, 1995.

McClintock, Anne and Rob Nixon. "No Names Apart: The Separation of Word and History in Derrida's 'Le Dernier Mot du Racisme.'" *Critical Inquiry.* 13:1 (Autumn 1986): 140–154.

Miller, Andrew. *The Imperial Archive: Knowledge and the Fantasy of Empire.* New York: Verso, 1993.

————. *Novels Behind Glass: Commodity Culture and Victorian Narrative.* Cambridge: Cambridge University Press, 1995.

Mills, Sara. *Discourses of Difference.* New York: Routledge, 1991.

Minh-ha, Trinh. *Woman, Native, Other: Writing, Postcoloniality and Feminism.* Bloomington: Indiana University Press, 1989.

Monk, Una. *New Horizons: A Hundred Years of Women's Migration* London: HMSO, 1963.

Munich, Adrienne Auslander. "Queen Victoria, Empire, and Excess." *Tulsa Studies in Women's Literature.* 6:2 (1987): 265–281.

———. *Victoria's Secrets.* New York: Columbia University Press, 1997.

Nightingale, Florence. *Cassandra.* Introduced by Myra Stark. New York: Feminist Press, 1979. Originally published 1852.

Nixon, Rob. "Refugees and Homecomings: Bessie Head and the End of Exile." In E. Ann Kaplan, Roman De La Campa, and Michael Sprinker, eds. *Late Imperial Culture.* New York: Verso, 1995.

Nord, Deborah Epstein. "'Neither Pairs Nor Odd': Female Community in Late Nineteenth-Century London." *Signs.* 15 (1990): 733–754.

Oliphant, Margaret. "The Condition of Women." *Blackwood's Edinburgh Magazine.* 83 (February 1858): 139–154.

Orr, A. "The Colonial and Indian Exhibition." *The Westminster Review.* 126 (July 1886): 29–59.

———. "The Future of English Women." *The Nineteenth Century.* 3:181 (July 1886): 1010–1032.

Parr, Joy. "The Skilled Emigrant and Her Kin: Gender, Culture, and Labour Recruitment." *Canadian Historical Review.* 68:4 (1987): 529–551.

Paton, Walter, ed. *Handbooks on British Colonies—Issued by the Emigrants' Information Office.* London: HMSO, 1906.

Perkin, Joan. *Victorian Women.* New York: New York University Press, 1993.

Pickens, K. A. "Marriage Patterns in a Nineteenth-Century British Colonial Population." *Journal of Family History.* 5:2 (1980): 180–196.

Plant, G. F. *Oversea Settlement: Migration from the United Kingdom to the Dominions.* London: Oxford University Press, 1951. Originally published 1903.

Poovey, Mary. *Uneven Developments: The Ideological Work of Gender in Mid-Victorian England.* Chicago: University of Chicago Press, 1988.

Pratt, Mary Louise. *Imperial Eyes: Travel Writing and Transculturation.* New York: Routledge, 1992.

"Proposed Emigration of Young Women to Canada." Advertisement, British Women's Emigration Society. Fawcett Library. *Scrapbooks.* 1/ BWE/ 3/2, BWEA Scrapbook 2.

Rammsack, Barbara N. "Cultural Missionaries, Material Imperialists, Feminist Allies: British Women Activists in India, 1865–1945." In Nupur Chaudhuri and Margaret Strobel, eds., *Western Women and Imperialism: Complicity and Resistance.* Bloomington: Indiana University Press, 1992.

Richards, Thomas. *The Commodity Culture of Victorian England: Advertising and Spectacle, 1851–1914.* Stanford, Calif.: Stanford University Press, 1990.

———. *The Imperial Archive: Knowledge and the Fantasy of Empire.* London: Verso, 1993.

Roberts, Barbara. "Daughters of the Empire and Mothers of the Race." *Atlantis: A Women's Studies Journal.* 1 (Spring 1976): 114–15.

Robson, John M. *Marriage or Celibacy:* The Daily Telegraph *on a Victorian Dilemma.* Toronto: University of Toronto Press, 1995.

Romig, Evelyn M. "Twisted Tale, Silent Teller: Miss Havisham in *Great Expectations.*" *Dickens Quarterly.* 5:1 (March 1988): 18–22.

Ross, Adelaide. "Emigration for Women." *Macmillan's Magazine.* 45 (1882): 312–17.

Ross, Marlon B. "Contested Spinsters: Governessing an the Limits of Discursive Desire in the Fiction of I. Compton-Burnett." In Laura L. Doan, ed., *Old Maids to Radical Spinsters: Unmarried Women in the Twentieth Century Novel.* Chicago: University of Illinois Press, 1991.

Rubin, Gayle. "The Traffic in Women." In Karen V. Hansen and Ilene J. Philipson, eds., *Women, Class and the Feminist Imagination: A Socialist-Feminist Reader.* Philadelphia: Temple University Press, 1990.

"Rules." FMCES Pamphlets, 1880–82. Fawcett Library. Female Middle Class Emigration Society. Box 1/3.

Ruskin, John. "Of Queen's Gardens." In *Sesame and Lilies, The Two Paths and the King of the Golden River.* London: Dent, 1907. Originally published 1865.

Rye, Maria. *Emigration of Educated Women.* Reproduced from *The Englishwoman's Journal.* London: Victoria Press, 1861. Fawcett Library. Pamphlet #325.2.

———. "Middle-Class Female Emigration Impartially Considered." *The English Woman's Journal.* 10:56 (1862): 73–85.

Said, Edward. *Culture and Imperialism.* London: Vintage, 1994.

———. *Orientalism.* New York: Vintage, 1979.

Scott, Joan Wallach. *Gender and the Politics of History.* New York: Columbia University Press, 1988.

Scrapbooks. Fawcett Library. 1?BWE 3/1–3 Box 22.

Sharpe, Jenny. *Allegories of Empire: The Figure of the Woman in the Colonial Text.* Minneapolis: University of Minnesota Press, 1993.

"Shipping Off Domestic Servants." *Daily News,* May 2, 1890. Fawcett Library. *Scrapbooks* 1/BWE 3/1–3, Box 22.

Shires, Linda M. "Fantasy, Nonsense, Parody, and the Status of the Real." *Victorian Poetry.* 26 (Autumn 1988): 267–283.

Showalter, Elaine. *A Literature of Their Own.* Princeton, N.J.: Princeton University Press, 1977.

Sidney, Samuel. *Female Emigration As It Is, As It May Be; A Letter to the Right Honourable Sidney Herbert, M. P.* London: George Woodfall and Son, 1850.

"Single Women Wanted." Headline, *The Times,* 1894. Fawcett Library. *Scrapbooks* 1/BWE 3/1–3, Box 22.

Smith, Monika Rydygier. "The W/Hole Remains: Consumerist Politics in *Bleak House, Great Expectations,* and *Our Mutual Friend.*" *Victorian Studies Association of Western Canada.* 19:1 (1993): 1–21.

South African Committee. July 4, 1899. Fawcett Library. WBWEA Box 2/4 1/BWE/4/4.

South African Sub-Committee of the United British Women's Emigration Association. "Information and Suggestions for the Use of the Capetown Committee Regarding to Employers in South Africa Desiring to Obtain Servants Through the UBWEA." December 13, 1899. Fawcett Library. *UBWEA Minutes,* 5 May 1896–6 December 1901. Box 2/4, 1/BWE/4/4.

Spender, J. W. *Westminster Gazette,* December 9, 1897. Fawcett Library, *Scrapbooks* 1/BWE, 3/1–3 Box 22.

Sprinker, Michael. "Introduction." In Kaplan, De La Campa, and Sprinker, eds., *Late Imperial Culture.* New York: Verso, 1995.

Spurr, David. *The Rhetoric of Empire: Colonial Discourse in Journalism, Travel Writing, and Imperial Administration.* Durham, N.C.: Duke University Press, 1993.

The Standard, 1894. Fawcett Library, *Scrapbooks* 1BWE 3/1.

Stone, Marjorie. "Bakhtinian Polyphony in *Mary Barton:* Class, Gender, and the Textual Voice." *Dickens Studies Annual: Essays in Victorian Fiction.* 20 (1991): 175–200.

Strobel, Margaret. *European Women and the Second British Empire.* Bloomington: Indiana University Press, 1991.

Tennant, Margaret. "Maternity and Morality: Homes for Single Mothers 1890–1930." *New Zealand Women's Studies Journal.* 2:1 (1985): 28–49.

Thompson, David. *England in the Nineteenth Century: 1815–1914.* New York: Penguin Books, 1978.

Thornton, A. P. *Doctrines of Imperialism.* New York: John Wiley & Sons, 1959.

To Intending Emigrants. Leaflet advertisement distributed by the Australian government's emigration agency in London. Fawcett Library, *Scrapbooks* 1BWE 3/1.

Travellers Aid Society Report for 1887. Pamphlet distributed at ports and on ships. Fawcett Library. 4TAS, AR (1) 1886–1895.

Tregear, Edward. "Compulsory Emigration." *Westminster Review.* 130 (September 1888): (378–88).

Trollope, Joanna. *Britannia's Daughters: Women of the British Empire.* London: Pimlico/Random House, 1983.

Turner, Wesley. "80 Stout and Healthy Looking Girls." *Canada: An Historical Magazine.* 3 (December 1975): 37–49.

———. "Miss Rye's Children and the Ontario Press, 1875." *Ontario History.* 68:3 (1976): 169–203.

Van-Helten, Jean Jacques, and Keith Williams. "'The Crying Need of South Africa': The Emigration of Single British Women to the Transvaal, 1901–1910." *Journal of South African Studies.* 10:1 (Oct 1983): 17–38.

Van Keuren, David K. "Cabinets and Culture: Victorian Anthropology and the Museum Context." *Journal of the History of Behavioral Sciences.* 25:1 (1989): 26–39.

Van Vugt, William E. "Prosperity and Industrial Emigration from Britain During the Early 1850s." *Journal of Social History.* 22 (1988): 339–354.

Vicinus, Martha. *Independent Women: Work and Community for Single Women, 1850–1920.* Chicago: University of Chicago Press, 1985.

———. *A Widening Sphere.* Bloomington: Indiana University Press, 1977.

————, ed. *Suffer and Be Still: Women In the Victorian Age*. Bloomington: Indiana University Press, 1972.

Weber, Adan Ferrin. *The Growth of Cities in the Nineteenth Century: A Study in Statistics*. Ithaca, N.Y.: Cornell University Press, 1968. Originally published 1899.

"What Women May Do." *Woman*. 123 (May 4, 1892). Fawcett Library. *Scrapbooks*. 1/BWE, 3/1–3, Box 22.

Williams, Raymond. *Problems In Materialism and Culture: Selected Essays*. New York: Verso, 1980.

Wills, W. H. "Ships: Safety for Female Emigrants." *Household Words*. 3 (1851): 228.

Wilson, Lady. *Letters from India*. Introduction by Pat Barr. London: Century, 1984.

Wittig, Monique. *The Straight Mind and Other Essays*. Boston: Beacon Press, 1992.

WOMAN—For Women and Girls "Forward! but not too fast." 123 (Wednesday, May 4, 1892). Fawcett Library. *Scrapbooks*. 1 BWE 3/1.

Women's Branch of the Oversea Department. "The Opportunities Offered to Women." *Britain's Call from Overseas: The Need and Scope for British Women in the Dominions and Colonies*. In *London III, Miscellaneous Institutions*, 1929. Originally published 1897.

Woolcock, Helen R. *Rights of Passage: Emigration to Australia in the Nineteenth Century*. London: Tavistock Publishers, 1986.

INDEX

ABOUT THE AUTHOR

R ita S. Kranidis is Assistant Professor of English at Radford University in Radford, Virginia, where she teaches a variety of courses including Women's Literature and Victorian and Cultural Studies. She has a BA in English and Women's Studies from Mount Holyoke College, an MA from C. W. Post–Long Island University, and a Ph.D. from the State University of New York at Stony Brook. She is author of *Subversive Discourse: The Cultural Production of Late-Victorian Feminist Novels* (St. Martin's Press, 1995) and editor of *Imperial Objects: Victorian Women's Emigration and the Unauthorized Imperial Experience* (Twayne Macmillan Publishers, 1998).